Tourism and Poverty

Routledge Advances in Tourism

EDITED BY STEPHEN PAGE, *University of Stirling, Scotland*

Tourism and Poverty

Regina Scheyvens

Routledge
Taylor & Francis Group
New York   London

First published 2011
by Routledge
711 Third Avenue, New York, NY 10017

Simultaneously published in the UK
by Routledge
2 Park Square, Milton Park, Abingdon, Oxon OX14 4RN

Routledge is an imprint of the Taylor & Francis Group, an informa business

© 2011 Taylor & Francis

First issued in paperback 2013

The right of Regina Scheyvens to be identified as author of this work has been asserted by her in accordance with sections 77 and 78 of the Copyright, Designs and Patents Act 1988.

Typeset in Sabon by IBT Global.

Library of Congress Cataloging-in-Publication Data

Scheyvens, Regina.
   Tourism and poverty / by Regina Scheyvens.
      p. cm. — (Routledge advances in tourism)
   Includes bibliographical references and index.
   1. Tourism.   2. Tourism—Government policy.   3. Poverty—Government policy.   I. Title.
   G155.A1S272 2011
   339.4'6—dc22
   2010034408

ISBN13: 978-0-415-99675-4 (hbk)
ISBN13: 978-0-415-85167-1 (pbk)

I dedicate this book to Sophie, Jessie and Harry,
who bring joy into my life every day.

Contents

Tables

Figures

Photographs

Boxes

Abbreviations

ADB	Asian Development Bank
ASSET	Association of Small Scale Enterprises in Tourism (the Gambia)
AusAID	Australian Agency for International Development
BEE	Black Economic Empowerment
CBT	Community-Based Tourism
CSR	Corporate Social Responsibility
DANIDA	Danish International Development Agency
DFID	Department for International Development (UK government aid agency)
ECPAT	End Child Prostitution Child Pornography and Trafficking of Children for Sexual Purposed
ESCAP	Economic and Social Council of the United Nations
FDI	Foreign Direct Investment
FTTSA	Fair Trade in Tourism South Africa
GDP	Gross Domestic Product
GNI	Gross National Income
GTZ	Deutsche Gesellschaft für Technische Zusammenarbeit (German technical cooperation agency owned by the federal government)
IFC	International Finance Corporation (part of the World Bank Group)

IIED	International Institute for Environment and Development
IIPT	International Institute for Peace through Tourism
IMF	International Monetary Fund
IUCN	International Union for the Conservation of Nature and Natural Resources
LDC	Least Developed Country
MDGs	Millennium Development Goals
MFAT	Ministry of Foreign Affairs and Trade (New Zealand)
NGOs	Non-government Organizations
NZAID	New Zealand Agency for International Development
ODA	Official Development Assitance
ODI	Overseas Development Institute
OECD	Organization for Economic Cooperation and Development
PATA	Pacific Asia Travel Association
PPT	Pro-Poor Tourism
SNV	Netherlands Development Organization
ST-EP	Sustainable Tourism—Eliminating Poverty (a UNWTO programme)
UNCTAD	United Nations Conference on Trade and Development
UNDP	United Nations Development Program
UNEP	United Nations Environment Program
UNESCO	United Nations Educational, Scientific and Cultural Organization
UNWTO	World Tourism Organization (2003 ouwards name)
WTO	World Tourism Organization (pre 2003 name)
WTTC	World Travel and Tourism Council

Acknowledgements

This book would not have been possible with the support, guidance and input of a wide range of people, all of whom I have enjoyed working with at different times. John Overton, long-time friend and mentor, told me it was about time I wrote another book, then Stephen Page added his encouragement and I was away! I have also had a particularly supportive Head of School, Henry Barnard, and some wonderful colleagues at Massey University, whose good humour I really appreciate. I'm inspired by the excellent teachers and researchers with whom I work.

Thanks to funding from both NZAID and Massey University I have been able to conduct fieldwork on tourism and development in a number of different countries. I have also worked with some excellent researchers when collecting data for case studies included in this book. Thank you, Bronwyn Tavita Sesega (Samoa) and Azmat Gani and Adi Vale Bakewa (Fiji), for providing cultural insights and working closely with me when I was conducting fieldwork in your countries. Many thanks also to Matt Russell, who transcribed numerous interviews, collected secondary sources of data and enthusiastically assisted with the writing up of the Fijian research. I would particularly like to extend my thanks to all people, from villagers to tourism officials, NGO staff and hotel managers, who agreed to share information with me during my research in the Pacific.

Thanks to all of the academics and writers out there whose work has helped me to gain a better understanding of the issues presented in this book. I sincerely hope I have not made any errors of interpretation or attribution when dealing with primary and secondary data in this book. Thank you, Max Novick of Routledge—you have been a patient, friendly and really supportive editor who showed particular consideration when my father was ill.

Finally, I want to thank my family, especially my partner, Craig, who encourages me in my work even when he knows I'm taking on something that seems beyond the bounds of possibility. Thanks also to our three kids who are lots of fun and provide a great distraction from work, and my parents, Harry and Josie, who help out in all sorts of wonderful and practical ways.

1 Introduction

THE PROMISE OF TOURISM AS A TOOL FOR POVERTY ALLEVIATION

This book addresses a critical question facing many aid agencies, academics, governments, tourism organisations and conservation bodies around the world: can tourism work as a tool to overcome poverty? In recent years many proclamations have been made about the actual and potential contributions tourism can make to developing countries, perhaps none more audacious than that of the president of Counterpart International, Lelei LeLaulu, who asserts that tourism represents 'the largest voluntary transfer of resources from the rich to the poor in history, and for those of us in the development community—*tourism is the most potent anti-poverty tool ever*' (eTurboNews 2007—emphasis added).

While most advocates of 'Pro-Poor Tourism' (PPT) are more balanced in their assertions, they do agree that tourism can indeed alleviate poverty. This proposition is alluring as we are told tourism is a significant or growing economic sector in most countries with high levels of poverty (Roe et al. 2004). We are also presented with figures on the centrality of tourism to the economies of many developing countries: for example, in 2006 65.9 percent of the Maldives' export earnings came from tourism, while Vanuatu earned a massive 73.7 percent of its export dollars from this sector (ESCAP 2007: 4). When we hear of village families in Indonesia who earn less than $8 per month in cash and struggle to meet their basic needs, yet they are within close vicinity of a tourist attraction (Schellhorn 2007: 177), it is hard to overlook that tourism might provide them with opportunities to enhance their well-being.[1]

However, academic views on the relationship between poverty and tourism have varied widely over the past half century, with the industry being soundly criticised for many years. While in the 1950s tourism was identified as a modernisation strategy that could help newly-independent developing countries to create jobs and earn foreign exchange, in the 1970s and 1980s many social scientists argued that poor people and poorer countries are typically excluded from or disadvantaged by what tourism can offer.

During this time tourism was widely critiqued as an industry dominated by large corporations which exploit the labour and resources of developing countries, cause environmental degradation, commodify traditional cultures, entrench inequality and deepen poverty (see e. g. Britton 1982; Pleumarom 1994). Given the strength and vigour of this critique, it is fascinating to see how there has been a concerted push towards a reversal of this thinking coinciding with the development industry's global focus on poverty alleviation from the 1990s onwards.

Tourism has been identified as a promising economic sector through which to develop poverty alleviation strategies thanks to some persuasive statistics. Developing countries now have a market share of 40 percent of worldwide international tourism arrivals, up from 34 percent in 2000 (UNWTO 2007: 4). For over 50 of the world's poorest countries tourism is one of the top three contributors to economic development (World Tourism Organization 2000, cited in Sofield 2003: 350). Tourism is also growing rapidly in a number of countries with least developed country status. Tourism accounts for 8.9 percent of employment in the Asian and Pacific region, that is 140 million jobs; in Pacific Island countries, tourism accounts for almost 1 in every 3 formal sector jobs (ESCAP 2007: 4–5). There has been 110 percent growth in arrivals to the least developed countries between 2000 and 2007 compared with an overall increase in worldwide international arrivals of 32 percent for this period (UNWTO, cited in PATA 2008). Furthermore, it is suggested that the approximately $68 billion given in aid annually pales in significance compared with revenues from tourism which are around $153 billion (Ashley and Mitchell 2005, cited in Christie and Sharma 2008: 428).

Telfer and Sharpley (2008: 2) claim that 'the most common justification for the promotion of tourism is its potential contribution to development, particularly in the context of developing countries'. These benefits are summarised in Table 1.1. Firstly, tourism can purportedly bring 'economic benefits' which contribute to the well-being of the poor directly through: generation of jobs—the tourism industry in 2009 employed over 235 million people world wide, which accounts for 8.2 percent of all jobs (WTTC 2010: 7); provision of income-earning opportunities for many others who provide goods and services to the industry; and collective community income such as lease money paid by resorts based on communal land or a share of gate takings at a national park going directly to a resident community. By enhancing local livelihood options, tourism can enable some rural communities to thrive rather than undergoing serious decline due to continuous out-migration of their youngest and brightest members (ESCAP 2003: 28; Scheyvens 2007b). Tourism can also bring 'non-cash livelihood benefits' to the poor, including conservation of natural and cultural assets, opportunities for the poor to get training and develop further skills, and also indirect benefits through tax revenues which governments use to support infrastructural development such as roading and water supplies, and to provide basic services, including education and health care (Ashley and Roe 2002; Goodwin et al. 1998). Finally, there may be 'policy, process and participation' benefits for the poor whereby the government puts in place policy frameworks which encourage more direct participation by the poor in decision-making, where partnerships between the public and private sectors are encouraged, and where communication channels are improved so poorer peoples have better access to information.

There are also strong claims that tourism as a sector has performed better than other sectors in recent years, so that it offers more promise in terms of development strategies. Thus UNCTAD (1998) refers to tourism as the 'only major sector in international trade in services in which developing countries have consistently had surpluses'. Many countries are being forced to look beyond their traditional agricultural exports (e.g. bananas, cocoa, coffee and sugar) because of the declining value of these products or their diminishing viability due to the demise of traditional trade agreements which had offered preferential access to markets. Comparing the value of export crops with tourism receipts for South Pacific countries over a 20 year period, it has been found that 'in every case the value of these primary products in real terms has declined and the only sector to demonstrate a continuous upward trend has been tourism' (Sofield et al. 2004: 25–26).

Even if we put aside exaggerated claims, such as that cited in the opening paragraph of this book that 'tourism is the most potent anti-poverty tool ever', the promise of tourism as a tool for poverty alleviation is clearly compelling and the potential benefits extend well beyond the economic sphere (see Figure 1.1). As such it would be negligent to cynically dismiss tourism's potential here, and this may also do a disservice to the millions of poorer people around the world who, in struggling to enhance their well-being, are looking to tourism as an area of promise.

It is important to consider what these people seek to gain from tourism. As noted by members of the Pro-Poor Tourism Partnership, a small group of academics and researchers who have advocated for PPT, this goes well beyond jobs and business opportunities (Roe et al. 2002). Rather, poor people hope that tourism will achieve many of the following: improve infrastructure in the area, including water, roads and health facilities; make their area safer for all, because tourists do not visit places plagued by crime and insecurity; improve communication facilities, thus giving them greater access to outside ideas and information; enhance community income via lease fees, profit sharing arrangements from joint ventures or donations from tourists; lead to greater pride and optimism due to planning together for tourism, revitalising cultural traditions and welcoming visitors from afar (Roe et al. 2002: 2–3).

However it is also vital that we examine whether unrealistic expectations are being raised, an issue highlighted by the downturn in tourist numbers resulting from the recent global economic recession, and that we seek to

Table 1.1   Pro-Poor Strategies to Provide Economic and Other Benefits

Strategy focus	Examples
Economic benefits	Expansion of employment and wages through job creation and training for the poor. Expansion of business opportunities for the poor through entrepreneurial opportunities. Development of collective community income through e.g. lease fees, donations, equity dividends and cooperatives.
Non-cash livelihood benefits	Capacity building, training and empowerment. Mitigation of environmental impacts of tourism on the poor. Equitable management of resources between tourists and local people. Improved access to services and infrastructure.
Policy, process and participation	Supportive policy frameworks at the national and local level that enable participation by the poor. Increased participation by the poor in decision-making. Encouragement of partnerships between public and private sectors. Enhancement of communication and the flow of information among all stakeholders.

Source: Based on Ashley (2002: 20)

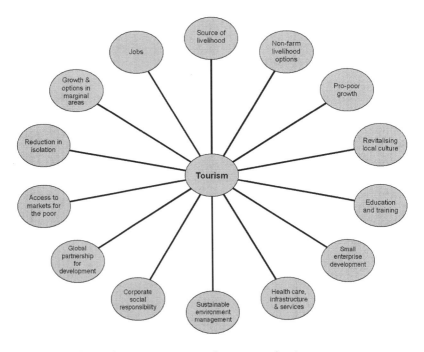

Figure 1.1   Linkages between tourism and poverty reduction.
Source: PPT Partnership (2004), in ESCAP (2007: 8)

understand the agendas of various stakeholders currently endorsing tourism as a tool for poverty alleviation.

THE NEED FOR CAUTION

Over 35 years ago Turner and Ash warned in their landmark book, *The Golden Hordes: International Tourism and the Pleasure Periphery,* that 'tourism has proved remarkably ineffective as a promoter of equality and as an ally of the oppressed' (1975: 53, cited in Higgins-Desbiolles 2006: 1193). Is there any reason for us to believe that things have changed radically due to the emergence of the PPT concept?

There could be a danger that, like a number of trends before it (e.g. 'ecotourism', PPT is something of a fad, a new way of dressing up the tourism industry to reclaim its credibility not just as an engine of growth but also as a 'soft' industry that is both socially beneficial and environmentally benign. Tourism industry players put on 'green lenses' in the 1990s, and along with a revival of interest in the environment due to the rising profile of climate change issues, a commitment to poverty reduction seems to have been a key focus for the industry in the first decade of the new millennium.

To date there has been relatively little in-depth critical exploration of the claim that tourism is an effective poverty alleviation strategy.[2] On the contrary, most reports have preached enthusiastically about the potential of PPT to contribute to poverty-reduction in a wide range of countries and contexts. There is some cynicism about PPT however, as seen in the following comment from the Director of the NGO Tourism Concern: 'The mantra of this international financial community has become "pro-poor tourism", in the extraordinary fantasy that tourism as it currently operates will lead people, Moses-like, out of poverty' (Barnett 2008: 1001). The over-enthusiasm for PPT has led others to comment that PPT may be yet another passing trend: ' . . . within the tourism industry pro-poor tourism has become the latest in a long line of terms and types to attract attention, funding and energy' (Mowforth and Munt 2009: 335). As the major players in this industry, as in any industry, are still concerned with profit maximisation, we need to consider whether PPT is just 'window dressing', or tokenistic, or, like transformations made under a 'green agenda' before it, intended mainly to reduce costs and/or enhance the positive publicity for the agencies concerned. While other writers are more optimistic in their assessment of PPT they tend to conclude that pro-poor tourism ' . . . is easier said than done' (Van der Duim and Caalders 2008: 122).

Thus in the process of exploring the poverty-tourism nexus this book will critically examine a number of questions.

- Firstly, what are the motives of various agencies that have jumped onto the pro-poor tourism bandwagon? Brennan and Allen (2001: 219) contend that 'Ecotourism is essentially an ideal, promoted by well-fed whites'—could the same be said of PPT, or does this have substance as an approach to development?

- Secondly, moving beyond the hype about Corporate Social Responsibility, can an industry driven by profits ever be expected to prioritise the interests of the poor?
- Thirdly, is a pro-poor approach to tourism likely to impact significantly on the extent and severity of poverty? To date, a number of benefits from pro-poor tourism have been claimed but the changes seem somewhat limited. As Ghimire and Li have noted (2001: 102), tourism has brought economic benefits to rural communities in China, as evidenced by a proliferation of televisions and satellite dishes. However living conditions have not improved on the whole. Ghimire and Li thus question whether poverty can be seen to have been alleviated in this context where there is still a lack of potable water, energy sources are unreliable and sanitation and health care facilities are poor (2001: 102).
- Fourthly, and related to the previous point, can PPT effectively work on a large scale, influencing mainstream tourism initiatives? Even in South Africa, where government agencies have demonstrated a strong commitment to promoting fair trade in tourism, the government is struggling to get the industry to commit to any significant changes (Briedenham 2004).
- Fifthly, can PPT effectively challenge inequitable institutions and structures that are in place, to a greater or lesser extent, in every country? It may, for example, be very difficult for well-intentioned and well-designed PPT initiatives to be implemented effectively if corruption is rife, there is racism and sexual discrimination, and powerful elites are used to capturing the benefits of development interventions.
- Finally, and fundamentally, can PPT help to overcome the inequalities between tourists and local people, when international tourism is to some extent based upon, and highlights, the vast inequalities between the wealthy and the impoverished? This is no more apparent than when viewing tourists' leisure pursuits: 'Golf courses and enormous pools are an insult to more than 1.3 billion people denied access to clean water' (UNDP 1999, cited in Richter 2001: 50).

TRENDS IN TOURISM

Tourism is one of the world's largest industries. In this section, the significance of tourism is discussed noting trends in terms of overall growth of numbers and revenues from tourism, particularly in less developed areas, and projections for the future. The nature of tourism to the developing world is also explored, specifying the types of experiences being demanded by tourists and the ways in which this may vary across different markets, including domestic, regional and international tourists.

International Tourism

As the figures below attest, international tourism has grown rapidly in recent years showing the increasing importance of developing country destinations as a market for international tourists (Table 1.2).[3] Even though Africa attracts a comparatively small proportion of international travellers, since 1995 tourist numbers here have increased two and half times, while the traditionally strong tourist destination of the Americas has seen by far the smallest rate of growth of all of the regions (28 percent). International arrivals in Asia and the Pacific have also more than doubled since 1995 and thus this region has overtaken the Americas to receive the second highest number of international arrivals after Europe. The development of new airlines and marketing strategies has paid off for the Middle East region, which has seen almost a tripling of tourist arrivals in the past 15 years. These trends are supported in Table 1.3, which forecasts the market share of tourism that these regions will have in 2020. This suggests that Europe's percentage share of international tourism will decline significantly by 2020 while Asia and the Pacific, Africa and the Middle East will all considerably increase their market share. Overall the prominence of developed countries as tourism destinations is declining as developing countries provide increasingly popular destinations.[4]

Factors contributing to the growth in international tourism to developing country destinations indicated in Tables 1.2 and 1.3 include tourists' increasing amounts of disposable income, improved airline schedules and transportation services, the emergence of low cost airlines, the development

Table 1.2   International Tourist Arrivals by Region (in millions)

Region	1995	2000	2005	2009[5]	Change 1995–2009
Europe	309.1	392.2	441.0	460.0	49%
Asia/ Pacific	82.0	110.1	153.6	180.9	121%
Americas	109.0	128.3	133.3	140.0	28%
Africa	18.6	26.1	35.3	45.9	147%
Middle East	13.7	24.9	37.8	52.9	286%

Source: UNWTO (2010: 3)

Table 1.3   Market Share of International Tourist Arrivals by Region

Region	Market share %	
	1995	2020
Europe	59.8	45.9
Asia/Pacific	15.1	26.6
Americas	19.3	18.1
Africa	3.6	5.0
Middle East	2.2	4.4

Source: UNWTO (2009)

of new source markets including India and China, and the marketing by tour companies of holiday packages which minimise the uncertainties of travel to developing countries (Akama 1999; ESCAP 2007). There are also 'push' factors at play, particularly people's desire to escape from growing urban congestion. In addition, tourists are increasingly seeking 'difference' in their holiday experiences whether this means exotic cultures, unique landscapes, pristine natural areas, or the availability of niche products such as ecotourism and cultural tourism which appeal to the postmodern tourist (Awaritefe 2004; Munt 1994; Urry 1990). Developing countries often have a comparative advantage here. Not content to just seek out difference, more tourists now are seeking to travel responsibly (WTO 1998: 9), and 'make a difference' as well, thus there has been rapid growth in the volunteer tourism market whereby tourists combine travel and leisure with the opportunity to work on conservation or development projects (Urry 1990).

The generally higher rates of growth of tourism in regions dominated by developing countries noted above does not necessarily translate into good growth in revenue for developing countries. Figure 1.2 shows that Africa receives a very small amount of tourism revenue. As 33 of the 49 least developed countries are located in Africa, increasing revenues from tourism to this region should seemingly be a priority to those promoting PPT. Similarly, World Tourism Organization (UNWTO) data indicates that in 2006, while developing countries as a whole claimed a market share of almost 40 percent of international arrivals, the least developed countries (LDCs) only received 1.3 percent of international arrivals despite achieving high rates of growth, as noted earlier (UNWTO 2007: 4). Table 1.4 shows that the increase in revenues gained in all developing countries was considerably higher than for the high income countries. This revenue is very significant for the poorer countries. For example, foreign tourists contributed over $1 billion in foreign exchange to the Tanzanian economy in 2008, which is almost one third of all goods and services sold by Tanzania abroad (Mitchell et al. 2009). Nevertheless as Table 1.4 reveals, even though the international tourism receipts to LDCs have almost quadrupled since 1990, they are *minute* when compared with receipts earned by low to middle income and high income countries.

This could be taken two ways. As tourist arrivals and tourist revenues are currently rather low in the LDCs and the African region generally, it could be suggested that the claims of PPT proponents that tourism can eliminate poverty are overstated. Alternatively, it could be argued that with such high rates of growth in arrivals to the LDCs and much 'untapped potential' for tourism development, tourism is a very promising industry which could, if managed well, bring many benefits to poorer people living in the LDCs.

Domestic and Regional Tourism

Figures on international tourist arrivals are deceptive, however. In fact, approximately 80 percent of tourists are *not* international tourists, they are domestic tourists (Boniface and Cooper, 1994: 56), with some suggesting domestic tourism flows may soon be ten times larger than international flows (Ghimire 2001: 2). In particular countries, the figures are even more skewed towards domestic tourism: for every international tourist in China, there are an estimated 26 Chinese tourists, and in India this ratio is one international tourist for every 100 domestic tourists (ESCAP 2007: 3). There has been a rise in both domestic and regional tourism, especially in Asia where growing middle classes along with the emergence of 'no-frills' airlines have contributed to rapid growth in these forms of tourism (Brown and Hall 2008). 78 percent of all international travel in Asia and the Pacific

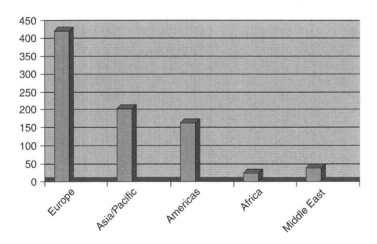

Figure 1.2 International tourism receipts by region ($ billion).
Source: UNWTO (2010: 5)

Table 1.4   International Tourism Receipts in Developing and High-Income Countries ($ billions)

Country categories	1995	2000	2005	Average annual growth 2000–2005 %
50 LDCs	1.1	3.0	5.3	12
Other low- & low-middle income economies	22.7	63.0	102.1	10.2
Upper-middle income economies	25.8	60.1	102.1	10.1
High income	223.8	356.81	476.6	6.0

Source: UNWTO (2006b: 3)

in 2003 was accounted for by intra-regional tourists: this amounted to 94 million visitors (ESCAP 2007: 2).

Developing country governments often place little emphasis on domestic or regional tourism, as international tourism is associated with higher spending, it earns export revenue, and it also has a more glamorous reputation. Growth of domestic tourism in the next twenty years is expected to be particularly strong in developing countries, as is growth of intraregional tourism within Asia and Africa; thus it would seem timely for developing country policy makers to look at what benefits such forms of tourism could bring to their countries (UNWTO 2007; WTTC 2010).

Domestic and regional tourism is important for a number of reasons. Such tourists account for a large proportion of the overall market. Domestic and regional tourists are also less fickle than international tourists in the face of seasonality, security or health scares, and they travel to a wider geographical range of places than international tourists thus bringing their money to more economically depressed areas (Scheyvens 2007b). Overall domestic tourists account for three to four times as much spending as international tourists (WTO 1998: 4). In some countries there are certain traditions which help to spread the benefits brought by domestic tourists; for example, in Thailand it is common practice for tourists to bring back specialist items from the regions visited, such as confectionary or fruit, as gifts for family and friends. This supports small-scale vendors who set up roadside stalls (ESCAP 2007: 3).[6]

Fluctuations in Tourism

While it is by now clear that growth in domestic, regional and international markets is stimulating increasing tourism in developing counties, there are also key factors threatening the growth of tourism. Tourism is an industry uniquely sensitive to a variety of internal and external influences, such as natural disasters, terrorist activity, global economic downturn or simply changes in fashion (Telfer and Sharpley 2008: 185). Natural hazards and freak weather events regularly lead to damage to tourism and related infrastructure and to cancellations of air travel to affected destinations long after the clean-up after an event. Many countries seem to be experiencing more extreme weather patterns than in the past and this could have a long-term impact on tourism in tropical destinations in particular. In a related point, the climate change mitigation policies put in place in richer countries are likely to lead to higher costs for air travel, which could lead to a decline in arrivals to some countries. The UNWTO is concerned that this could seriously reduce transfers of wealth to developing countries dependent on tourism (Gössling et al. 2008).[7]

The interdependence between political stability and tourism success has been widely recognised (Rao 2002; Sonmez 2000). Violent crime, terrorism, political upheaval and socio-political turmoil in particular threaten the viability of tourism destinations. Between 2001 and 2004, up to 5 million jobs in tourism were estimated to have been lost worldwide when a crisis in world tourism was triggered by the September 11 terrorist attacks (Beddoe 2004). Neumayer's (2004) cross-national study of acts of political violence found they could lower tourist arrivals in the long-term by up to one quarter, whereas more general political instability could result in a long-term decrease between one fifth and one quarter. For example, the 2000 coup in Fiji led to a 30 percent reduction in tourist numbers for the year compared with record levels in 1999, the hotel sector experienced a 44 percent reduction in employment, and real GDP declined by 11.1 percent (Chand and Levantis 2000; King and Berno 2002). This is a significant loss when tourism provides around one third of Fiji's GDP (Australian Department of Foreign Affairs and Trade 2000). Longer-term impacts included an 8 percent reduction in GDP and a significant decline in government savings as revenue was needed to reconstruct damaged infrastructure (Prasad and Narayan 2006). There have been fluctuations in tourist arrivals in the usually stable 'land of smiles'—Thailand—in 2009 and 2010 due to internal conflict. The 2002 terrorist bombing in Bali not only had devastating economic consequences for the island's economy, which at that time depended on tourism for approximately 40 percent of direct employment—it also lowered visitor arrivals throughout Indonesia (Telfer and Sharpley 2008: 185).

There are also major economic events which have seriously disrupted tourism flows. Around 1997 it was the Asian financial crisis that hit the tourism sector very hard. Although the average growth rate of international tourist arrivals in the East Asia/Pacific region reached 9.6 percent in 1995–1996, the crisis led to an average growth rate of -0.01 percent in the 1996–1997 period (WTO 1998: 6). The year 2009 was a particularly difficult one for tourism. The UNWTO reported that while tourism fared better than many other industries, the global economic downturn combined with additional uncertainties brought on by the influenza A (H1N1) took a heavy toll. International travel declined by 4.3 percent in 2009, and there was an associated decline of 5.8 percent in international tourism receipts (UNWTO 2010).

Government responses to the global recession have varied. Countries like Thailand and Malaysia have reduced visa fees and worked with airlines, hotels and tourist sites to reduce prices (Adams 2009: 3), while other governments have focused on stimulating domestic travel. In China, local authorities distributed domestic-travel coupons nationwide (Adams 2009: 2). The Fijian government decide to invest further in tourism, almost doubling its budget for this sector from F$12 million in 2008 to F$23.5 million in 2009. Most of the increased budget was spent on marketing. The Cook Islands meanwhile took almost the opposite stance, rebranding themselves as a 'Recession-Free Oasis', offering 'romantic and secluded escapes' for middle and high-income New Zealand couples.[8]

While insurance claims, foreign aid and good marketing plans help some destinations to 'bounce back' quite quickly from the impacts of natural disasters and political and economic events than in the past, this does not diminish the fact that the livelihoods of thousands of people can be undermined for a period of time (Ashley 2005). In these situations employment losses are usually most intensely concentrated among lower-skilled and socially weaker workers (Chok et al. 2007: 48), and vulnerability to such factors can be compounded in states with a heavy reliance on tourism. It has been generally noted that, because of the high import levels and relative dependence on export markets characteristic of many small island states, they are particularly vulnerable to global economic conditions (Briguglio 1995: 1616; Pelling and Uitto 2001).

TRANSFORMING MASS TOURISM

While figures were cited previously about the growth in tourist numbers and the significance of tourism revenues, we must look more deeply and consider whether the *nature* of tourism might influence its impact on poverty. Often crude generalisations have been made about 'mainstream' or 'mass' tourism versus 'alternative' tourism. Mass tourism has then been slammed for producing negative social, economic and environmental impacts, while alternative forms of tourism such as ecotourism and community-based tourism have been touted as offering ethically superior products which bring wide-ranging benefits to local people and places.

Yet an interesting aspect of PPT is its focus on tourism 'at all levels and scales of operation' (PPT Partnership 2005b: 1)—this marks it out as distinctive from views that 'alternative' forms of tourism provide the answer to overcoming the negative impacts of tourism and delivering more positives. Rather, it is asserted that mainstream tourism can bring direct benefits to the poor as well. In one respect this offers much promise as the reality is that 'much of third world tourism today is not small-scale, eco-logically oriented, or even broadly participatory' (Clancy 1999: 5), rather, it is of the mass variety. Furthermore, alternative forms of tourism can readily develop into mass tourism, as seen with the institutionalization of backpacking tourism (Aziz 1999; Cohen 1987), and the boundaries are often blurred when we see resort tourists providing the main customers for 'ecotours' such as sea-kayaking in southern Thailand (Kontogeorgopo-ulos 2004). Weaver (1999: 809) suggests that such sea-kayakers are 'passive and casual' ecotourists and that, because of sheer numbers, this group has far more potential than 'hardcore' ecotourists to impact on local econo-mies. This accords with the views of PPT protagonists who are advocating reforms to mainstream tourism.

For this reason, and due to the fact that proponents of PPT are particu-larly keen to see more focus on gaining benefits for the poor from mass tourism, this book will not just focus on small-scale, alternative tourism as providing the main opportunities for poverty alleviation. Rather, it will explore the idea that 'mass tourism itself can be practised in ways that min-imise and mitigate its obvious disbenefits' (Husbands and Harrison 1996: 1). This quote is instructive: it is the *way in which tourism is practised* which must change if the poor are to gain more from this industry, not just the rhetoric the industry uses to promote itself. It has become some-what fashionable to purport to be an ethical business—thus, for example, 'responsible tourism' has recently been adopted as something of a main-stream industry slogan in Europe after years of being sidelined or ignored. The 2008 London Travel Market was reportedly taken over by responsible tourism speak.[9] Careful analysis is needed to understand whether this is leading to meaningful changes in the industry which will result in greater benefits for the poor.

EXPLANATION OF KEY TERMS

Some of the key terms used in this book need to be clarified before the main discussion commences. The relatively popular use of 'North' versus 'South' in writing on development issues is not used in this book as this makes a geographical division out of what is really a social, economic and political division (Hadjor 1993: 11). In the past (Scheyvens 2002) I have opted to use 'Third World', drawing on Alfred Sauvy's explanation that the term was coined to mean that third of the world (set apart from the capitalist and communist blocs) which was 'excluded from its proper role in the world by two other worlds' (Hadjor 1993: 11). This 'Third World' was never meant to be associated with inferior status, but rather to denote countries left out from the realms of political and economic power. This term seems less appropriate today, however, given that the 'Second World' has had its sta-tus transformed since the 1990s with the fall of communism in Europe, while some of the 'Third World' countries have achieved staggering rates of economic growth and have become donors in their own right, for example, South Korea and Taiwan.

For simplicity, in this book I will use the term 'developing countries' to cover those countries which are net recipients of official development assistance (ODA) via bilateral or multilateral aid.[10] All countries listed by the Development Assistance Committee of the OECD as ODA recipients have a gross national income (GNI) per person of no more than $11,455, with the majority receiving less than $3,705 per capita.[11] This includes the 49 least developed countries (LDCs), a category developed by the United Nations that enables poorer countries to qualify for additional development assistance. LDCs are designated as such based on three criteria: low GNI (less than $750 per capita); human resource weakness (based on indicators of nutrition, health, education and adult literacy); and economic vulnerability (United Nations 2010).

Developing countries then all have lower GNI per capita than OECD countries, they generally have poorer socio-economic statistics than OECD countries, and most do not wield great power on the world stage. Many share undeniable similarities which stem largely from their histories of colonialism and imperialism. However, they are otherwise rather diverse. Some are 'upper middle-income countries' (including Eastern European countries) which are economically much stronger than the LDCs. Some developing countries are increasingly powerful on the global stage: with a third of the world's population between them and growing economies, India and China are wielding considerable influence now in international affairs. For example, as one of the five permanent members of the UN Security Council, China cannot be said to be politically marginalized. It has also become a significant aid donor to certain countries, but as China received $1,489 million in ODA in 2008 (OECD 2010), it is still categorised here as a developing country. Malaysia, Argentina, Brazil, Chile, Mexico and others have also shown significant improvements in a range of development indicators. The IMF chooses to designate developing countries with Telfer and Sharpley's stronger definition of 'developed countries' as 'those that are technologically and economically advanced, enjoy a relatively high standard of living and have modern social and political structures and institutions' (2008: 4–5).

The terms 'poverty' and 'the poor' are also used extensively in this book. Poverty is discussed in detail in Chapter 2, where I assert that it is best understood as a multidimensional concept embracing not just people's access to money or assets, but their ability to live life with dignity, to understand their rights, to participate fully in the opportunities life may bring and to be free of exploitation. I use 'the poor' with greater caution, however, based on the awareness that to many individuals and communities, this is a rather derogatory label. There is often controversy over the use of the term 'poor' in the Pacific Islands, for example, although the Head of Pacific Studies at Victoria

University in New Zealand, Teresia Teaiwa, herself part-Fijian, argues it does have meaning for Pacific peoples but not in the conventional economic sense: rather, to be poor is to lack food, lack family or lack belonging to a community (personal communication, 2009). It is not about a lack of money or personal possessions, as commonly assumed by outsiders. Similarly, Andean people living along the Inca trail are disturbed that outsiders sometimes judge them as being 'poor' (see Box 2.1, Chapter 2).

FOCUS AND OUTLINE

It is important to identify that my main interest in examining the potential contribution of tourism to poverty alleviation is based on a fundamental belief that the continued presence of high levels of inequality and poverty in our world is an affront to humanity. This is a stance championed by Nelson Mandela who challenged world leaders with the following statement at the launch of the Make Poverty History campaign in 2005:

> Like slavery and apartheid and apartheid, poverty is not natural. It is man-made and it can be overcome and eradicated by the actions of human beings.

Thus I am primarily interested in whether tourism can uplift the well-being of the poor. I am not so interested in ESCAP's claims that that pro-poor tourism can 'enhance a country's international profile', 'open the door to new investment', and 'stimulate economic growth' (2003: 2), as such outcomes *might* benefit the poor, but, I would argue, they do not inherently lead to enhanced well-being of those living in poverty.

Chapter 1 has introduced the reader to the supposed potential of PPT, as well as raising concerns about enthusiastic proclamations about what PPT can achieve. It has also discussed trends in global tourism, highlighting how few tourists travel to the LDCs at present but how there is much potential in the growth of tourism to developing countries as a whole in recent years. To follow, Chapter 2 provides a detailed discussion of the meaning of poverty in all its dimensions and approaches to tourism which seek to address poverty, unearthing a range of perspectives concerning the relationship between tourism and poverty alleviation. Chapter 3 then reviews evidence of the ways in which tourism has undermined development prospects in specific places, as expressed by advocates of political economy, dependency and anti-globalisation thought. The logic here is that tourism is structured in such a way that it creates or perpetuates poverty and inequality in the developing world. While acknowledging that tourism can lead to a range of negative impacts, in this chapter I query whether such criticisms have been overstated and suggest bringing more balance back into our discussions of tourism as a tool for development and poverty alleviation.

Chapter 4 then takes an unusual approach, suggesting that poverty itself attracts tourists. Postcolonial and postmodern writers explain why some tourists want to visit 'cheap' locations, and how tourist marketing often exploits 'difference', such as the fact that tourists like to explore 'traditional' villages, experience 'authentic' culture and the like. This raises the concern that there is little incentive to ensure that tourism alleviates poverty, as tourists want things to stay just the way they are. However, Chapter 4 also explores a new breed of tourists, the 'voluntourists', who also like to visit poorer places but who are keen to donate their time and labour to assist the people in these communities. The rising popularity of voluntourism has led to claims that it is more about the ego of the tourists than the well-being of the people in the places visited, a position not fully supported by this author. Ways in which tourism can engender greater understanding of global inequalities and build linkages between distant peoples are also explored in a discussion on 'justice tourism'.

In Chapters 5, 6 and 7, I move on to consider positive ways in which tourism industry players, governments and development agencies are connecting tourism and poverty alleviation. In Chapter 5, it is apparent that most positive views on the potential of tourism to alleviate poverty come, somewhat surprisingly, from the tourism industry—despite the fact that their aim is to generate profits, not to assist the poor. We see pro-poor rhetoric at the local level with individual hotels and resorts claiming to have a strong commitment to social development goals, but also at the supranational level with the likes of regional tourism industry associations (e.g. PATA) and also the Fair Trade in Tourism movement. In Chapter 5, I will consider whether support for pro-poor tourism is leading to meaningful change within the industry, and better outcomes for the poor.

The governments and development agencies discussed in Chapters 6 and 7 could be seen as positioned more appropriately than industry to advocate for tourism as a tool for poverty alleviation, and indeed some of them are making major efforts in this regard. Chapter 6 stresses that governments have a central role to play in planning for and controlling the development of tourism in such ways that it will deliver greater benefits to the poor. To date, however, many governments have been attracted to tourism more in terms of its potential to contribute to economic growth and they have assumed that benefits will automatically trickle down to the poor. In Chapter 6, I provide a range of examples of governments which have taken a more holistic approach to tourism development, involving careful regulation of the sector but also partnership with private sector institutions, mechanisms to connect local suppliers to tourism businesses, support for building capacity of local people, and delivering communal benefits to poor people living in areas of tourism development. Chapter 7 considers a range of development agencies, from multilaterals such as the UNWTO and World Bank, to bilateral donors and NGOs, which are working hard to find ways of making tourism more pro-poor. There are a number of innovative examples of pro-poor strategies that will be discussed, especially showing how particular agencies have moved beyond an approach of simply supporting local-level community-based tourism initiatives and are now mainstreaming poverty reduction into their tourism programmes at a range of levels. Limitations to the effectiveness of the PPT work of such agencies will also be discussed along with the need for them to devise innovative ways of supporting change in the tourism industry.

The conclusion to this book, Chapter 8, returns to questions raised about PPT in this chapter, with the overall aim of evaluating the potential of PPT to bring wide-ranging benefits for the poor. It concludes with suggestions for 'ways forward' for governments and development and tourism industry personnel who are committed to providing more opportunities for the poor to benefit from tourism development.

2 Poverty and Tourism Unpacked

INTRODUCTION

At the start of the twenty-first century we were being constantly reminded of the amazing rates of progress in our world, from the consistently high economic growth rate in China to the technological revolution which has seen Bangalore named as India's 'silicon valley'. Meanwhile, Airbus launched its A380, which could transport larger numbers of people (up to 853 in an all-economy class configuration) over long distances, and Richard Branson enthused that the world, and beyond, was our oyster as Virgin airways made plans to commercialise flights to the moon.

Then in a relatively short space of time several factors converged to call into question the inevitability and impacts of such 'progress'. An energy crisis was sparked amid concerns about peak oil, demonstrated by a spike in oil prices from less than $60 a barrel at the start of 2007 to $147.30 a barrel in July 2008; a food crisis emerged, doubling the price of staple foods like rice and wheat in some markets in early 2008, sparking food riots; and due to what some see as incessant corporate greed there was a collapse of major lending organisations and related businesses, which led to a global economic crisis from 2008 to the present.[1]

The world thus needs to face up to some major challenges to the ideology of 'progress'. Our drive for economic growth has seriously compromised the quality of the natural environment in many places, an extreme example being BP's oil spill in the Gulf of Mexico, which spewed up to 100,000 barrels of oil per day into the Gulf of Mexico contaminating the surrounding sea and coastline.[2] Poverty is rife. The number of countries with LDC (least developed country) status has grown from 25 in 1971 to 49 in 2010. Every day around 18,000 children die of hunger or malnourishment,[3] despite the fact that globally food production doubled in the last quarter of the twentieth century (World Bank 1997: 5). And despite numerous medical advances, approximately 2 million children die each year due to diarrhea, which is often caused by lack of access to safe drinking water.[4] There is mobile phone coverage in remote corners of Africa, but this does not help the poor who have no way to pay to transport their sick to hospital. While the maternal mortality rate in New Zealand has plummeted to 1 woman in every 5,900 births, women in Afghanistan face a 1 in 8 lifetime chance of maternal death (Save the Children 2010). The village store sells Coca Cola, SIM cards for mobile phones and miniature tubes of Colgate toothpaste, but the women who live there still have to walk seven hours a day to fetch water during the dry season. Preventable diseases like malaria and HIV/AIDS continue to be rife, robbing children of parents and communities of their most productive members. What is most disturbing in all of this is the realisation that so much of this human suffering is preventable. It is politics and economics, not 'natural causes', that are most to blame for the continuing high rates of poverty in our world.

Some may thus query, how can a supposedly frivolous, hedonistic, profit-driven industry like tourism hope to seriously address poverty issues? We need a better understanding of the complex relationship between tourism and poverty alleviation:

> while there are a great number of reports rendering prominent the link-ages between tourism and poor people . . . few in-depth studies have been carried out to understand the complexity of these interrelation-ships. (Gössling et al. 2004: 132)

In particular, none of the smattering of academic publications on pro-poor tourism to date has included a substantive discussion of the term 'poverty'. A fundamental weakness with pro-poor tourism, consequently, may be that it is dislocated from a theory of poverty. The closest it comes to this is its sustainable livelihoods roots (e.g. Ashley and Roe 1998). This chapter thus begins by unpacking the term 'poverty'. It then moves on to discuss the 'poverty consensus' which has had a major influence on the development industry from the 1990s onwards. The evolution of pro-poor tourism as an approach to development is the focus of the third section of this chapter, and finally there is a theoretical analysis of various perspectives of the tourism/poverty relationship.

The approach taken here is based on the premise that a thorough discussion of the term 'poverty' should be conducted *prior* to analysis of pro-poor tourism. In fact, a critical discussion of poverty is needed before we can consider whether there is real meaning in the notion of PPT, and whether PPT has the potential to transform the way in which governments, the private sector and development agencies are working to ensure that tourism is actually resulting in greater benefits for the poor.

POVERTY UNPACKED

The Meaning of Poverty

The *Concise Oxford English Dictionary*'s (Thompson 1995: 1071) definition of poverty includes 'the state of being poor', 'want of the necessities of life', and 'scarcity or lack', where 'poor' is defined as 'lacking adequate money or means to live comfortably' (1995: 1062). Certainly a central aspect of poverty is the lack of access to basic needs, such as food, safe drinking water and adequate shelter. While a lack of material well-being and the inability to earn a sufficient income are closely associated with the state of poverty, they fail to provide us with a full understanding of the meaning of this term. It is now commonly accepted that poverty is not simply an economic concept, rather, it is multidimensional in nature (Akindola 2009; Osmani 2003; Sultana 2002): 'Poverty never results from the lack of one thing, but from many interlocking factors that cluster in poor people's experiences and definitions of poverty' (Narayan et al. 2000: 32).

Denis Goulet articulated that in addition to basic needs, development includes two other key criteria: freedom (of expression, or from servitude) and dignity/self-esteem (cited in Todaro and Smith 2003: 52–54). Goulet's ideas could thus lead us to question whether employment in the tourism industry necessarily equates with pro-poor development. Thus is the bonded employment of a 10-year-old boy in an Indian hotel where he must work at least 16 hours per day every day of the week, is allowed to visit home once a year, and is faced with regular verbal and physical abuse, really an example of tourism employment contributing to the alleviation of poverty? In this case, the hotel may provide the boy with all of his basic needs, while trampling on his fundamental freedoms and self-esteem. While this example may seem extreme, there are many others from around the world of a lack of labour rights in the tourism industry, as seen in evidence from Tourism Concern's campaign on 'Sun, Sand, Sea and Sweatshops'.[5]

Similarly, the tourism industry has driven displacement of thousands of people from their ancestral lands, whether for the creation of national parks and wildlife reserves in African countries, or coastal resorts in Asia (Carruthers 1997; Goodwin et al. 1998). The livelihoods of such people are directly undermined by such tourism development, which removes or limits their prior freedom to hunt, fish, collect medicinal plants and meet multiple other needs from the natural environment. The new opportunities which tourism offers them are typically limited by comparison. Even if they can later earn a little money from the sale of souvenirs to tourists, the fact remains that their land rights have been systematically ignored and their communities may start to disintegrate as the young and more educated migrate away in the hope of finding better opportunities. Those who remain behind often become impoverished. These two examples serve to explain that poverty is not just about a lack of basic needs.

Now we move on to consider how people living in impoverished conditions describe poverty. A World Bank research project, Voices of the Poor, based on a participatory poverty assessment whereby over 20,000 people in 23 countries were asked about their perceptions of poverty, revealed the following:

> Poverty definitions give prominence to problems with securing food and difficulties finding safe and predictable sources of livelihood. What

is striking however is the extent to which dependency, lack of power and voice emerge as core elements of poor people's definitions of poverty. Powerlessness and voicelessness also underlie discussions of a heightened sense of vulnerability and the inability of poor people to protect themselves from shocks. . . . (Narayan et al. 2000: 51)

The key findings of this World Bank study are shown in Figure 2.1, highlighting that lack of physical necessities, assets and infrastructure are key problems for the poor, but also revealing that poverty has direct psychological and sociological dimensions as the poor clearly articulate that they are abused by those in power, that institutions can be disempowering, and that lacking power and voice is humiliating for them and can place them in a position where they are vulnerable to exploitation. This may be why Bebbington (2007: 813) asserts that ' . . . chronic poverty is a socio-political relationship rather than a condition of assetless-ness'. Note also that income did not feature as the central economic concern of those in the Voice of the Poor study:

The poor tend to mention income only infrequently relative to assets such as membership within kinship and social networks, health, labor power, land, and other resources that make self-provisioning possible. (Narayan et al. 2000: 51)

This study suggests also that the pain people feel in not being able to meet social expectations (such as attending festivals, participating in ritual gift-giving, or even providing a cup of tea for guests) is an affront to their personal dignity, and can harm social relations (Narayan et al. 2000: 26). This may in turn undermine social capital (Putnam 1995), the bonds between a community and with others outside the community which can be drawn upon in times of need.

We can gain further insights into the social and political dimensions of poverty in the writing of several authors whose work is summarised in Table 2.1. Firstly, I turn to ideas related to sustainable livelihoods. Chambers and Conway (1992), Carney (1998) and a number of others have urged us to understand the realities of the poor in relation to the diverse livelihood strategies they may adopt. Chambers and Conway's (1992) model of sustainable livelihoods recognises that the resilience of the poor to withstand shocks and stresses is determined by the diversity of their livelihood strategies, their capabilities and the assets they have: the latter can include tangible resources as well as intangible assets such as claims they can make on others. Thus as opposed to conventional approaches to poverty, rather than seeing the poor as lacking in 'basic needs' which should then be provided by an outside agency, the livelihoods approach explicitly recognises the assets they possess which can help them to attain a livelihood (Osmani 2003: 14). Under a livelihoods

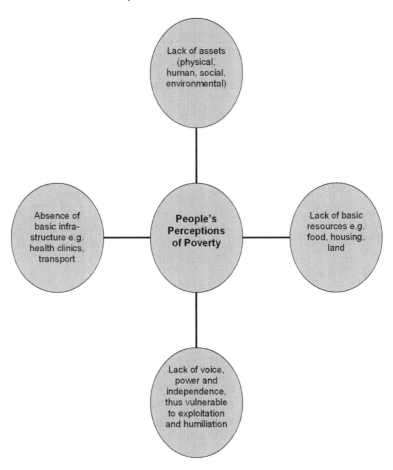

Figure 2.1   Key findings from the World Bank's 'Definitions of Poverty' study.
Source: Derived from Narayan et al. (2000)

approach to development, although resource conservation is an environmental imperative, continued resource use is also recognised as an essential aspect of human livelihood systems (Chambers and Conway 1992). An integrated livelihoods approach recognises the need to secure, and develop, people's livelihood capacities through a diversity of strategies, one of which may be tourism.

Secondly, John Friedmann's work on empowerment is considered. Poverty is often closely related to social exclusion (Osmani 2003), which Friedmann (1992) referred to as 'disenfranchisement'. As noted in Box 2.1, to the Indians of the Inca trail to be an 'orphan' of one's own society means that one is excluded from their people and thus is poor. When people are disenfranchised they lack the ability to participate fully in social life, they lack positive connections to other people, and thus they find it difficult to access resources such as information or education, and are excluded from positions of political power. Socio-cultural factors related to gender, ethnicity, class and caste, among others, can lead to social exclusion of some groups of people and be implicit in their poverty. Thus for example, in some societies widows are stigmatized, meaning they are more likely to live in poverty because they are not well respected or supported. Friedmann's (1992) answer to overcoming their disenfranchisement is for the poor or excluded to be empowered, and here he explicitly considers the social, political and psychological dimensions of power:

- Social power: access to bases of household production including financial resources, information, knowledge and participation in social organisations;
- Political power: access of individuals to processes used to make decisions that impact on their well-being—'the power of voice and of collective action';
- Psychological power: self-confidence and a 'sense of personal potency' (Friedmann 1992: 33).

A focus on empowerment and disempowerment enables the conceptualisation of poverty and inequality in terms other than the reductively economic (Schilcher 2007a; Sofield 2003). It also accords with people's analysis of their own situation. For example, respondents in a study conducted in Oyo state, Nigeria, saw lack of empowerment as one of three key components in their understanding of poverty (Akindola 2009). It can thus be argued that development is a process which requires active participation and empowerment of the poor so they can determine their own futures and put in place strategies to achieve their goals. They may demonstrate empowerment through transforming existing structures and forming their own social movements for change. The poor can be *active agents* of change rather than *passive beneficiaries* of processes determined by others. Friedmann argues though that 'Genuine empowerment can never be conferred from the outside. In the struggle against poverty and for political inclusion, the role of external agents is to provide support in ways that encourage the disempowered to free themselves of traditional dependency' (1992: 77).

Thirdly, Amartya Sen has inspired much thinking (and action) around rights-based approaches to development. Sen introduced the concept of 'development as freedom', whereby the poor should have the freedom or opportunities to enhance their well-being (Sen 1999). Sen's proposition, which would also be supported by Friedmann's (1992) ideas about empowerment, is that the development process should help to activate the individual agency of poor peoples so that they can claim their rights (Mowforth and Munt 2009: 44).[6] As laid out in the 1986 UN Declaration on the Right to Development: 'A fundamental human freedom is freedom from want.

Box 2.1   Who is 'Poor' in the Andes?

Annelies Zoomers conducted research along the Andean 'Inca route' between Peru
and Bolivia, which has become very popular with western tourists. She noticed that
while tourists often constructed the resident Andean people as impoverished, this
contrasted sharply with Andean people's own views of their situation. The term
'poverty' apparently only emerged in the south of Peru in the 1990s when NGOs
came to work on 'poverty alleviation' in the area. To the older generations, it is a
nonsense that their people are now considered to be poor. As one research partici-
pant noted:

*My father used to say to me: How can they consider us (pueblo) poor, since we are
the ones who supply food to the neighbouring districts and even to the capital of the
province? We have sufficient food, livestock and even money ... we produce the
best potatoes, the best maize, and the best livestock. (cited in Zoomers 2008: 978)*

In fact, there is no word for 'wealth' or 'poverty' in the Quechua language. Instead,
there are two terms which relate to rich and poor:
- 'Qhapaq' means to be rich in possessions, rather than money.
- 'Waqcha' means orphan, equating to a situation whereby one's isolation from family and community relations means a person misses out on communal resources and
cannot benefit from systems of reciprocal exchange. Ironically, this is how foreign
backpackers in the region are sometimes seen: 'The tourists feel sorry for the locals
who live in poor houses, have no electricity, and few possessions, while the locals
pity the tourists who travel alone (they are w'acha – orphans) and have no family or
children (not even animals). Lonely backpackers are often seen as poor people, as
socially isolated' (Zoomers 2008: 979).

Poverty is a human rights violation, and freedom from poverty is an inte-
gral and inalienable right' (emphasis added). A rights-based approach to
development builds on this right:

> A rights-based approach holds that someone, for whom a number of
> human rights remain unfulfilled, such as the right to food, health, edu-
> cation, information, participation, etc., is a poor person. Poverty is
> thus more than lack of resources—it is the manifestation of exclusion
> and powerlessness. (Mikkelsen 2005: 204)

Also fundamental to Sen's ideas is the concept of capability which refers
to a person's ' ... actual ability to achieve various valuable functionings
as a part of living': what people can do is therefore more important than
who owns what (Sen 1993: 30). An individual's functionings might include
the ability to earn an income, but also include other things they value such
as being educated, being secure and living a dignified life. People should

ideally then be able to choose and achieve what is important to them in life, including physical needs, self-worth and participation (Sen 1999).

Fourthly, and strongly linked to Sen's ideas, is the rights-based approach to development which sees poverty not as a state of deprivation which then requires development actors to provide assistance, but as a fundamental denial of human rights. The key focus then should be to ensure that the poor are empowered and that they have the resources and opportunities to claim their rights (Hamm 2001). A prime example of this approach was in the 2000 Human Development Report (UNDP 2000).

Ideas from key contemporary thinkers on poverty are summarised in Table 2.1. Note that all appreciate the multidimensional nature of poverty, and there are significant overlaps and complementarities between these ideas with common threads being capabilities, empowerment, sustainable livelihoods and rights. For example, Friedmann and Sen have similar ideas on freedom, while a rights-based approach requires empowerment of citizens to claim their rights. The focus on overcoming vulnerability in the sustainable livelihoods approach can also be traced back to Sen's (1981) early work on famine.

This discussion of the multidimensional nature of poverty leads to some direct challenges to those agencies advocating that tourism is a tool for poverty alleviation. Rather than focusing narrowly on whether tourism can foster economic growth and provide jobs and income, we need to consider if tourism results in the following:

- Provides alternative livelihood strategies which help to *reduce the vulnerability* of poor communities, *enhance their well-being* and *increase their self-reliance*
- Helps poor people to build up their capabilities and assets
- Facilitates the *empowerment* of poor peoples and helps them to lead *dignified lives* in which they have *greater control* over their own well-being
- Leads to poor people *securing their rights.*

Now that the meaning of poverty has been thoroughly discussed, the chapter moves on to consider how tourism came to be seen as a tool for poverty alleviation under the pro-poor tourism approach.

THE POVERTY AGENDA

It is no coincidence that the term 'Pro-Poor Tourism' (PPT), which was coined to mean 'tourism that generates net benefits for the poor' (Ashley and Roe 2002: 62), was first used in the development literature in 1999 (see Deloitte and Touche 1999). It was inspired broadly by the development industry's move in the 1990s to establish poverty alleviation as the

Table 2.1   New Thinking about Poverty

Key ideas and thinkers	Explanation
Empowerment *John Friedmann (1992)*	Friedmann argued that development is about empowering disenfranchised people (i.e. those that face social exclusion – from political processes, the labour market, educational opportunities, etc). When they are empowered they will have opportunities to have greater control over their own lives and well-being. He identified three key aspects of empowerment: social (access to resources and participation in social institutions), psychological (sense of dignity and self-esteem, e.g. pride in one's culture), and political (freedom from servitude, freedom of expression). To overcome poverty, the poor must not be seen as victims or as beneficiaries, but as active agents of change.
Sustainable Livelihoods *Chambers and Conway (1992)*	A livelihood comprises the capabilities, assets and activities required for a means of living. Poor people are particularly vulnerable to shocks and stresses when they do not have a diverse range of livelihood strategies to draw upon. Thus a sustainable livelihoods approach seeks to build resilience of poor communities and focuses on the agency of communities; the approach is people-centred and participatory.
Capabilities Approach/ Development as Freedom *Amartya Sen (1999)*	This is sometimes referred to as 'development as freedom' because, as Sen explained, people should be free to enhance their well-being and thus avoid illiteracy, hunger, etc. This well-being may be premised upon access to food, shelter or less-tangible things, such as capability to take part in an important ritual or freedom to access education. The poor, then, are those who are restricted from accessing the means to improve their well-being.
Rights-Based Approach *UNDP (2000)*	Poverty constitutes a denial of human rights. International human rights law grants all people the right to participate in the life of a community. State laws and policies also protect the rights of citizens, who therefore have entitlements they should be able to claim. A rights-based approach thus suggests that the best approach is to argue for resources, access and opportunities for the poor based on the fact that these are rights of every citizen.

number-one development agenda. Thus before explicitly discussing the evolution of PPT, it is important to gain an understanding of what has been driving the global development industry in recent decades.

Despite billions of dollars donated to charities, decades of development planning, aid projects and programmes, grants and loans, by the end of the 1980s it was clear that limited progress had been made in eliminating poverty (Cling 2003). Particularly strident criticisms were directed at structural adjustment programmes (SAPs) which had been imposed on many developing countries from the late 1970s onwards. SAPs were driven by the logic that structural reforms could lead poorer countries out of indebtedness and put them on the road to economic recovery. In fact the impacts of SAPs on many societies were extremely harsh due to requirements such as reductions in government support for domestic industries and the requirement of fiscal constraint (particularly, cuts in social spending), meaning poverty was in some cases entrenched (Dent and Peters 1999).

It is in this context that poverty alleviation was made the leading development agenda in the 1990s and 'pro-poor' discourse came to the fore. This focus on poverty proved alluring: 'It has provided a powerful rallying cry—a new development mantra—for those in development practice and charged with garnering flagging political and financial support for aid programmes' (Storey et al. 2005: 30). The World Bank and UNDP came out in favour of this approach in 1990, followed by the Development Assistance Committee of the OECD, which established International Development Targets (the precursors of the Millennium Development Goals) in 1996. Concurrently a number of multilateral and bilateral donors also came on board to endorse the poverty agenda as their central aim, for example, DFID in 1991, and AusAID in 1997. By 1999 the IMF introduced Poverty Reduction Strategy Papers (PRSPs) as a more participatory, poverty-focused alternative to SAPs. Interestingly, in 80 percent of PRSPs tourism is identified as an important economic sector (Mann 2005: iv), leading to the suggestion tourism can be effectively directed towards benefiting the poor.

This period was characterised by what many see as a consensus on poverty, including the belief that poverty results from poor governance and protected economies, and that globalisation offers a path out of poverty. Thus blame for economies that were failing was placed squarely with those countries themselves rather than recognising the roles that outside structures and institutions, historically and contemporarily, play in producing the conditions for poverty (Erbelei 2000). Contemporary poverty analysis has thus overlooked the underlying causes of poverty (Green and Hulme 2005; Hickey 2008). The 'poverty consensus' has also been criticised in terms of its heavy focus on economic development, while overlooking important environmental, social and political issues: 'the pro-poor development paradigm . . . is considerably circumscribed in its premise of economic growth as the foundation of development' (Mowforth and Munt 2003: 34). Storey et al. (2003: 30) contest the notion that there is now a 'new poverty agenda' in place, suggesting that ' . . . a poverty focus merely represents a different path to the same ends (i.e. political reform and economic adjustment)'. These authors are essentially criticising the neoliberal logic behind the poverty agenda, something that will be discussed in more detail near the end of this chapter.

The Millennium Development Goals (MDGs)

Associated with the poverty consensus are the Millennium Development Goals, a set of eight goals that are almost universally supported, having been agreed upon by all 191 Member States of the United Nations:

- Eradicate extreme poverty and hunger
- Achieve universal primary education
- Promote gender equality
- Reduce child mortality
- Improve maternal health
- Control HIV/AIDS, malaria and other diseases
- Ensure environmental sustainability
- Develop a global partnership for development

While gaining widespread support and being lauded for identifying a single, unifying goal for development agencies, the MDGs have also been criticised because, as Hickey notes, ' . . . the focus on targets and the narrow politics of securing quick wins has sidelined a more thorough consideration of the institutional arrangements and political processes required to move towards these goals' (2008: 355). Such targets are quantitative, and distract from important related issues. For example, by the year 2015 there may be millions more children in primary school than 15 years earlier, helping to achieve MDG 2; however, what is the *quality* of the education they receive, and does this education always lead to improved life outcomes for them?

Bond (2006) argues that the development of the MDGs has been led in a top-down fashion by countries and organisations whose policies directly compromise the well-being of the poor in much of the world, namely, the G8, World Bank, International Monetary Fund, World Trade Organization and developing country elites. If we look closely at some of these organisations, there are clear examples of a significant mismatch between rhetoric and reality with relation to their commitment to poverty alleviation. The IMF, for example, demands budget surpluses yet this conflicts with possibilities for social spending (Öniş and Şenses 2005). We can also consider the World Trade Organization's policies with respect to agriculture. As Torres and Momsen (2004) note, agriculture ideally should be able to compliment tourism. However the World Trade Organization has effectively undermined the agricultural sector in many countries by allowing dumping of food surpluses from protected western markets into developing country markets at prices lower than cost, and supporting the removal of trade barriers. This thus allows large agribusiness companies to dominate agricultural production in some areas while undermining small farmers, and prevents developing country governments from providing economic support to local farmers (Bond 2006).

Furthermore, Mowforth and Munt are concerned that no fundamental changes are being suggested under the MDGs, rather, neoliberal reform and economic growth are still the focus of development efforts:

> it is interesting to note that all the rhetoric about poverty reduction and elimination that has emanated from the supranational institutions in recent years has assumed that there will be and can be no change in the prevailing model of development. The point is not that the intentions to adjust policy are ill-inspired, but that they are contingent upon a system which has manifestly failed to date to deliver development to a majority of the world's population. (2009: 339)

Thus some authors feel that an emphasis on poverty reduction is a means of window dressing which may deflect criticism of the dominent neoliberal policies, when the orthodoxy on which the operations of many development-related organisations are based has barely changed: ' . . . one gets the strong impression that the Bretton Woods institutions are using the poverty issue as a pretext for broadening and deepening the neoliberal agenda' (Öniş and Şenses 2005: 280).

Nevertheless a number of agencies have joined the ranks of governments and international agencies all around the world in endorsing the MDGs: in fact, ESCAP, the Green Hotelier and the UNWTO all suggest ways in which the travel industry specifically can address the MDGs (see ESCAP 2007: 9–10, and Mowforth and Munt 2009: 339–341). Thus according to the UNWTO,

> For poor countries and small island states, tourism is the leading export—often the only sustainable growth sector of their economies and a catalyst for many related sectors. It can play a key role in the overall achievement of the Millennium Development Goals by 2015. (Francesco Frangialli, Secretary-General of the UNWTO, cited in Asia Travel Tips 2005)

It is important now to consider how the evolution of PPT is linked to this consensus on poverty.

THE EMERGENCE OF PRO-POOR TOURISM

The emergence of pro-poor tourism (PPT) is strongly associated with the development industry's 1990s-onwards global focus on poverty alleviation described previously.[7] Thus Mowforth and Munt (2009: 99) contend that PPT is 'Out to capture the emerging development consensus on poverty reduction by generating net benefits for the poor'. Considerations of poverty in relation to tourism were seen creeping into international initiatives in the 1990s as well as the World Tourism Organization's 1997 *Global Code of Ethics for Tourism,* which stated that local people should have an equitable share of the social, cultural and economic benefits of tourism. Similarly, support for alternative forms of tourism grew through the 1980s and 1990s, although this did not always prioritise the needs or interests of the poor: 'One reason that *pro-poor* tourism was initiated was that the "people" elements often fell to the periphery in responsible and sustainable tourism discussions, particularly within business' (Ashley and Haysom 2004: 2–3).

While the preceding explains how the general environment was conducive to the emergence of PPT in the late 1990s, it evolved specifically out of UK-sponsored research on sustainable livelihoods in southern Africa (see for example, Ashley and Roe 1998), and a comparative study of tourism, conservation and sustainability issues in protected areas of Indonesia, India and Zimbabwe (Goodwin et al. 1998). Tourism was identified as an industry which had considerable potential to improve the well-being of rural communities in some parts of the world, thus the UK's Department for International Development (DFID) together with the Department for Environment, Transport and the Regions commissioned a paper to be written on sustainable tourism and poverty elimination (Goodwin 1998). Goodwin cites this as the initial paper written on tourism and poverty elimination (personal communication 2009), however the concept of 'pro-poor tourism' was first used in a report commissioned by DFID in 1999 (Deloitte and Touche 1999).

The British delegation to the 1999 meeting of the UN Commission on Sustainable Development (CSD7) then used this information to get tourism as a means of poverty alleviation on the agenda. This was in line with the sentiments of the 1992 Rio conference, which had emphasised the need to consider both development and the environment when devising strategies for sustainable development. Thus it was felt there was a need to move beyond ensuring that tourism was environmentally friendly and instead to ensure 'that the "social" elements' were central (Ashley and Haysom 2006: 267). After CSD7, governments were urged to 'maximise the potential of tourism for eradicating poverty by developing appropriate strategies in cooperation with all major groups, indigenous and local communities' (IIED 2001: 41).

Following this, in 2000 the Overseas Development Institute (ODI) initiated a research project focused on analysing the theoretical basis of PPT and examining case studies of tourism in practice (Ashley et al. 2001). This project was conducted by the Pro-Poor Tourism Partnership, a collaboration of Harold Goodwin (International Centre for Responsible Tourism), Dilys Roe (International Institute for Environment and Development) and Caroline Ashley (ODI—Overseas Development Institute). Since then the PPT Partnership has been responsible for a wide range of studies on PPT, funded in the early years by DFID (see for example, Ashley and Roe 2002,

Roe et al. 2002) and, after DFID's priorities changed and their funding to PPT ceased, mainly by the ODI but also occasionally by others, such the Travel Foundation. One major programme the PPT Partnership engaged in was the 'PPT Pilots' programme in South Africa, which worked with a small number of private sector tourism enterprises to develop more pro-poor initiatives and linkages (e.g. procurement from small, locally-based enterprises) (PPT Partnership 2005a). The PPT Partnership has thus been extremely influential, with Ashley, Goodwin and Roe authoring many of the early reports on tourism as a tool for poverty alleviation and its website providing a clearing house for research and other information related to PPT.[8] While other agencies and individuals have since put their own spin on PPT, it is the PPT Partnership that really defined and drew attention to this approach to tourism.

Members of the PPT Partnership stress that PPT is not a product; it is an *approach* to tourism which seeks to bring social, environmental and cultural benefits to the poor in addition to economic benefits. PPT does *not* aim to expand the size of the sector, but to 'unlock opportunities for the poor within tourism, at all levels and scales of operation' (PPT Partnership 2005b: 1). This is interesting, as it does not focus on growth of tourism, and it does not focus just on the community level. As noted in Chapter 1, the people behind the PPT Partnership firmly believe that it is important to bring about changes in mainstream tourism, including challenging corporations to change the way they operate, rather than to establish numerous community-run bungalow ventures with dubious business prospects. They assert that a wide range of stakeholders, from local entrepreneurs to government officials and international tour companies, will need to make concerted efforts if poverty reduction is to occur:

> Pro-Poor Tourism is about changing the distribution of benefits from tourism in favour of poor people. It is not a specific product. It is not the same as ecotourism or community-based tourism, nor is it limited to these niches. Any kind of tourism can be made pro-poor. PPT can be applied at different levels, at the enterprise, destination or country level. (Pro-Poor Tourism Partnership 2005a: 1)

Associates of the PPT Partnership have a broad, holistic notion of poverty alleviation which is inspired at least in part by alternative development theory. For example, as indicated in Table 1.1 in Chapter 1, they draw attention to the value of a number of non-economic benefits of PPT such as the development of new skills, better access to education and healthcare, and infrastructural improvements in terms of access to potable water and improved roads or transport. They also explain how intangible benefits of tourism can make a significant difference to the lives of the poor, including greater opportunities for communication with the outside world and improved access to information, better knowledge of market opportunities, strengthening of community institutions, and enhanced pride in one's culture and the skills and knowledge which exist within the community (Ashley and Roe 2002).

The next major player to take on board the idea of PPT was the World Tourism Organization, which, together with UNCTAD, initiated its ST-EP programme ('Sustainable Tourism—Eliminating Poverty') at the World Summit on Sustainable Development in Johannesburg in 2002. The World Tourism Organization had been established as an organ of the United Nations in 1975 with the understanding that tourism could make a major contribution to development, but it was not until 2003 that it was formally made a United Nations agency (UNWTO).[9]

ST-EP has four key components, which will be discussed further in Chapter 7: capacity-building seminars, research and publications, ST-EP projects supporting sustainable tourism, and dissemination of information and awareness-raising. A $5 million donation from the government of the Republic of Korea in 2003 led to the ST-EP Foundation being based in this country. The UNWTO has since established a Trust Fund for ST-EP which aims to attract funds from multiple donors and to use these funds for technical assistance towards tourism development that aims to reduce poverty. SNV, the Netherlands development organisation, was the initial founder, contributing €2 million for 2005 and 2006, while the Italian government provided a smaller contribution for 2005 (PPT Partnership 2005a).

A review of PPT practices in 2006 revealed seven key strategies that could directly enhance the well-being of the poor:

- Employment of the poor in tourism enterprises
- Supply of goods and services to tourism enterprises by the poor or by enterprises employing the poor
- Direct sales of goods and services to visitors by the poor (informal economy)
- Establishment and running of tourism enterprises by the poor, e.g. micro, small and medium-sized enterprises or community-based enterprises
- Tax or levy on tourism income or profits with proceeds benefiting the poor
- Voluntary giving/support by tourism enterprises and tourists
- Investment in infrastructure stimulated by tourism also benefiting the poor in the locality (UNWTO 2006a)

Harrison, reflecting on the roles of donors, academics and others in the field prior to PPT emerging in the late 1990s, notes:

Clearly, the focus on tourism as an alleviator of poverty is not new. . . . Nevertheless, specifically PPT approaches . . . seem to have led to a popular, simple, sharper and more appealing moral focus on the links poorer residents in destinations have with tourism enterprises. (2008: 855)

Indeed, Brown and Hall (2008: 842) suggest that the concept of PPT emerged ' . . . perhaps as a way of demonstrating that tourism need not be as inequitable as it often appears'. This may be why it has become seemingly more acceptable for a range of other development agencies to put tourism directly on their agendas, when in the past they were concerned that this sector was best left to private business. Agencies that have demonstrated a commitment to PPT include: donors (e.g. German agency GTZ and the Danish agency DANIDA); tourism industry organisations (e.g. Pacific and Asia Travel Association—PATA); NGOs (e.g. IUCN—the World Conservation Union); research centres/universities (e.g. the Cooperative Research Centre for Sustainable Tourism in Australia, Asian Institute of Technology in Bangkok, George Washington University and London Metropolitan University); and multilateral organisations (e.g. the Asian Development Bank). Other UN agencies supporting poverty alleviation through tourism include the UNDP, UNCTAD, ESCAP and UNEP.

Table 2.2 lists a range of initiatives regarding tourism as tool for poverty alleviation. The UNWTO and others have adopted their own term for PPT. Others vary in terms of what they focus upon: some focus more on tourism as a fairly traded activity emphasising both awareness of consumers and a fair deal for tourist service providers (Fair Trade in Tourism; Fair Trade in Tourism South Africa); others see it as a means to overcome oppression of disadvantaged groups (Empo-Tourism); and others again seem to emphasise combining development opportunities for the poor with environmental and business sustainability (ST-EP, Anti-Poverty Tourism and Tourism Against Poverty). Some of the organisations behind these initiatives will be examined in more details in later chapters.

The focus for the remainder of this chapter, however, will be to unpack what theoretical perspectives may be informing those agencies which have a stated commitment to using tourism as a tool for poverty alleviation.

DIVERGENT PERSPECTIVES ON THE TOURISM-POVERTY RELATIONSHIP

Clearly PPT has, in a relatively short period of time, attracted attention from a wide range of institutions including those in the public, private and civil society sectors. In this context it is wise to consider motivations behind the push for pro-poor tourism: for example, is this coming more from organisations seeking to improve the image of the tourism sector and provide additional impetus for the growth of the sector in the face of criticism of its ill effects, or from agencies that genuinely want a redistribution of the benefits of tourism to improve the well-being of the poor? In order

Table 2.2   Selection of Initiatives Linking Tourism and Poverty Alleviation

Initiatives Linking Tourism and Poverty Alleviation	Organisations
PPT (Pro-Poor Tourism)	The foremost driver of PPT is the PPT Partnership, which involves three organisations: the Overseas Development Institute (UK), the International Institute for Environment and Development (London) and the International Centre for Responsible Tourism (Leeds Metropolitan University). They conduct research on ways in which tourism can bring benefits to the poor. The PPT Partnership has a website which provides a repository of information on PPT, and it makes its studies all available here. It stresses that PPT is an approach to tourism, not a product, and that PPT can be enacted by a wide range of agencies at a wide range of scales, from the local to national and international initiatives.
ST-EP (Sustainable Tourism – Eliminating Poverty)	Launched in 2002 by the World Tourism Organization and UNCTAD and funds both research and development projects that link tourism and poverty alleviation.
Tourism Against Poverty (TAP)	International Council of Tourism Partners – this organisation of travel industry providers promotes socially responsible and sustainable travel, supports the Millennium Development Goals and showcases tourism 'best practice' on its website.
APT (Anti-Poverty Tourism)	Devised by Zhao and Ritchie (2007) as a term which refers to any form of tourism development which has poverty alleviation as a central objective. These authors identify three themes to APT: destination competitiveness, destination sustainability and local participation.
Fair Trade in Tourism	A UK partnership of Tourism Concern, Voluntary Service Overseas and the University of North London which promotes ethical trading practices by facilitating the exchange of ideas between tour operators, tourists and destination communities.
Fair Trade in Tourism South Africa	FTTSA is currently the most active national movement to support fair trade in tourism. It certifies tourism businesses and thus provides a guarantee for consumers regarding a business's ethics.

Continued

Table 2.2   Continued

Empo-tourism	Term coined in South Africa during the development of Spatial Development Initiatives (see Koch et al. 1998) but not in current usage. It centres on using tourism to facilitate empowerment and to bring economic benefits to impoverished South Africans who were discriminated against under apartheid (Ashley and Roe 2002: 63).

to explore the thinking behind the wave of interest by diverse agencies in PPT, this section discusses ways in which the relationship between tourism and poverty alleviation has been conceptualised over time.[10] Table 2.3 summarises the ideas to be discussed, focusing on several theoretical approaches: liberal, neoliberal, critical, alternative development and post-development. These approaches have, to varying degrees, contributed to the growth of interest in PPT.

Liberal Perspectives

The early liberal approach to tourism is epitomised by the logic of modernisation theory, which informed development practice particularly from the 1950s through to the 1970s. From this perspective tourism is regarded as 'a catalyst for modernization, economic development and prosperity in emerging nations in the third world' (Williams 1998: 1), an industry which generates jobs and foreign exchange, while also bringing beneficial socio-cultural change in terms of demonstrating 'modern' ways of life to people living in traditional cultures. A basic premise of this approach was that people's traditional ways of life contributed to their poverty. This approach thus endorses tourism as a means of bringing development to poorer countries and as such it accords with what Jafari (2001: 29–30), in his analysis of scholarly work that has dominated thinking on tourism at different stages, calls the 'advocacy platform'.

Critical Perspectives

When it became clear that economic growth often did not 'trickle-down' to benefit the poor, there was a backlash against liberal development thought from scholars inspired by dependency and political economy theory. Adopting explicitly critical perspectives, these scholars suggest that the prospects for international tourism to erode inequalities between people in different parts of the world are slim, and that in fact tourism in many cases exploits, highlights and entrenches these differences (Britton 1982; Brohman 1996). They also stress the harmful socio-cultural and environmental impacts of tourism. Numerous studies have made these points, with texts from the

1970s which signified a major shift in thinking away from the idea that tourism automatically led to poverty alleviation (e.g. de Kadt 1979; Nash 1977; Smith 1977), through to contemporary studies still drawing heavily on dependency theory (e.g. Akama 2004; Manyara and Jones 2007; Mbaiwa 2005; Weaver 1999).

Postcolonial writers also contribute to this critical stance on tourism in developing countries, demonstrating how contemporary tourism is anchored in colonial and postcolonial relationships, demonstrating how neocolonial ideas still resonate in tourism marketing, and questioning, for example, the power relations implicit in images and text used to promote tourism (Akama 2004; Hall and Tucker 2004). They thus note that certain places and peoples have appeal because they are seen as 'unspoilt' to the middle and upper classes of the west and the emerging economies (Jaakson 2004; Wels 2004). 'Unspoilt', however, often equates with poverty: while resorts and luxury lodges have every convenience, those living in the 'picturesque' villages nearby may lack basic amenities such as access to clean drinking water and sanitation services, and health facilities and schools may only be available to those who can afford transportation and fees. Other tourists are attracted to the 'cheap' holiday which is possible in poorer countries, overlooking the fact that their 'great deal' is due to the low price of labour and lack of unionisation and labour rights.

The critical perspectives of tourism concur with what Jafari (2001: 29–30) refers to as the 'cautionary platform', a particular body of tourism scholarship which proclaims that tourism has a wide range of negative impacts, including cultural commodification, social disruption and environmental degradation. In addition, it is argued, the economic benefits of tourism are minimised because foreign companies, which dominate many developing countries, repatriate their profits.

Critical perspectives may have driven people to look to new forms of tourism development that are less harmful, but they have not played a very strong role in the actual development of PPT initiatives, perhaps due to the fact that they focus on critique. As Oppermann (1993) observed, such perspectives tend to stop short of considering effective strategies whereby developing countries could work to secure greater benefits of tourism development. However not all writers inspired by dependency and postcolonial theory are philosophically opposed to tourism. Useful contributions have been made by writers who could be said to take a 'post-dependency' approach which recognises that international tourism can bring developmental benefits when there is strong, state-led tourism development which prioritises national interests (Clancy 1999; Potter 1993; Telfer 2002) (e.g. see case studies on Bhutan and Cuba in Chapter 6). For example, the state could focus on building up the national economy prior to planned penetration of international tourists, and through this they could enhance domestic services and infrastructure, leading to greater economic self-reliance (de Kadt 1979; Simms 2005: 47). The state could also promote domestic tourism both in respect of the rights of citizens to leisure time whereby they can enjoy their own country's attractions, and building nationalistic sentiments (Ghimire 2001; Scheyvens 2007b).

Alternative Perspectives

While acknowledging the concerns of those coming from a critical perspective, some scholars have suggested that tourism can contribute to development if it is approached in an alternative way (Smith and Eadington 1992). Indicative of early publications in this field was Dernoi's (1981) 'Alternative tourism: towards a new style in North-South relations'. Support for alternative tourism was 'driven by "a sense of outrage" over the misuse of nature, the costs of materialism and the loss of culture' in tourism destinations' (de Kadt 1990: abstract).

The alternative approaches to tourism as a means of development and poverty alleviation are informed by a number of bodies of thinking. Alternative development perspectives centre on grassroots development and embrace ideas on participation, equity, gender-sensitivity and empowerment (Telfer 2002). Zhao and Richie (2007) specify empowerment as a key condition for tourism to be able to contribute to poverty alleviation as it aims to enhance and strengthen people's participation in political processes and local decision-making, as well as removing the barriers that work against the poor and building assets which allow them to engage effectively in markets. Timothy (2007: 203) shows how decentralising decision-making power by empowering 'people locally on the ground' can lead to more effective development outcomes. Cole (2006) and Sofield (2003) also apply empowerment to their analysis of tourism and development, arguing that it is a key to achieving sustainable tourism. Certainly alternative development strategies have been inspired by thinking on sustainable development since people and poverty, not just the environment, have become central to sustainable development discourse (Neto 2003), as evidenced by discussions at the 2002 World Summit on Sustainable Development in Johannesburg. As noted earlier, a sustainable livelihoods perspective has influenced PPT in that tourism is seen as another means of diversifying the livelihood options of the poor.

Incorporating the preceding ideas, alternative approaches to tourism generally support small-scale or locally-based tourism initiatives which attempt to bring benefits to poorer communities, minimise harm to the environment and to local communities, and aim to build good relationships between 'hosts' and 'guests' (Krippendorf 1987). They also support the notion that local residents should play an active role in tourism planning and decision-making forums (Murphy 1985), and support tourism that is fair, just and equitable (Scheyvens 2002). This thinking accords with Jafari's notion of the 'Adaptancy Platform' (2001: 31), whereby community-focused forms of tourism are proposed as an alternative to the excesses of mainstream tourism. Some of the alternative forms of tourism proposed include 'soft tourism', 'green tourism' (Dann 2002), 'altruistic tourism' (Singh 2002), 'volunteer tourism' (Wearing 2001), and 'justice tourism' (Scheyvens 2002).

Alternative development advocates have provided a strong critique of forms of tourism dominated by outside interests and offered some viable alternative ideas on tourism development which is more in line with local interests. They have been less effective, however, in tackling the need for change in the most important market, mass tourism. As Jafari (2001) notes, while alternative forms of tourism are well-intentioned, they account for only a small proportion of the total tourism product. For pro-poor tourism to be successful, it must help to transform mainstream tourism as well.

Endorsement of alternative tourism is coupled with an assumption that communities will not want to pursue mass tourism (De Kadt 1992; Jafari 2001), when in practice this can be seen as more manageable and profitable and less invasive than alternative forms of tourism (Butler 1990; Thomlinson and Getz 1996). Thus, argues Burns,

> Exhortations to "leave only footprints" . . . carry an ironic and unintentional truth because footprints with no dollars attached do little to develop the industry to a level of critical mass that can supply large-scale employment and a reliable stream of tax revenues to be used to implement beneficial government policies including health, education, and welfare. (2004: 25)

Furthermore, alternative forms of tourism can ' . . . deflect attention away from the more specific question of how far tourism *does* alleviate poverty' (Harrison 2008: 853). In this respect we need to understand the constraints to poorer people participating in tourism. Typically they lack information, resources, skills and power in relation to other stakeholders in the tourism process, thus they are vulnerable to exploitation (McLaren 1998). It is not sufficient to be able to cite a few cases whereby tourism has resulted in positive impacts on a community: alleviating poverty is a greater challenge altogether.[11]

While the alternative perspectives thus prioritise local interests of resident communities, the neoliberal perspectives discussed next tend to prioritise global interests of corporations and large development agencies, and sometimes government interests at the national level.

Neoliberal Perspectives

The liberal approach discussed earlier was followed, from the late 1970s onwards, by a surge of support for neoliberalism. This is the approach closely aligned with the poverty agenda that became so popular in the development community in the 1990s (Storey et al. 2005). While it certainly sounds honourable that donors are seeking to make poverty alleviation central to every aspect of their work, when approached from a neoliberal perspective, poverty alleviation ' . . . is considerably circumscribed in its premise of economic growth as the foundation of development' (Mowforth and Munt 2003: 34). Policies which have been introduced under neoliberalism, including efforts to privatise basic services such as electricity and water, or to individualise ownership of communally held resources, can be seen as contrary to the interests of the poor in many circumstances. Neoliberalism stresses the importance of economic rationalism and efficiency, market liberalisation, and a small role for the state, whose institutions are seen as interfering with free market processes (Öniş and Şenses 2005). It was recognised, however, that due to the failure of structural adjustment programmes in the 1980s, targeting of the poor and some form of social safety net or social protection was needed (Schilcher 2007a). Such policies, packaged together and based on an 'unquestioning belief in the benefits of the free market', came to be known as the 'Washington Consensus' on poverty alleviation (Hart 2001: 286),[12] or, as it was simply referred to earlier in this chapter, as the poverty consensus. Key financial institutions such as the World Bank and IMF were foremost among advocates of such neoliberal thinking, as it rose to the fore in the face of the indebtedness of many developing countries.

International tourism was seen to accord nicely with a strategy of encouraging indebted countries to grow the economy and trade their way out of poverty (Brohman 1996):

> The tourism industry per se fits very well in such a growth-focused neoliberal approach. . . . tourism has been proven to accelerate economic growth particularly in countries and regions deprived of alternative means of economic development . . . [and] tourism is a direct beneficiary of neoliberalism, as it tends to flourish in an open economic environment that facilitates the free movement of capital, labour and consumers. (Schilcher 2007a: 58)

This connection applies regardless of whether one is referring to large, vertically integrated, multinational hotel chains, or small-scale community or ecotourism businesses, as the latter ' . . . may draw previously self-sufficient communities into the global economic system' (Schilcher 2007a: 59).

But what of a pro-poor tourism approach? Surely that is different and may not be so well aligned with the growth rather than redistribution ethos of neoliberalism. In practice, PPT does not seek to disconnect from a capitalist framework, rather, ' . . . strategies derived from a PPT perspective are formulated to incorporate the poor into capitalist markets by increasing the employment and entrepreneurial opportunities, and more collective benefits, available to them' (Harrison 2008: 855). Such comments lead Hall and Brown to seriously question the potential of PPT: 'does PPT simply offer another route by which economic imperialism, through tourism, may extend its tentacles, or is it an appropriately liberating and remunerative option?' (2006: 13).

A neoliberal agenda dictates that governments should take a 'hands-off' approach to the economy, instead implementing an 'enabling environment' in which market-led growth can occur. The market, however, bows to the interests of consumers, not to the interests of the poor; thus if governments fail to 'interfere' by setting in place appropriate policies, restrictions, and so forth, the poor will once again miss out on the benefits of development. For example, an outward-oriented approach whereby state action is heavily influenced by the neoliberal agendas of multilateral institutions to whom they are indebted, has meant government decisions sometimes conflict with the interests of local communities (Carbone 2005). With regards to tourism planning, this can mean that tax breaks are given to foreign investors developing large resorts, while small-scale local entrepreneurs find it difficult to access credit or training needed to improve their enterprises. In Fiji, for example, developers of resorts worth over F$10 million have waivers for corporate tax on profits for 10 to 20 years, yet these resorts still source most of their food inputs from overseas because of a lack of support for local farmers to access this lucrative market (Author's fieldwork, June 2009). Tourist resorts worldwide rely on a lot of branded international food products, from breakfast cereals through to dairy products and even in places where abundant local produce is grown (see Photo 2.1) they may import more standardised fruit and vegetables from abroad.

Thus neoliberal orthodoxy was challenged later in the 1990s as it became clear that inequalities between developed and developing world economies were growing. Liberalisation of economies did not automatically lead to enhanced economic growth, rather, it often left a vacuum in terms of the state's capacity to manage development and thus corruption increased (Öniş and Şenses 2005). Meanwhile studies revealed that the 'miracle' of growth in certain East Asian economies was spurred, in part, by interventionist state strategies and protection of infant industries. Thus there is now talk of a 'new poverty agenda',[13] supported by the major financial institutions which have shown willingness to respond to some critiques of global neoliberalism (Hart 2001; Öniş and Şenses 2005; Storey et al. 2005). The new poverty agenda is characterised by an emphasis on enhancing the role of the state, rather than letting markets rule unimpeded, an appreciation of the importance of strong institutions, support for democratic governance, and a move to more effectively target the poor and vulnerable (Öniş and Şenses 2005: 273–275). With relation to tourism, we see this 'new poverty agenda' reflected in renewed interest in the role of the state in regulating tourism development and facilitating linkages between the private sector and local communities (Sofield 2003).

Photo 2.1 Fijian woman wearing a resort branded *lavalava* returns home after harvesting produce from her gardens: it is very difficult for smallholder farmers to market their produce to tourist resorts.
Source: Author

While neoliberal perspectives have been pushed by multilateral agencies and adopted by many donors and governments of developing countries, the post-development perspectives discussed next have so far mainly been advanced by researchers and civil society activists.

Post-Development Perspectives

Post-development thinking embraces postmodernist, postcolonialist and post-structuralist thought.[14] While advocates of these perspectives often eschew the labels associated with them, all question that 'development' is an inherently 'good' project, they contest the value of grand theories of development that suggest single ways of understanding the world, and all share an interest in power relations: 'Much post development work involves analysing and critiquing the knowledges, languages and meanings within development industries, particularly focusing on how they may serve to shape or perpetuate power relations' (Beban-France and Brooks 2008: 77). Some are particularly interested in how people and places are socially constructed for tourism (e.g. Pritchard and Morgan 2000), and in issues of representation, identity-formation, and ideology (e.g. Hutnyk 1996). This is explained further in Chapter 4, which discusses ways in which poverty itself has become a drawcard for tourism.

Those influenced by post-development thought tend to reject reductionist views of the world which see tourism as either a force of good or evil. Many tourism researchers still essentialise identity categories and use power binaries to frame their analysis, suggesting for example that foreign investors are 'exploitative' while local communities work together for the good of all. However, the reality is far more complex. An example of this is the relationship between resorts in Fiji and nearby communities, which will be explored in Chapter 5. There are also ways in which traditionally exploited groups, such as indigenous peoples, are gaining greater power due in part to their human rights being supported in law. Thus in Namibia the government devolved tenure rights to communities so they can make decisions regarding their resources and have market power. Now communities which establish conservancies get conditional use of wildlife, and some have developed effective tourism enterprises based on this right (ODI 2000: 28).

Post-development views appear to accord with Jafari's fourth and final platform of scholarly knowledge on tourism, the knowledge-based platform (2001: 31–32). Researchers coming from this perspective are interested in a holistic view of the structures and functions of the tourism industry, rather than focusing on 'impacts' (like the advocacy and cautionary platforms) or on alternative forms of tourism, as occurs under the adaptancy platform. It is thus suggested that we need detailed studies of systems, processes, places and interactions between people, in order to understand how culture and power influence the actions of tourism stakeholders (Cheong and Miller 2000; Davis 2001). Teo (2003: 460), commenting on the global system as a whole, argues that it should be conceived as a 'multi-layered and intricate web of structures, agents and interactions that interweaves external conditions with local ones in both cooperative as well as competitive ways'. In this way we can consider how communities engage in tourism in ways that reflect their interests as well as those of other tourism stakeholders.

They are not simply victims of a destructive global industry, rather, they have power to respond to tourism, adapt it, embrace it or reject it. Malam (2005) demonstrates this clearly in her research on the microgeographies of power and identity in Koh Phangan, Thailand, as played out in relationships between young Thai male workers and young western female backpackers. Rather than positing the young men as less powerful actors in their romantic/sexual relationships with the backpacker women, Malam clearly articulates how the power balance varies over time and space, and that it is predicated by axes of education, gender, culture and economics. Thai male bar and bungalow workers have used the space of the beach bar to exert their masculinity even though they are effectively a poorly paid group of migrant workers.

Post-development thus encourages us to develop a nuanced understanding of the links between tourism and poverty reduction: tourism is neither a panacea nor the root of all problems for developing countries. As noted by both Jafari (2001) and Sofield (2003), tourism is a system involving multiple levels and dimensions, and a wide range of actors, from the private and public sectors and civil society. This then provides the opportunity for tourism to be directed by social and environmental motives, rather than just neoliberal economic motives (Wearing et al. 2005), and to be more centred on the needs of the poor. Wearing et al. (2005) thus assert the need for a 'decommodified research paradigm' in tourism that is not directed by neoliberal thinking, while Higgins-Desbiolles (2006) pushes the notion that tourism is best understood as a social force, as opposed to neoliberal discourse which commonly presents tourism as an 'industry':

> Tourism is in fact a powerful social force that can achieve many important ends when its capacities are unfettered from the market fundamentalism of neoliberalism and instead are harnessed to meet human development imperatives and the wider public good. (Higgins-Desbiolles 2006: 1192)

Inspired by the writing of Turner and Ash (1975), Higgins-Desbiolles asserts that mass tourism, as first promulgated by Thomas Cook's tours, was indeed tourism for the masses but not just to achieve business goals. Rather, Cook wanted to offer the working class 'more wholesome leisure activities' (e.g. an alternative to hard drinking) and he also subsidised politically motivated trips, such as bringing 1500–1600 people to support a demonstration of working men in Paris (Higgins-Desbiolles 2006: 1193).

When unshackled from its connection to 'industry', it is certainly easier to appreciate the wide range of ways in which tourism can be connected to development opportunities well beyond the economic, such as advancing political aims, encouraging understanding across cultures, improving the well-being of both visitors and those visited, contributing to an awareness of global citizenship, and promoting other social and environmental goals.

Another important contribution of post-development is its recognition of the value of social movements and alternative voices: ' . . . processes of social mobilization become central to any discussion of chronic poverty because they are vehicles through which such relationships are argued over in society and potentially changed' (Bebbington 2007: 793). As argued by Storey et al. (2005), who criticise the existence of a 'poverty consensus' among donors, there should be vigorous debate among both scholars and practitioners concerning questions of poverty. It is thus imperative that we hear the debates about tourism development, the critical voices, especially from local residents, environmental groups and people's organisations in areas most affected by tourism development, but also by international labour organisations, NGOs, or lobby groups. Tourism Concern's work in advocacy, such as their campaign against travel to Myanmar related to known human rights abuses in that country, can be seen as a post-development expression. This is in line with Bond's (2006) argument that advocates of poverty reduction should pay attention to the pleas of a wide range of justice and anti-poverty movements around the globe, supporting 'organic' social struggles such as resistance of communities to certain developments (e.g. golf courses, tourist resorts), anti-debt movements and labour strikes. Under post-development approaches we are urged to work with 'an active civil society' to identify appropriate paths for tourism development (Burns 2004: 25).

Furthermore, post-development perspectives encourage us to examine the culture of powerful development institutions, and to unpack the ways in which this influences their approach to development, their practices and their relationships with 'partners' (Radcliffe 2006). This was evident in Schilcher's (2007b) study of supranational organisations involved in the governance of tourism, which she examined through a case study of the European Union's influence on tourism development in the Pacific. Her research showed that the European Union's approach was influenced by member countries' colonial relationships with Pacific Island states, and that at every level of interaction the European Union sought to play the dominant role and to expand its own interests. In Samoa, the policy influence of the European Union was likely to lead to less local ownership and control over the industry (ibid). It would be interesting to see further in-depth studies of the ways in which organisations such as the UNWTO, WTTC and others approach tourism as a tool for poverty alleviation.

The theoretical perspectives discussed above are summarised in Table 2.3. They have all, in various ways, informed the chapters to come in this book.

Another way of understanding the forces motivating advocates of PPT is represented in Figure 2.2. This figure indicates how agencies may be influenced to varying degrees by political, economic and social ideologies when deciding to support tourism as a means of alleviating poverty. For example, tourism industry organisations—to be discussed in Chapter 5—are more likely to be driven by neoliberal logic regarding benefits of the expansion of tourism for developing country economies, so they are located at the

Table 2.3 Theoretical Perspectives on the Relationship between Tourism and Poverty

Liberal/neo-liberal	Critical	Alternative Development	Post-Development
1950s–1960s · Tourism can contribute to modernisation through economic growth, employment generation and the exchange of ideas; benefits will trickle down to the poor. 1980s onwards · Tourism offers a way out of indebtedness: 'trade your way out of poverty'. It encourages foreign investment and private sector development while providing employment and generating foreign exchange. Late 1990s onwards · Tourism is promoted hand-in-hand with free trade, democratisation and anti-poverty agendas. · Investment in tourism in developing countries gives foreign companies a presence in major or growing markets. · Poverty Reduction Strategy Papers identify tourism as an economic sector that can reduce poverty. Public–private partnerships encouraged. · Tourism is seen as a means of helping to overcome the poverty and inequality which can breed terrorism. · 'New poverty agenda' sees the state as having a critical role in providing an 'enabling environment' to encourage growth of tourism, and to more effectively target poorer groups in society.	1970s–1980s · Tourism is associated with enclave development, dependence on foreign capital and expertise, growing social and economic disparities, and repatriation of profits. It can undermine local cultures, social networks and traditional livelihoods, e.g. when people are resettled so national parks can be created. Tourism is often neocolonial in nature, with dark-skinned 'natives' serving up an 'exotic' experience for pale-skinned visitors. 1990s onwards · Anti-globalisation lobby sees tourism as a means of advancing the forces of capitalism into more remote places and cultures. · Postcolonial writers comment on the allure of the 'other'— poverty attracts tourists as poor places are associated with 'authentic' experiences of culture and nature. Strong class differences between 'hosts' and 'guests' are noted.	Late 1970s onwards · Alternative forms of tourism that are small-scale, involve education of tourists and more local control over tourism, are seen as worthy of promotion,. e.g. justice tours, conservation tours. 1980s onwards · The 'green agenda' of the 1980s and the UN Summit in Rio in 1992 lead to renewed emphasis on the environment including ecological and social sustainability. Ecotourism comes to the fore. 1990s onwards · Tourism offers poor communities a means of diversifying their livelihood options. · Community-based tourism seen as particularly worthy. · Communities can actively participate in tourism and be empowered through their experiences.	1990s onwards · Rejects reductionist thinking: tourism is neither 'good' nor 'bad'. Stresses the need to take a holistic view which sees tourism as a complex system in which local people can exert agency/power: they may be able to resist, subvert, manipulate or transform tourism to their own benefit. · Rights-based approaches can ensure greater resources and power for traditionally disadvantaged groups. · Acknowledges importance of dissenting viewpoints. · Some support a more active role for the state in directing development towards the interests of the people.

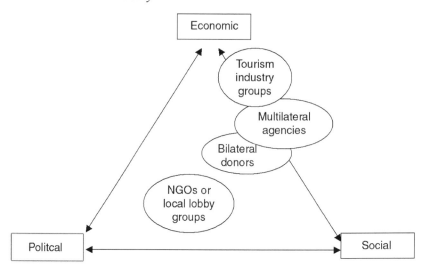

Figure 2.2   Forces motivating advocates of tourism as a tool for poverty alleviation.

economic apex of the triangle. We should not, therefore, confuse any proclamations of a commitment from tourism industry associations such as WTTC to assist the poor with a genuine concern for the social upliftment and political empowerment of poorer peoples. Multilateral and bilateral development agencies such as the ADB, SNV, NZAID and GTZ, however, whose work will be discussed in Chapter 7, are shown as attempting (to varying degrees) to balance an interest in social and economic well-being of the poor, thus they are located between these two corners of the triangle. Meanwhile, only NGOs and local lobby groups are identified as being significantly influenced by a political agenda. Examples include the tourism watchdog organisation Tourism Concern, which has campaigned on the rights of tourism sector employees, and Equations in India, which empowers local communities to monitor large-scale tourism development.

CONCLUSION

This chapter provided a thorough discussion of poverty, showing it to be a complex, multidimensional phenomenon which thus needs to be addressed using well-conceptualised, context-specific strategies that deal with people's social, economic and political realities. Poverty will never be solved by simply transferring economic resources from richer to poorer states. Indeed, the figures show that the developing countries consistently send more money to western countries in the form of debt repayments than they receive in the form of aid.[15] Along with a focus on economic benefits through offering alternative livelihood strategies, PPT should also assist the poor to lead dignified lives: that is, to be respected members of their community rather than being ashamed of their means of earning a livelihood, and to be able to contribute to and participate in family and other social group events. Furthermore, effective PPT strategies should aim to build up the capabilities of the poor and facilitate their empowerment, and it should assist them to secure their rights and thus gain greater control over their lives. The solution to poverty requires nothing less than solid political commitment to prioritising the needs, rights, and well-being of the poor along with transformation of inequitable structures that constrain them.

There are systems and institutions in place that sustain poverty, locally and internationally. Global environmental, economic and security crises in recent years have highlighted the entrenched nature of poverty and inequality in our world: poverty remains despite the fact that most economies are growing. Those agencies supporting tourism as a tool for poverty alleviation cannot, therefore, do so lightly. If tourism is to make more than just a token contribution to poverty alleviation, it will have to tackle systems of inequality head-on. This may be very difficult when tourism is entrenched within a capitalist system that is often seen as being built on the backs of poorer classes. When this book considers the role of tourism in contributing to poverty alleviation, therefore, I will pay particular attention to those who have the power to make a difference: governments, large tourism companies, development agencies and tourism organisation bodies. They have to show political will if tourism is to make serious inroads in addressing critical poverty-related issues still facing our world.

Tourism is one of the world's largest industries, and there is definitely potential to direct more of its benefits to the poor. Whether PPT can deliver on its aims may depend on the approach driving advocates of PPT. We have seen in this chapter that theoretical approaches like neoliberalism focus almost exclusively on economic considerations, ignoring the multidimensional nature of poverty and sometimes undermining the power of developing country governments to act in ways which comprehensively promote their people's interests. Thus innovative approaches which engage with political and social challenges to inequality need to be adopted by proponents of PPT.

3   Tourism Entrenches Poverty

INTRODUCTION

Chapters 1 and 2 discussed the growth of interest in tourism as a tool for poverty alleviation, while also drawing attention to the theoretical underpinnings of pro-poor tourism. While many claims are now being made about the potential of tourism to deliver greater benefits to the poor, as noted in Chapter 1, there is a need for caution. Some advocates of tourism are also prone to exaggerate claims for what tourism can achieve. These claims extend well beyond rosy economic projections for tourism earnings, with some suggesting that tourism is a universal panacea for overcoming poverty, inequality and even conflict (see IIPT 2004). Thus Chapter 3 takes the discussion on tourism and poverty to another level, focusing on major critiques of tourism in developing countries that emerged in the 1970s and continue to this day. Table 2.3 labelled these the 'Critical Perspectives'. These critiques are multifaceted, coming from local activist groups formed to oppose the cultural erosion and social disruption they see occurring in the wake of major tourism developments, through to sociologists exposing the core-periphery relationships that have developed when foreign investors reap the majority of the rewards of investment in developing country tourism hotels and resorts.

The purpose of this chapter then is to raise awareness of barriers or constraints that need to be addressed if tourism is to be able to work more effectively in the interests of the poor. In addition, this chapter also explains that supporting alternative forms of tourism is not necessarily the best way to circumvent such negative impacts and bring more benefits to the poor. While Chapter 3's intention is to remind readers of the very real constraints which may impede tourism from contributing to poverty alleviation, it does not finish on a negative note. Rather, the chapter concludes by reflecting on all of the criticisms wielded at the tourism sector, noting that tourism is often incorrectly blamed for causing a wide range of problems. It is thus important that we provide more careful analysis when weighing up the merits of tourism against the potential harm it can cause.

The overall tone of the book in the remaining chapters will be positive, however. Note that Chapters 5, 6 and 7, in particular, will focus more on tourism's actual and potential contributions to poverty alleviation.

CRITICAL PERSPECTIVES ON TOURISM

In the 1970s and 1980s, after many years of tourism being put forward as a panacea for underdevelopment and being pursued with a passion by numerous governments, the industry started to face heavy criticisms from a wide range of observers. As noted in Chapter 2, these critics argued that tourism was more likely to exploit developing country peoples and environments and deepen inequalities rather than alleviating poverty. There was then a tangible shift in thinking about tourism as a tool for economic growth at this time: ' ... an earlier simple faith in the merits of economic growth as such has given way to questions about the balance of that growth and the distribution of material benefits' (de Kadt 1979: xi). The following discussion starts by tracing the early critiques that emerged from both social scientists and tourism monitoring and activist groups in a number of developing countries. It later moves on to the anti-globalisation critiques of the 1990s.

Early Critiques of Tourism by Watchdog Groups and Academics

In Chapter 2 it was noted that post-development approaches pay particular attention to the voices of dissidents, such as activist groups which emerge to oppose certain forms of development. Such groups have played an important role in alerting wider audiences to problems associated with tourism in their home countries and communities. The Consumers' Association of Penang was a particularly active organisation in the 1980s, when its members raised concerns about the impacts of large-scale tourism development in Malaysia and the ways in which this often upset local social and cultural norms. To publicise their concerns, they published, *See the Third World While it Lasts: The Social and Environmental Impact of Tourism with Special Reference to Malaysia* (Hong 1985). This book criticises, among other things, tourists who take photos without asking and who 'invade' traditional long houses, and businesses which put pictures of partially dressed indigenous people on the front of postcards. Meanwhile, Ron O'Grady wrote, *Third World Stopover: The Tourism Debate* in 1981 on behalf of the World Council of Churches. His book sought to temper enthusiasm for this growth with concern for the social, economic and environmental consequences of tourism. A year later the Ecumenical Coalition on Third World Tourism (ECTWT) was formed, aiming to raise awareness about tourism issues and to stimulate debate about how tourism can become more equitable. Thus they initiated a number of conferences and reports related to issues such as sex tourism and implications of the spread of golf tourism, and sponsored publication of the book, *Alternative Tourism* (Holden 1984).

Much lobbying of the tourism industry and governments was been carried out by NGOs specifically concerned with sex tourism, including the Asian Women's Association of Tokyo, End Child Prostitution in Asian Tourism (ECPAT) in Thailand, and the Coalition on Child Prostitution and Tourism. They effectively exposed the global market for sex which saw westerners exploiting the cheaper sex options in an 'exotic' destination where they could be more anonymous than at home. This work has led to changes in legislation in a number of western countries so they can now prosecute citizens for engaging in illegal sexual activities abroad, particularly sex with minors.

Similar concerns about the social and cultural impacts of tourism were also raised by academics. In 1978 the anthropologists had their say in the edited collection by Valene Smith, *Hosts and Guests: The Anthropology of Tourism*. The following year, Emmanuel de Kadt made an enduring impression with his oft-quoted book, *Tourism: Passport to Development?* (1979) which looked both at the potential of tourism to bring development and at concerns about the negative impacts of tourism, particularly on vulnerable peoples. Accordingly to Harrison (2008: 853), de Kadt's critique is ' . . . as valued now as three decades ago'. The concerns of the early tourism academics, as well as others who have most likely been inspired by them but have written more recently, are explored further in the sections to follow.

A number of social and cultural problems thus came to be associated with tourism in the developing countries (Harrison 1992), including denigration of important spiritual or cultural sites by tourists, drug abuse, crime and prostitution among the local population in destination areas, and a rapid undermining of the values and norms of societies in the destination area (de Kadt 1979). Similarly, serious concerns were raised about the pressure of rapid tourism development on unique ecosystems, and problems associated with the inadequate disposal of waste from tourists. Perhaps the major concern raised at this time was economic disparities in the spread of benefits from tourism. It was found that many of the benefits of tourism accrued to foreign investors and multinational corporations, while local benefits were cornered by a minority of elites (Britton 1982). Some thus suggested that tourism in developing countries was a form of neo-colonialism.

Tourism as a Form of Neo-colonialism

Krippendorf (1987) furthered the arguments against tourism by lending a political angle to debates which rested on economic dependency, claiming that tourism was colonialist in nature and that this undermined the autonomous decision-making power of local people. Momsen agreed:

> Tourism seeks consciously and specifically to capitalise on differences between places and when these include differences in levels of economic development then tourism becomes imbued with all the elements of

domination, exploitation and manipulation characteristic of co
ism. (1994: 106)

Such views were endorsed by activists within developing countries, such as
Rohan Seon who wrote the calypso song 'Alien'. This song expresses the outrage of St Lucian people over resort developers who buy up beautiful stretches
of coastline and then forbid Caribbean people from enjoying these beaches
unless they buy an expensive day pass. This led St Lucian people to question
the nature of such 'progress', as it was leading to alienation of land: 'Like an
alien/in we own land/I feel like a stranger' (cited in Pattullo 1996: 80–81).
Such criticisms emerged in the midst of concern about corporate greed, lack
of consideration for local benefits, and, not least, exclusion of local people:
'. . . there is the social and racial divide created when white-skinned tourists
are protected by armed hotel guards from dark-skinned locals, which leads
them to become demonised' (Farrington 1999: 11). As such, tourism was
seen as a new form of imperialism, just another way in which the West is
exploiting the physical and human resources of the developing countries.

Other writers who continued in this vein included Britton and Clarke
(1987), Lea (1988) and Harrison (1992), who suggested that developing
countries had been 'underdeveloped' because of the way in which they were
tied to western capitalist countries. Kenyan academic, John Akama, summarises these views nicely:

> the establishment and development of tourism in most Third World
> countries is usually externally oriented and controlled, and mainly
> responds to external market demands. In consequence, the nature of
> international tourism as a 'luxury and pleasure seeking industry' usu-
> ally entails rich tourists from the metropolis (mainly from developed
> Northern countries) visiting and coming to enjoy tourist attractions
> in the periphery (mainly the poor and resource scarce countries in the
> South). These forms of tourism development accentuate the economic
> structure of dependency on external market demand, and also lead to
> 'alien' development (i.e. the establishment of tourism resorts in Third
> World countries) to which local people cannot relate and respond, both
> socially and economically. (Akama 1999: 7–8)

Development of the 'core' capitalist countries was seen as occurring at the
expense of 'peripheral' developing country societies, which in turn contributed to enclave development, dependence on foreign capital and expertise,
and repatriation of profits.

Neo-colonialism can also be seen in the ways in which lower-end jobs
tend to go to local staff, while expatriate staff dominate management positions. Even where local people have a relatively high level of education, it
may be difficult for them to rise up to positions where they are managers,
or owners of their own enterprise: 'School trained people often end up in
the hospitality sector. It does give them hope—but not hope that people can

rise to the top and run a business in their own right' (Hassan Khan, Fiji Council of Social Services, 11 June 2009, personal communication).

Many of the criticisms of tourism were directed at leakages. [1] There is still plenty of evidence to support these views, which were inspired by dependency theory and political economy approaches. The direct loss of the economic benefits of tourism to a host country is particularly evident when individuals book their travel through Western travel agencies, use Western airlines, stay in accommodation that is part of a multinational hotel chain, and eat mainly imported food and drink. Potter (1993: 102) and Milne (1990, cited in Khan 1997: 989) claim that leakages of tourist spending back to western countries can be as high as 70 percent, while McCulloch et al. (2001) suggest it is between 55 and 75 percent. Meanwhile, Dieke (1993) asserts that in the early 1990s in the Gambia, leakages from charter operations reached 77 percent. Leakage of tourist dollars often occurs when multinational tourism companies follow centralised purchasing procedures which impede local managers from buying supplies locally (Brown 1998). Where transnational corporations dominate, they can exert considerable power over those supplying goods and services to tourism (Hall and Brown 2008). All-inclusive resorts exemplify this type of tourism, with international travel, domestic transfers, accommodation, meals and entertainment on site, all included in the price of a package holiday. Such deals may certainly bring more tourists to a destination but this does not necessarily contribute to the alleviation of poverty. All-inclusive holiday packages minimise economic opportunities for local providers of transport, food, sellers of handicrafts and so forth. Leakages from tourism are also particularly high in countries with small and/or weak economies. The small size of the economy in most small-island states also means they have difficulty producing all the goods and services required by the tourism industry, and it is hard for them to compete with external suppliers (Meyer 2007). This is clear in the Gambia, where most hotels import eggs because to produce eggs domestically, chicken feed must be imported and this pushes up the price of domestic eggs (Sharpley 2007).

Another problem associated with foreign domination of the tourism sector is that developing country governments do not always earn good tax revenue from tourism. It can be very difficult for governments to collect tax revenue when tourists book their tours through a foreign company and a company's financial records are audited outside of the country where tourism occurs. Thus in Botswana, it is estimated that the government collects tax only from 11 percent of tourist companies (Mbaiwa 2005: 165). Furthermore, investment incentives to foreign companies investing in tourism in developing countries often include reduced import duties or 'tax holidays' of 10 to 20 years, which effectively takes away potential government revenue which could be used for the provision of services for the poor. For example, in Kenya there is no duty on imported construction materials and a 10 year holiday on corporate tax, and in Tunisia there is low tax on imported items and a reduced company tax rate (UNCTAD 2007: 98; 101). In Fiji the government offers significant incentives for the development of five-star hotels, including the following: 100 percent write-off on all capital expenditure in any one year during an initial period of eight years; carry forward of losses of up to six years; duty-free import of all capital equipment, machinery and plant in the development phase, with the exception of motor vehicles and furniture; and a waiver on corporate tax on profits for 20 years for capital investments over F$40 million, and a 10-year waiver for investments of F$10 million to F$40 million (Narayan 2000: 17). This has contributed to the situation that only 6 percent of 132 tourism ventures implemented between 1988 and 2000 were locally owned (Narayan and Prasad 2003).

It is notable that of 41 countries which provided tax incentives to attract investment in services, 39 were developing countries, and all 30 of those providing duty-free inputs or duty-free zones were developing countries (UNCTAD 2007: 103). Despite the implications, developing countries are competing with each other to attract foreign investment in tourism.

ECONOMIC DISPARITIES

The preceding arguments criticised the nature of tourism development as a neocolonialist endeavour. In this next section, more general points are made about the way in which tourism development can enhance economic disparities between the rich and poor.

Involvement of the poorer classes has been generally ignored in tourism policy except in cases where it is asserted they will benefit from job creation or the assumed 'trickle-down' of any economic benefits which occur. Many governments are of the mindset that any negative effects of tourism will be offset by these positive developments. In reality, the opposite may occur. Government money is often invested in establishing infrastructure for tourism while the basic infrastructural needs of citizens for utilities like water and electricity are pushed aside. The tourism industry can also have direct negative economic impacts through its influences on other economic sectors within a country (Nowak et al. 2003). Thus, for example, primary production may suffer as a result of land, labour and capital being invested in tourism, significantly threatening the livelihoods of some groups of people (Mowforth and Munt 2003: 273). In some locations competition for beach space has undermined the fishing industry. Competition for labour also impinges on local agriculture especially if the high season for tourism coincides with the busy season in agriculture. Loss of agricultural labour may result in sub-optimal production levels.

Development of tourism can also encourage land speculation and have inflationary effects not only on land prices, but prices for food, rent and basic utilities such as electricity and water (James 2004). At its worst, this may be led by the government. In Cambodia, for example, there have been a number of forced evictions of people from areas of land slated for commercial development, such as resorts. Amnesty International claims that in the case of the burning down of Mittapheap 4 village, the government did not consult these people before the evictions and nor did it seek to settle the land dispute prior to ordering that the village be demolished. An international company plans to build a resort and casino in this area (New Frontiers 2008).

Both Weaver (1998) and Akama (1999) argue that core-periphery relations not only occur between western and developing countries, rather, they can exist within a state: 'Internally induced core-periphery dynamics . . . have been neglected as a framework for the analysis of Third World tourism, as if domestic involvement in the national tourism sector were somehow assumed to be either implicitly benign, or negligible' (Weaver 1998: 292). In Kenya, the spatial concentration of tourism facilities and infrastructure increases the likelihood of negative impacts in tourism areas, and also precludes other areas from sharing in the benefits that tourism may bring (Akama 1999). As Burns and Holden (1995) noted, tourism development can lead to 'islands of affluence' in a sea of poverty.[2] Some might suggest that this is the case in the Indian Ocean destination of the Maldives (Box 3.1). This explains how an outwardly successful model of tourism development brings millions of dollars into the economy of the Maldives every year, yet the government cannot manage to lift a population of only less than 400,000 people out of poverty.

Box 3.1   **Luxury Tourism but Persistent Poverty in the Maldives**

In some ways the Maldives epitomize the dilemmas of small island states engaging in tourism as a means to achieve development. The government restricts tourism to uninhabited islands, and the natural environment has been protected through regulations requiring, for example, that all resorts treat their own wastes, that coastal development must not unduly disturb coastal ecology, and that indigenous vegetation may not be removed (Domroes 2001: 129–130). Presumably this is an excellent example of sustainable tourism in practice and as such the Maldives has been lauded by the World Tourism Organization (Lyon 2003: 15). The Maldives are heavily reliant on international tourism revenue. Tourism accounts for 20 percent of GDP, as opposed to 18 percent from the second most import economic sector, fishing, and less than 3 percent from agriculture, which is declining (Masters 2006: 27). Tourism brings in around 70 percent of foreign exchange earnings (MoTCA 2007: 26) and provides half of all paid employment through a wide range of occupations including construction, transport, handicraft manufacture and sales, and employment in resorts (Abdulsamad 2004). In 2006, 35.3 percent of government revenue, over $ 147 million, came directly from tourism (MoTCA 2007: 25, 36).

Superficially, development levels seem quite high in the Maldives. The life expectancy rate is 72 years, over 97 percent of the population are literate (UNDP 2009)

Continued

Box 3.1   Continued

and tourism has contributed significantly to the Maldives' $3,756 GDP per capita figure, which is considerably higher than their South Asian neighbours (India - $1,043; Sri Lanka - $2,099) (IMF 2008). However, due to inequities in the spread and ownership of resorts, the way tourists have been discouraged from visiting inhabited islands, and high levels of leakage, tourism has exaggerated existing inequalities between Maldivians: many outer islanders live on $365 per annum while average incomes in Male', the capital, are three times atoll incomes (UN 2002: 3), and 21 percent of the population lived below the poverty line in 2004 (European Union 2008).

Of greatest concern, tourism revenues do not benefit those who need them most. The resorts cater largely for higher spending, luxury tourists, and most of the provisions on the resort islands need to be imported as there is little arable land in the Maldives. Tourism has certainly generated employment, around 14,000 formal positions, however 6,000 of these jobs are filled by foreigners. This includes both highly skilled positions and more menial positions. Maldivians often choose to stay on their home islands rather than residing for eleven months of the year hundreds of kilometres away from their families on a resort island where they are required to work 12 hours a day, six and a half days of the week (Maldivian waiter, personal communication: August 2005). Worker accommodation is typically cramped, with up to 15 people in one room, and there are reports that workers are often not paid for several months at a time if 'business is slow' (Haynes 2004: 3). Maldivians are also paid less than other nationalities for doing the same types of work. In 2001 a foreign house keeper was paid 165 percent compared with a Maldivian house keeper, a tour guide 207 percent and a waiter 133 percent (MOT 2001, cited in Yahya et al. 2005: 40).

While generating essential revenue for the government and for a small number of influential families who own many of the resorts, tourism has exaggerated existing inequalities between Maldivians. Many outer islanders live on $365 per annum, earning around one third of that earned by residents of thecapital Male' (UN 2002: 3), and 21 percent of the population lived below the poverty line in 2004 (European Union 2008).

Despite the millions of dollars tourism brings into the economy every year, service delivery to outer islands is poor, with 40 percent of the population living on islands without access to healthcare (UN 2002). Around one quarter of atoll populations receive electricity for less than 6 hours a day, and 12 percent of the population does not have access to potable water (UN 2002: 2; 8). Most Maldivians cannot grow fresh fruit and vegetables due to the lack of suitable soils. Thus while resort buffet tables are laden with a wide range of largely imported fruits and vegetables, 30 percent of Maldivian children under the age of 5 are malnourished, and one quarter of them suffer stunted growth (UN 2002: 4). This is the basis of the claim that 'Maldives faces a nutritional situation more acute than that of sub-Saharan Africa' (UN 2002: 21).

Tourism Concern started a campaign against tourism in the Maldives in 2004 (Haynes 2004), motivated primarily by a concern with the relatively high levels

Continued

Box 3.1   Continued

of poverty in a country where tourism was bringing in enormous riches. A briefing on the campaign, named 'Lost in Paradise', highlighted another issue related to the poor of spread of the benefits from tourism, that is, the lack of good governance in the Maldives:

The income from the resorts rarely reaches those who need it and benefits the select few, including the government in the form of taxes. State management of tourism protects these systems and ensures local communities are denied access to the benefits of tourism. Local people are unable to speak out due to the repressive government and conditions where they are faced with imprisonment and possible torture for having a voice. (Haynes 2004: 1)

There is hope of change, however. A new, democratically elected government came to power late in 2008 bringing with it promises of a fairer spread of economic benefits in the Maldives.

THE LIMITS OF GLOBALISATION AS A DEVELOPMENT STRATEGY

Tourism is integrally entangled with globalization processes, and this often compromises development outcomes for poorer communities. Since the 1990s, a number of commentators have challenged the way in which developing countries have been incorporated into the global economy:

> The growth of tourism to developing societies has not come without controversy. . . . When developing countries promote this trade—the provision of tourism-related goods and services to foreign visitors—they are, in effect, embracing greater integration into the world economy. It is the terms of this integration, and the direct economic and political effects stemming from them, that invite this controversy. (Clancy, 1999: 2)

Globalisation is closely aligned with neoliberal doctrine, which aims to maximise opportunities for economic growth through encouraging minimal barriers to trade and increased volumes of trade between countries as individual countries seek to capitalise on their comparative advantage. One problem with this logic, however, is that social and environmental well-being may be sacrificed in order to produce products cheaply for the global market, or to encourage foreign investment. Thus as Carruthers notes ' . . . to offer investors the most attractive terms, the natural incentive is toward downward harmonization of environmental, labor, and public health standards' (2001: 102). This is what can occur too with tourism destinations. For example, Tourism Concern's research on tourism employment in Bali, Dominican Republic, Mexico, Egypt, Kenya and the Canary Islands revealed a wide range of problems including: lack of job security and high use of uncontracted, casual staff; poor wages; long hours of work and unpaid overtime; lack of opportunities for progression, e.g. to supervisory or management positions; and mediocre training opportunities (Barnett 2008: 1001). The fact remains, however, that low wage rates in a particular country can attract foreign investment.

Neoliberal policies encouraging tourism development can certainly lead to economic growth, but this does not automatically translate into benefits for the poor. In Peru, for example, neoliberal policies implemented under Fujimori's rule in the early 1990s led to a tripling of tourism arrivals between 1992 and 1996. While there were macroeconomic benefits from this, Desforges (2000: 190) suggests they were largely offset by concurrent shrinkage of the agricultural sector, entrenchment of poverty, and marginalisation of many people from the benefits of tourism. Similarly in Ghana, there was an increase in tourist arrivals from approximately 85 thousand in 1985 to 286 thousand in 1995, and tourist receipts increased from $20 million to $233 million over the same period. It was claimed that these great improvements were driven by adoption of neoliberal policies of structural adjustment programmes. However, at the same time spatial disparities in Ghana became entrenched, the quality of life of many Ghanaians declined, and there were high rates of leakage due to increasing foreign ownership of tourism infrastructure (Konadu-Agyemang 2001). And while we are often given evidence of the miracle of economic growth in China, we are not informed that growth of international arrivals (at 14 percent per annum on average between 1980 and 2006) has led to increasing economic disparities both between inland China and the coast, and in terms of economic indicators such as GDP per capita and household income (Wen and Sinha 2009).

A key aspect of economic globalisation has been the increasing power in the hands of a small number of travel and tourism companies with a high degree of vertical integration, leading to oligopolistic control within the industry (Brown 1998; Cater 1995; Schilcher 2007a: 58). Continuing high levels of competition can mean sustainability is not a priority for those that survive:

> Competition leads to international mergers and acquisitions, while smaller operators often survive on narrow margins in the face of continuous new product development and aggressive marketing through lower prices from the major groups. The resulting instability of the sector makes it difficult for enterprises at all levels to plan for a more sustainable future and to act responsibly. (Hall and Brown 2008: 1024)

operators based in the West have inherent advantages over their devel-
country counterparts as the majority of the world's international-
sts derive from western countries:

> It follows that such companies have become predominant in the con-
> trol of international tourist movements. . . . In addition, their expertise,
> marketing connections and capital resources give them an overwhelming
> competitive advantage over local tourism operators. (Cater 1995: 200)

The influence of foreign tour operators is clear in a country like the Gambia, where most air traffic consists not of scheduled flights, but of charter
flights for tourists: thus 'tour operators remain highly influential in the
development of tourism . . . ' (Sharpley 2007: 57). The tour operators can
negotiate very low contract prices for bed and breakfast with hotels, aver-
aging between 10 and 12 pounds per night, meaning most hotels struggle
to make a profit (Nyang 2005, cited in Sharpley 2007: 57).

Similarly, transnational companies based in the West can dominate the
international transport sector because of superior technology, sophisticated
marketing strategies and established links with tour operators, making it
difficult for developing country carriers to compete (Cater 1995). They can
also seek to influence the policies of countries which are keen to attract
tourists. In Panama, for example, the shipping company Carnival Line pressured the government to change the law which required all crew to have a
compulsory day off each week: now, whether or not they get a day off is up
to the discretion of the employer (cited in Hall and Brown 2008: 1025).

Large tour companies have the power to simply shift thousands of clients from one destination to another if the conditions in a particular country are seen as unsuitable (Akama 1999). This is what happened in the
Gambia when in October 1999 the government put in place a ban on all-
inclusive resorts in order to promote forms of tourism which were more
integrated with the local economy. They reversed this ban in December
2000 because of a large decline in the number of tourists. In this case,
tour agencies directed their clients to all-inclusive resorts in other countries,
including the Caribbean (*In Focus* 2000, 38: lift out Campaigns Update).
Thus powerful travel companies can shift thousands of clients from one
destination to another when the conditions in a particular country no longer suit them (Akama 1999). This could result in the collapse of a small
developing country economy while the profit margins of the tour company
are maintained.

Overseas companies and investors which come into a country under
pro-globalisation policies (e.g. tax breaks and other investment incentives)
can push out small, local investors or businesses which find they cannot
compete. Deregulation, privatisation and trade liberalisation all favour
MNCs, which then attract local capital which could have been invested in
smaller, indigenous enterprises (James 2004: 12). In Fiji, for example, F$80

million from the country's compulsory superannuation saving scheme was invested in the development of a Marriott resort at Momi Bay, which—only partially completed—went into receivership in 2008 (author's fieldwork, June and December 2009). And when multinational companies and international agencies loan funds for infrastructure development for tourism, they gain increasing control over the industry in the destination area (Telfer 2003: 100).

An interesting example of such control emerged from a high-profile case of environmental damage as a result of resort construction which hit the headlines in the Maldives in 2005. The Dhivehi Observer reported that fully-grown coconut palms, topsoil and sand had been removed from an inhabited island, Mandhoo, it order to beautify the exclusive Hilton Maldives Resort and Spa complex in adjacent Rangali and Rangalifinolhu islands. The Hilton worked together with a local company, Crown Company Pvt Ltd, to lease land on Mandhoo on which to construct large warehouses. However they never asked for permission to remove soil or vegetation from Mandhoo to their resort island. When Mandhoo islanders started to complain about the operations of the Hilton and Crown, Hilton no longer gave its tourists the option of day trips to Mandhoo and consequently the incomes of souvenir sellers diminished (Dhivehi Observer 2005).

The power of foreign companies can also make it difficult for governments to enforce environmental regulations, or to implement progressive labour force policies as investors can then threaten to take their money elsewhere. For example, small island states offer similar sun, sea and sand experiences, thus they compete to attract investors. If one offers better pay rates and labour conditions for tourism workers, they may not remain competitive (James 2004). Most developing countries do not have the power to bargain effectively with foreign investors; therefore it is unlikely that globalisation of tourism will lead to more enlightened labour force policies (Richter 2001: 49). Tourism investors are sometimes attracted to poor countries due to lax environmental regulations, building codes and the like, which can make establishment of a hotel or resort comparatively cheaper for them.

Neoliberal growth strategies which prioritise attracting overseas investment can also lead to displacement of local peoples from their land. In some cases coastal redevelopment in the name of tsunami recovery has resulted in people who derived their livelihoods from the sea being relocated inland—up to several kilometres in some cases—while the prime coastal land they used to occupy is leased to resort owners (Rice 2005). In this way poor fisherpeople have been taken advantage of when they are at their most vulnerable.

Box 3.2 provides an example of how globalisation and associated neoliberal growth discourse has been used to put pressure on Pacific Island states to convert communal land tenure systems to freehold land, which could lead to impoverishment of the people while making investors rich.

Box 3.2   Pressure to Reform Communal Land Tenure Systems in the Pacific in Order to Facilitate More Foreign Investment in Tourism

In the Pacific Islands, the dominant land tenure system involves communal ownership of customary land. In key tourism destinations, the vast majority of land is held this way: Fiji (83%), Samoa (81%) and Vanuatu (98%) (Rockell 2007). This customary land is what allows diverse livelihood systems to thrive and contributes to food security. It also draws on local skills, resources and capabilities, leading Fingleton (2005: 6) to assert: 'One of the greatest strengths of the Pacific Island societies is that nearly everyone still has access to their customary land. The security that provides is the glue that holds the societies together'.

Communal land is, however, often seen by outside commentators as a barrier to development; thus pressure has been put on these countries to change their systems of land tenure to allow for more foreign investment in tourism and other industries. Hughes (2004: 4) for example claims that the institution of customary land is 'the primary reason for deprivation in rural Pacific communities'. Meanwhile Jayaraman (1999: 9) argues that the effective supply of land is restricted by customary land tenure systems with 'adverse effects on long term investment plans'. It is assumed that traditional tenure systems discourage people from making improvements to their land, and individualization of land holdings is promoted as the only way to appropriately 'develop' resources (Silltoe 1997: 180).

In fact in most Pacific Island states land owners can agree to lease customary land to the private sector, or work in joint venture arrangements with private tourism businesses, so customary land can be used effectively to pursue tourism development. Leasing of land to private developers has brought significant benefits for local communities, and is the basis of continued foreign investment in small island tourism (Scheyvens and Russell 2010; Schilcher 2007b).

In line with liberalisation of the economy of Vanuatu, which earns most of its foreign exchange from tourism, a Comprehensive Reform Programme was enacted in 1997. This Programme included a commitment to encouraging foreign investment, especially in the tourism sector. This made the leasing of land by foreigners a more straightforward endeavour; however, it has taken advantage of landowners' poor understanding of the law and has systematically dispossessed them of their land, particularly on the main island of Efate (Slatter 2006). Now approximately 90 percent of coastal land on Efate has been alienated (Stefanova 2008: 2). Foreign investment properties often enclose the foreshore and block coastal access for communities.

Today, many leases are undertaken without the custom owners' full understanding of the land's market value, and while legal, are often arguably concluded under unfair conditions. Leases are generally granted for 75 years ... for a single, up-front cash payment (versus annual rent) set far below reasonable commercial rates. ... Many entrepreneurs arguably take advantage of locals' limited knowledge of the law by constructing contracts that only allow indigenous owners to recover their land at the end of the lease if they compensate the leaseholder for all improvements made. (Stefanova 2008: 2)   *Continued*

> **Box 3.2** Continued
> There is no way that a landowner will be able to have their land returned to them
> if they have to pay hundreds of thousands of dollars for such 'improvements'.

An issue of grave concern with relation to increasing global intercon-
nectedness, is that the players are not meeting on a level playing field:
'Countries, cities and individuals having the wherewithal to move with
globalization have much to gain, but many others not having the infrastructure or investment to be tuned in are bypassed and marginalized'
(Yeung 1998: 476). Thus while there are positive aspects to globalisation
such as opportunities for sharing information or technology and promoting cultural exchange, concerns have been raised that the power hierarchies
at play may see developing country economies and societies being undermined. For example, Cater notes that relationships between local people
and other tourism stakeholders are 'markedly skewed' in favour of the latter (1995: 207). Zoomers, who researched indigenous people living along
the Inca route, notes that while tourism can bring benefits to some, it tends
to leave many people struggling on the peripheries:

> While cultural tourism has incorporated Andean people in the con-
> sumer-oriented global economy, the majority remain socially margin-
> alized and without sufficient access to productive resources. (Zoomers
> 2008: 971)

This is why Ringer suggests that tourism is 'an industry that satisfies the
commercial imperatives of an international business, yet rarely addresses
local development needs' (Ringer 1998: 9). Even when the global spread of
tourism provides direct economic opportunities for people, this may only
be possible if they become economic migrants, potentially leaving their
families and communities behind—in a way, becoming socially impoverished. Hutnyk (1996: 211) reveals some of the contradictions which signify
the inequality between tourists and local people in developing country destinations such as Calcutta: 'The ISD stall near the Modern Lodge offers
instant phone connections home—it is run by an Orissa man who has not
seen his family in four months.' Note that in the aforementioned Maldives
case study, it was common for tourism sector employees to be away from
their home islands for 11 months of the year.

Examples of the relative lack of power of local communities compared
to tourists and outside companies with whom they come into contact show
that while,

> globalization opens new doors of opportunity and affluence . . . its
> pernicious effects have to be fully tackled before it can be accepted
> as a benign influence that propels the world and its peoples forward.
> (Yeung 1998: 477)

World Trade Regulations

There are concerns that global trading agreements which epitomise the sorts of economic relationships pursued under globalisation may undermine the ability of states to protect the interests of local people involved in tourism development. Advocates of free trade are using the current global recession to leverage further collaboration around speeding up trade talks. Concern has been expressed, in particular, about the General Agreement on Trade in Services (GATS) which is administered by the World Trade Organisation. The GATS seeks to liberalise the trade in services so that member countries would have to allow foreign-owned companies free access to their markets, and no favouritism could be shown to domestic investors. Under GATS governments could not legislate to protect national interests by, for example, providing subsidies or preferential loans to support domestic tourism businesses because this would be seen as 'trade-restrictive' (Mowforth and Munt 2003: 266). Similarly the WTO Agreement on Trade-Related Investment Measures (TRIMs) would not allow performance requirements to be placed on foreign interests investing in tourism or other sectors (UNCTAD 2007: 113). This could presumably mean an end for the Dominican Republic's requirements that foreign companies employ Dominicans in at least 80 percent of positions, and that foreign equity participation is only allowed up to 49 percent of capital (UNCTAD 2007: 98). Kalisch (2001) is also concerned that governments would not be able to control the practices of foreign companies even if their actions resulted in significant negative social, environmental and cultural impacts. Pera and McLaren claim that for indigenous communities, free trade ' . . . will limit countries' abilities to put conditions on the type of investment they receive, will give more rights to foreign investors and will only increase the leakage of profits out of the host country' (1999: 4).

Such agreements are more likely to benefit large companies and investors which come into a country under pro-globalisation policies (e.g. tax breaks and other investment incentives) as they have more buying power and better technologies, while thwarting the opportunities open to small investors and informal sector actors. The latter typically require support to be able to compete with larger interests and protection from the state to avoid being bought out by larger companies (Kalisch 2001). Thus, for example, why would an island resort buy fish from residents of an adjacent island when they can get the quantity and quality they want, and have credit extended, by buying from a national or international supplier?

Fickle Nature of the Tourism Industry

While globalisation offers great opportunities for global connectedness, as noted previously, it can mean increasing vulnerability for tourism-dependent communities when travel plans are interrupted due to consumer whims, terrorist acts, political conflict or health concerns.[3] Telfer and Sharpley (2008: xiii) question why developing countries ' . . . are attracted to such a volatile industry as a preferred development tool', while Harrison (2003: 7) warns ' . . . tourism is seen to be crucially, even cruelly, influenced by external factors far beyond local control'. For example, the global economic recession deterred travellers and this meant that around 30 percent of the Tanzania's 3,000 tour guides lost their jobs between late 2008 and mid-2009, often causing extreme hardship for their families (eTurboNews 2009c).

As most developing countries constitute 'medium-haul' or 'long-haul' destinations to their most lucrative tourist markets, they tend to suffer significant declines during periods of international or regional terrorism (for example, 9/11 and the Bali bombings), and when there are health threats (such as SARS, swine flu and bird flu) in their broader regions. Some 5,000 tourism employees were made redundant on Bali in 2002/3 as a direct result of the first Bali bombings followed by the SARS epidemic (James 2004: 13), and it is still unclear whether the industry here will ever fully recover after the second bombings in 2005. As the authors of an article on the vulnerability of beach vendors' livelihoods in Bali after the bombings in 2002 and 2005 reflected:

> tourism is a risky strategy, prone to fluctuation, often with the minimum of warning. There is thus an irony about the promotion of an industry which, in theory, could be of economic benefit to many of the world's poorest countries but which, if circumstances were to become unfavourable, could leave those involved even more vulnerable than they were before tourism was introduced. (Baker and Coulter 2007: 249–250)

They later conclude:

> We are . . . prompted to question the wisdom of encouraging tourism as a significant vehicle for socioeconomic development in the world's poorer countries, particularly where economic diversification is limited, where threats of disruption from a range of shocks, both external and internal, are always possible, and the means to cope with these are simply unavailable. (Baker and Coulter 2007: 262–263)

Tarplee further notes that the most vulnerable people in Bali turned out not to be those employed by large companies and hotel chains—who were able to some extent to absorb the shock—but rather those at the peripheries of the tourism industry: part-time and casual employees, the 'suppliers' of tourist businesses such as those involved in farming and agriculture, and informal workers (2008: 158). Thus, for example, beach vendors' incomes were cut by two thirds due to the bombings and their adaptive mechanisms were to sell assets and reduce costs, including their children's education (Baker and Coulter 2007). They also worked increasingly long days on the beach, from dawn until dusk, which compromised the parents' ability to meet their children's needs. As one beach vendor relayed:

> my wife used to spend most of her time working around the home and looking after our three children, but now she works with me on the beach the whole time. We leave our eldest child [11 years old] to look after the younger two [2 and 6 years of age], and the house. The two eldest children are given beads to sell to any tourists they see when they come down to the beach. (cited in Baker and Coulter 2007: 260)

This suggests that the social and economic costs of the bombings will be borne for some time to come.

In the face of health threats, economic downturn, natural disasters and political crises, it appears that developing countries can only exert a little control over the rise or decline in their international tourist numbers. For Tarplee, 'Diversity of income sources was one of the most effective preventative mechanisms for reducing vulnerability' (2008: 161), thus showing that a reliance on one main industry—tourism—can be a very unwise development strategy.

Conservation Before People?

A common criticism of tourism is its impacts on the natural environment, which often results in local people's well-being and livelihoods being undermined. Yet the irony is that tourism is usually trying to 'sell' beautiful, unique and preferably pristine environments in order to attract tourists. Furthermore, it uses the language of sustainability and environmental sensitivity to promote its products with little consideration for the implications this has for local communities:

> Notable weapons among this veritable armoury of marketing semantics have been 'green tourism', 'sustainable tourism', 'ecotourism', and 'soft tourism'. The legacy of this promotional ploy remains, not least in those areas of 'nature' tourism where local residents have been marginalized or even removed in the name of wildlife conservation. . . . Rarely have notions of 'sustainability' been interpreted or employed in holistic terms. Rather, sustaining the tourism industry and the resources upon which it depends has appeared all too often to be the major priority. (Hall and Brown 2008: 1024)

Conservationists and advocates of ecotourism often proclaim that conservation combined with tourism offers a win-win situation for communities living in, or adjacent to, conservation estates. Thus in Africa, the well-known catch-phrase of tourism based around protected areas is, 'Wildlife pays, so wildlife stays' (McNeely et al. 1992: 7), meaning that people will protect wildlife if they gain an economic return from it. The willingness of tourists to pay good money to engage in activities centred on natural attractions, for example, game viewing, trekking and diving, is supposed to help both national governments and local communities see that there is a value to conserving natural resources. However in practice creation of protected areas has often been detrimental to the well-being of local communities, directly undermining their livelihoods while failing to deliver on promised economic benefits (Adams and McShane 1992; Bonner 1993). Eco-dollars generated by the creation of the protected areas have traditionally benefited tour operators and the national government, with small amounts invested in wildlife conservation but little spent on the development of impoverished communities (Boyd 1997). Figure 3.1 thus depicts protected areas as 'islands of prosperity in a sea of poverty', as so many resources and so much expertise is invested in protected areas while the impoverished communities surrounding them have too often been overlooked and thus marginalised. Even when development projects based on protected areas explicitly aim to target the livelihoods of the poor, the effects are often disappointing. For example, Box 3.3 highlights how an Indonesian national park has certainly contributed to environmental conservation but has had very poor results in terms of community development.

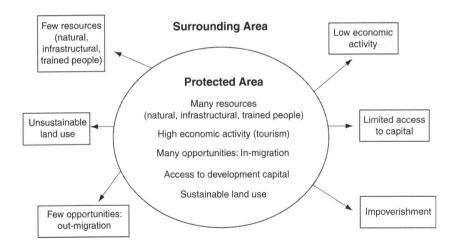

Figure 3.1 Protected areas as islands of prosperity in a sea of poverty.
Source: Author, drawing on Breen et al. (1992: 2)

Box 3.3 Conservation, Tourism and Impoverishment—A Case Study of Gunung Rinjani National Park, Indonesia

The Gunung Rinjani National Park Project (GRNPP) in Indonesia was founded on the idea of three interlocking concepts: conservation, community engagement and tourism. With regard to the second element, the specific objective was: 'Fostering community development on park boundaries by bringing benefits to rural women and men in recognition of the link between national conservation goals and local development goals' (David et al. 2005: 8). This objective referred to the fact that 42 villages with a population of 344,478 are located on the boundaries of the Rinjani park, and many of the residents are very poor. The most common activity is subsistence agriculture, but as up to 70 percent of families are landless, many encroach on the park's boundaries to utilise forest products. Thus 'Population pressure combined with landlessness are two of the most significant threats to the Rinjani ecosystem' (David et al. 2005: 12).

The impact of this project on poverty alleviation has been far less than would be expected. Almost NZ$3 million was invested in the project by a donor, NZAID, but only 2.4 percent of funding was spent on community development. Meanwhile the bulk of the funding (70%) went to the New Zealand–based company contracted as the MSC (management service consultant) to run the project (Figure 3.2). While mechanisms such as a rotational system for sharing trek bookings among trek organisers, guides and porters were established in order to promote sharing of the benefits, the system for this was not transparent and thus there have been suspicions and jealousy.

Overall, while entrepreneurship has been stimulated, the benefits are concentrated in the hands of a few (David et al. 2005; Japardy 2010). Thus while 817 individuals can be said to have benefited from the Rinjani project, over 600 of these are 'non-economic beneficiaries' (with increased knowledge, skills and confidence), 253 received 'limited economic benefit' (most from participation in a savings and loan scheme), and there have only been 43 individuals and their families who have experienced significant economic benefits from the project (David et al. 2005: 60).

Despite specific efforts to involve indigenous people and women in tour operations (including roles such as trekking guides, trek organisers and porters), by 2006 only 44 of the 235 people (19%) involved in tour operations in Desa Senaru, one of the main villages near to the park, were indigenous, and only 3 were women (1.3%) (Schellhorn 2007: 174). Meanwhile other potential economic opportunities for local people to engage with tourism have not been harnessed: for example, only 20 percent of fruit and 14 percent of vegetables purchased by guesthouses was sourced from Desa Senaru itself (Schellhorn 2007: 219).

The adat communities who live near the start of the Rinjani trek and who are the traditional guardians of the forests were particularly sidelined from the more lucrative tourism opportunities, as tour operators from the town of Mataram have the connections and skills (e.g. in English) to secure most of the potential clients (Japardy 2010). In addition, women living in the vicinity of the park

Continued

Box 3.3 Continued

tended to lose out on opportunities in tourism due to competition with men and recent transmigrants to the area. By comparison, the women had low levels of formal education and expressed that they were never really given a chance to participate in tourism (Schellhorn 2007: 225–226).

Butcher (2006) criticises environmental organisations which promote ecotourism in association with a protected area, as for most their top priority is conservation rather than the well-being of local people: 'it is very rare to find any ecotourism project funded by environmental NGOs that proposed ecotourism as a stepping stone to *greater* levels of development' (Butcher 2006: 308). Supposedly local people's continued impoverishment is the compromise needed to ensure the environment is protected. Cohen expands on this point with relation to cultural heritage as well, showing concern about ' . . . the possible misuse of the concept of sustainability . . . as a means of legitimising takeover of control over natural sites or cultural practices of local people by state agencies or private enterprises', all in the name of 'sustainable tourism' (Cohen 2002: 267). This can lead to the livelihoods of local people being undermined as their access to valuable sites is restricted due to concerns about sustainability: 'While serving the goal of environmental sustainability, such a policy is liable to infringe upon local participation and equity in the distribution of benefits' (Cohen 2002: 275).

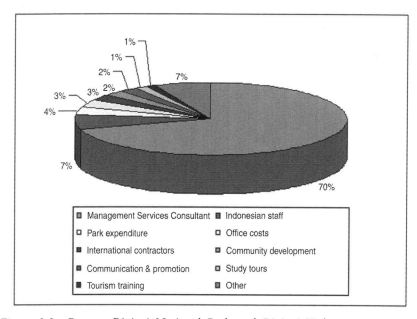

Figure 3.2 Gunung Rinjani National Park and Rinjani Trek ecotourism programme: allocation of NZAID funds.

IS ALTERNATIVE TOURISM THE ANSWER THEN?

Many of the foregoing criticisms are levelled at mass or conventional tourism that occurs in developing countries, which is in line with Shah and Gupta's (2000: 40) findings from their careful analysis of tourism case studies from around Asia: ' . . . mass tourism, especially that associated with luxury hotels and resorts, does not always bring the best returns and has significant negative social impacts on local communities'. At least partly in response to such critiques over the social, economic and environmental impacts of conventional, mass tourism, tourism providers have established a growing selection of alternative tourism products.[4] Such products go by a range of names, including the following: ecotourism, responsible tourism, green tourism, cultural tourism, soft tourism, ethnic tourism, alternative tourism, community-based tourism and sustainable tourism. It is not only the tourism industry which has espoused support for alternative tourism, as noted by Hall: ' . . . many governmental agencies and tourism academics have been caught up in the "sexy", supposedly "new", forms of tourism such as ecotourism and cultural tourism'. However, he urges us to be wary of uncritically embracing such alternative tourism: 'There is . . . a somewhat mistaken belief that these forms of tourism are somehow ethically superior' (Hall, in Hall and Butler, 1995: 105). Brohman too sounded a note of caution when he identifies 'alternative tourism' as 'one of the most widely used (and abused) phrases in the tourism literature' (1996a: 63).[5] Butcher (2003: 110) is meanwhile concerned that offering alternative, supposedly more ethical travel experiences to individuals fails to address more fundamental inequalities associated with global tourism:

> the individual solutions to social inequalities proposed by the New Moral Tourism lobby are deceitful. . . . to stay in a hotel or in a village, to enjoy the culture or just the climate, will make no difference to the broader inequality that exists between nations and peoples. More importantly, it is an agenda that discourages a critical examination of the causes of poverty by presenting individual behaviour as a strategy to bring positive change to the Third World. This makes for degraded politics . . . (Butcher 2003: 110)[6]

Munt thus suggested some years ago that we should be more critical of new, alternative forms of tourism: 'While mass tourism has attracted trenchant criticism as a shallow and degrading experience for developing country host nations and peoples, new tourism practices have been viewed benevolently and few critiques have emerged' (Munt 1994: 50). Since then a few authors have come forward to say that these 'new' forms of tourism do not symbolise a fundamental shift in approach; rather, they provide little more than a repackaging of mainstream products and they are part of the same profit-maximising tourism 'machine' that extracts major benefits for those who own and control the resources of the industry, while exploiting others (see for example, Butcher 2003; Butler 1990; Macleod 1998; Mowforth and Munt 2003).[7] Some suggest that alternative tourism merely provides a more socially and environmentally-friendly façade for continuing exploitation of developing country peoples and environments:

> 'Alternative' travel . . . works as a reassuring front for continued extension of the logistics of the commodity system, even as it masquerades as a (liberal) project of cultural concern, and despite the best intentions of its advocates. (Hutnyk 1996: 215)

There are thus a number of legitimate concerns about the potential of 'alternative tourism' to alleviate poverty. Fundamentally, alternative products sometimes involve merely repackaging old products using new labels. Also, alternative forms of tourism can be more culturally invasive than other forms of tourism because, as Butler notes, ' . . . alternative forms of tourism penetrate further into the personal space of residents . . . [and] expose often fragile resources to greater visitation . . . ' (1990: 41). In addition, alternative tourism cannot always deliver the same economic returns as mass tourism; thus it will not always be regarded by communities as more beneficial to them than mass tourism (Weaver and Oppermann 2000). As noted by Butcher (2003: 61), local people may not want fewer tourists, but more; they may feel there is 'not too much development, but too little'.

Community-based tourism is often upheld as a particularly good alternative to the excesses and inequalities of conventional tourism. However as Harold Goodwin, a leading advocate of responsible tourism, has noted, community ventures around the world have often been a failure due to a range of factors including lack of marketing, lack of business expertise among those running the venture, and a lack of viability of the business (due to factors which include remote location, lack of transport linkages and insufficient appeal of the product) (Table 3.1). In a study of community-based tourism enterprises in Kenya, for example, it was shown that while the enterprises did bring some communal benefits such as improvements to education and health services, they failed to significantly reduce poverty at the level of individual households. Furthermore, they were not sustainable: 'The current model of CBEs [community based enterprises] relies heavily on donor funding, thereby reinforcing dependency, an indicator of poverty' (Manyara and Jones 2007: 642).

The very focus of alternative development approaches on 'communities' has also been criticised because too often it is assumed that communities are homogeneous entities with shared interests, when in reality most communities are made up of distinct interest groups. Often communities are split into various factions based on a complex interplay of class, gender and ethnic factors, and certain families or individuals are likely to lay claim

Table 3.1   Constraints Facing Community-Based Tourism (CBT) Ventures

Lack of genuine community control.	Communities often do not have proprietorship over land or natural resources and lack other forms of capital, thus participation in tourism is limited to co-option in ventures controlled by outsiders.
CBT projects do not always provide appropriate tourism facilities for generating income.	For example, too many CBT initiatives rely on building lodges, which are capital intensive and need considerable maintenance, or walking trails from which it can be difficult to secure revenue.
CBT projects require skilled business people to run them effectively.	Appropriate skills, knowledge and resources for developing tourism ventures are often lacking at the community level.
CBT is often heavily dependent on donor funding.	In some cases donors invest hundreds of thousands of dollars in aid money into CBT projects which reap just a few hundred visitors a year, bringing benefits to a comparatively small proportion of the local community.
Few projects understand the need for commercial activities.	Local people must sell crafts, food, accommodation and wildlife or cultural experiences to tourists. This is the only way to ensure a sustainable supply of local income or conservation funds.
CBT projects are more successful when they engage with the private sector, including travel agents and tour operators.	CBT projects are more successful when they engage with the private sector, including travel agents, tour operators and the closer the partnership, the more likely it is to succeed.
Conservation is often prioritised over development.	Protected areas increasingly rely on money from tourists to pay for conservation initiatives. Local communities often have to compete with conservation projects for revenues.
Location is critical: for poor people to benefit, tourists must stay in or near to these communities, or visit them regularly.	Very few communities have tourism assets which are sufficiently strong to attract tourists – they rely on selling complementary goods and services. Tourists need to be close for this to happen.
The myth of community.	Communities are typically heterogeneous, comprising a range of different interest groups which may come into competition regarding the development of a potentially lucrative tourism venture.

Source: Based on Goodwin (2006), Koch (1997) and author

to privileges because of their apparent status. Elites may co-opt and come to dominate community-based development efforts and monopolise the benefits of tourism (Mansperger 1995; Mowforth and Munt 2003; Sindiga 1995). Indeed, the poorest of the poor may be excluded from community structures, thus making them very difficult to target if adopting a community-based approach.

Linked to concerns raised in the earlier section on 'Conservation before people', commonly alternative forms of tourism have been imposed on communities by overzealous outside interests groups who want to save the rainforests, or the marine environment, and promise communities compensation in the form of tourism revenues if they will just conserve their natural environment. Government agencies too such as provincial governments may wish to turn someone's village into a cultural attraction, and have lots of ideas on how this could bring benefits to community members, but typically they follow a flawed process of consultation and/or do not provide community members with adequate information or training to be able to understand what tourism could mean for them and how they could engage with tourism in beneficial ways. In the village of Bena in Indonesia, for example, government officials overlooked elders and instead worked with an elected village headman, who did not have the appropriate authority, and this led to resentment of the project in its early stages (Cole 2008: 106).

Alternative tourism, including community-based tourism, should thus be subject to the same critical scrutiny as conventional tourism.

DISCUSSION: IS TOURISM REALLY A NEGATIVE, UNSTOPPABLE FORCE?

For many years development agencies avoided supporting tourism for many of the reasons outlined in this chapter thus far: it is an industry associated with luxury and hedonism rather than one that directly addresses poor people's social and economic concerns; it is associated with ownership and control by foreigners and elites; and tourism has often led to negative social, economic and environmental impacts. However, it has been suggested that academics and donors have been too quick to write-off tourism and that they should no longer dismiss the potential of this industry (Scheyvens 2002a; Torres and Momsen 2004).

The Evidence is Mixed: Sometimes Tourism Does Contribute Effectively to Poverty Alleviation

While some research has reported that tourism leads to greater economic disparities between the rich and poor, this is contradicted by the findings of others studies. Thus a large-scale economic analysis of tourism in Brazil revealed that it benefited all income groups (Blake et al. 2008), but it was particularly advantageous to those on low incomes. In particular, tourism contributed 8.3 percent of the revenue earned by the lowest income households, and 7.1 percent of the income of low-income households, compared with only 5.1 percent of the income of high-income households (Figure 3.3).

Together, the low- and lowest income households received almost half of all household earnings from tourism (Figure 3.4). Furthermore, in contrast to the Brazilian economy as a whole, income earned in tourism accrues more to labour than to capital, and is particularly biased in favour of the

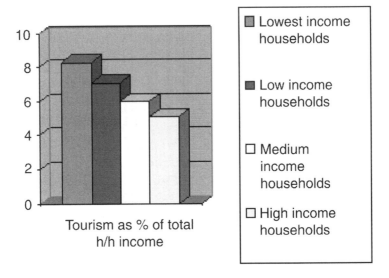

Figure 3.3   Tourism earnings as a share of total household income in Brazil, 2002.
Source: Blake et al. (2008)

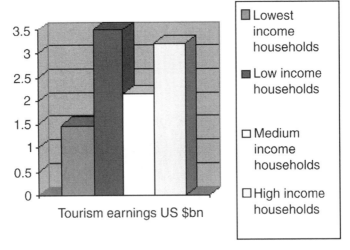

Figure 3.4   Tourism's contribution to household income in Brazil, 2002.
Source: Blake et al. (2008)

self-employed and also semi-skilled and unskilled work. These factors lead Blake et al. to conclude that ' . . . the industry can play an important role in poverty reduction in Brazil' (2008: 116).

Similarly, while academic literature tends to be critical of the lack of labour rights of tourism employees in many cases, and particularly notes discrimination against women, this does not mean that tourism itself is the problem. For women living near to Gunung Rinjani National Park in Indonesia, those that did gain work in tourism placed real importance on this:

> women value highly their own involvement in the tourism industry and see it as an opportunity to earn cash. Non-material aspects are equally important in this self-evaluation as respondents appreciate highly the opportunities to socialize, gain more knowledge, learn the English language and access information. (Schellhorn 2007: 223)

Change brought about by tourism in developing countries can then be positive. Even Nash, who generally writes of tourism as a form of imperialism, notes that several studies have found that tourism is ' . . . a benign and possibly beneficial agent of change' (Nash 1996: 22). More controversially, Butcher asserts that 'Some may bemoan the changes to community, but perhaps we should see this as a price worth paying' (2003: 92)—here he is referring to a price worth paying if development is to be achieved. While I do not necessarily concur with Butcher on this point, I would suggest that those bemoaning change are often outsiders, and that it is logical to expect that those living in poverty would *want* some forms of change. The key issue then becomes how they can possibly influence the nature of change that occurs through tourism.

Tourism as a Scapegoat

The impacts of tourism are, in reality, quite complex. In some cases tourism has been blamed for a multitude of ills for which it bears little responsibility, perhaps being criticised simply because it is such a visible industry (Crick 1989, cited in Brunt and Courtney 1999). For example, environmental damage may result from a combination of factors including overpopulation, poor resource conservation and inappropriate agricultural practices, rather than being solely attributed to tourism development (Hall and Page 1999: 134). Alternatives to tourism development such as cash cropping or establishment of other industries could be worse for local well-being: ' . . . the alternative to tourism development may be starvation and disease and, for many, a permanently damaged environment incapable of sustaining the existing communities' (Middleton and Hawkins 1998: 77). In other cases, without tourism, rates of out-migration would be much higher in many places (ESCAP 2003: 28; Macleod 2004), potentially undermining the viability of small communities or robbing them of their young, more educated populace.

Too often also tourism is blamed for social and political conditions that are caused by a much broader range of forces. For example, while Lepp (2008) originally thought that village tourism in Bigodi, Uganda, had led to dependency on westerners, his research found that external events which occurred well before tourism began in the village, such as creation of a nearby national park and civil strife under Idi Amin's government, were responsible for people's sense of dependency.[8] Furthermore, the dominant model of development in a country, not just its current tourism policy, can significantly impede the potential of tourism to assist the poor. Manyara and Jones note that, ' . . . Kenya's prevailing model for tourism development is anachronistic, colonial and narrowly based on safari and coastal products . . . This has been a major obstacle to economic development and poverty reduction' (2007: 629). Such factors mean that the benefits of tourism are not widely spread in Kenya and this contributes to the situation shown in Table 3.2, whereby poverty is greater in areas of high tourism development than in areas of high agricultural development.

The Kenyan example leads on nicely to the point that not all critics blame tourism *per se* for causing poverty and underdevelopment, rather, they are primarily concerned with the way in which it is developed and promoted. For example, Brohman (1996) criticises the narrow perspective taken by governments who encourage more visitors to a country to increase foreign exchange, without linking this specifically to wider development goals such as poverty alleviation or balanced regional development. He asserts that a key problem with tourism in the developing world is that it continues to be pursued as an outward-oriented development strategy, in line with a neoliberal rationale for development. Rather than encouraging domestic tourism or promoting tourism as a means for developing cross-cultural awareness, for example, for most developing countries tourism is explicitly being pursued as a means of earning foreign exchange. This

Table 3.2 Poverty Incidence in Selected Tourism and Agriculture-Dominant Areas of Kenya

Tourism		Agriculture	
Area	Incidence of poverty (%)	Area	Incidence of poverty (%)
Maasai Mara	50–60	Nyeri	20–30
Taita Taveta	50–60	Trans Nzoia	40–50
Laikipia	50–60	Kiambu	20–30
Kwale	Over 70	Uasin Gishu	40–50

Source: Manyara and Jones (2007: 629), compiled from Central Bureau of Statistics (2003)

is why, Brohman suggests, tourism in the developing countries has often left an unpleasant legacy including dependence on foreign investment and skills, environmental problems, cultural decay and spatial inequality. There has been insufficient focus on forms of development which build upon the skills and knowledge of local people (Blaikie 2000).

Criticisms are Based on Broad Generalisations

Other authors lament the generalisations made about foreign ownership, leakages and lack of local multiplier effects. Some supporters of PPT have been fighting back, suggesting that instead of focusing on, for example, the 50 to 70 percent of an international tourist's spend that does not reach their destination country (e.g. when airline tickets and a tour are paid for prior to departure), we should be focusing on how much of the in-country spend reaches the poor: 'The exaggerated claims divert attention from an important challenge at hand—boosting the linkages between tourism and the rest of the local economy' (Mitchell and Ashley 2007b: 2). In the Gambia, 14 percent of expenditure in-country reaches the poor. Mitchell and Ashley (2007b) argue this is much better than the 1.5 percent of the price of a cup of coffee in Europe that reaches the producer of the coffee bean.[9] Moreso in Tanzania, approximately 28 percent of tourist expenditure on Mount Kilimanjaro climbing package holidays reaches the poor (Mitchell et al. 2009).

While earlier sections of this chapter criticised foreign investment in tourism and foreign ownership of tourism ventures, an UNCTAD study of 32 hotel groups with 10,200 hotels, which examined the developmental impacts of FDI in tourism, suggests the concerns are overstated (UNCTAD 2007). In and of itself foreign investment need not be the problem, and it does not always dominate (Barrowclough 2007). In the Annapurna region of Nepal, for example, where thousands of trekkers venture annually, only around 10 of the almost 500 lodges had outside investors (Nepal 2007). This example reflects the reality that in developing countries 85 percent of accommodation capacity is actually provided by small and medium sized enterprises (Zimny 2006). Barrowclough, who works for UNCTAD, argues that in these contexts, the presence of internationally branded hotel chains is often sought out in order to attract the attention of foreign tourists: 'Tourism investors and managers . . . said that no national tourist board could compete with the loyalty schemes, corporate networks and direct mail promotions that reach millions of customers of a well-known brand' (Barrowclough 2007: 630).

Where TNC (transnational corporation) hotels *do* dominate, in some cases, is in the upscale four- and five-star establishments in major cities and in tourist areas. However even in such cases, often the TNCs are working on management contracts so while their brand and management style is applied to the hotel or resort, they do not own it. In the case of Hilton Hotels Corporation, they own only 3 percent of hotels; others they mainly franchise (73 percent), and manage (24 percent) (Endo 2006: 603).[10] In other cases, such as Bhutan, it is the foreign-owned hotels that have better linkages into the local economy than domestic ones (UNCTAD 2007: 117). Foreign hotels can often weather fluctuations in tourism more effectively than local firms due to their brand names which instill confidence in tourists, and due to having 'deeper pockets'. Furthermore, by introducing effective systems of management, accounting and so forth, foreign hotels can help to raise standards of hotel performance across the sector. The labour intensity is higher in four- and five-star hotels, meaning more staff are employed per guest and per room. They also offer better insurance and pension packages to employees (Barrowclough 2007: 626–627).

Thus it is not foreign investment in tourism *per se* which needs to be criticised, particularly as in many countries domestic capital is in short supply (Schilcher 2007a: 66), but the nature of this investment and how it is controlled. For example, we can query whether governments are giving generous tax breaks to foreign investors which then undermines the local economy (e.g. if they remove import duties from a range of items, this encourages foreign investors *not* to buy local, thus undermining local economic linkages). We could consider whether governments have incentives in place to encourage joint ventures rather than full foreign ownership, and we could look at how well governments protect employee rights and well-being. For some time it has been clear that 'employment conditions and standards in the tourism economy need attention' (Barrowclough 2007: 627). Thus rather than unreservedly supporting FDI in tourism, Barrowclough concludes that,

> FDI is not a panacea and can only be effective as part of an appropriate over-arching policy framework. FDI is best seen as a useful potential catalyst that can be a complement to domestic investment, but not a substitute. (2007: 629)

Thus governments have a key role to play in establishing an environment and policy framework that will determine whether developing countries maximise their benefits from tourism while limiting harm—this could include, for example, skills training, support to agricultural producers to improve the quality and supply of their produce, and support for domestic investors to build hotels and other tourism-related enterprises and to engage in equitable joint venture arrangements with outside interests (Barrowclough 2007). Such roles of governments will be explored further in Chapter 6.

The Agency of Local Communities

Early critics of tourism like Britton (1982) clearly did not consider the significant role that governments can play in managing the development of their tourism industries, but he also overlooked the potential for local communities to actively resist tourism and other 'projects' imposed on them from outside when this works against their interests.

It is too simplistic to suggest that tourism is an external force which erodes local cultures and undermines local economies and societies (Wood 1998). Put simply, 'traditional cultures and societies do not dissolve in the face of tourism' (Teo and Chang 1998: 124). Picard (1993) explains that tourism and culture are not independent of each other in many contexts. Instead, peoples respond to and interact with tourists and the tourism process in complex ways. Claims that tourism has 'destroyed indigenous culture' in a particular locality thus need to be examined carefully, as cultures are constantly evolving: 'The implicit notion of a pristine pre-tourist cultural baseline against which to measure tourism's "negative" impact is exposed as obfuscating at best and in a profound sense, meaningless' (Wood 1993: 63). Similarly, rather than seeing cultural adaptations that occur when people turn their traditional arts and crafts into products for tourist consumption as 'commodification' or 'exploitation', we need to appreciate the agency which people exert when they manipulate or adapt aspects of their own culture in the face of tourism development (Potter et al. 1999). A counter to all the criticisms of tourism as a destroyer of cultures is provided by Butcher, who notes that too often 'Culture becomes objectified; a romantic image cast in stone, rather than the creative subjectivity of the host' (2003: 93). Furthermore, westerners use double standards when assessing supposed cultural degradation caused by developing country tourism: ' . . . cultural change is less likely to be seen as destructive and more likely to be seen as creative in more developed societies' (Butcher 2003: 93–94).

Many of the criticisms of tourism earlier in this chapter suggest that local residents and particularly the lower classes/castes—the poor—*will lack agency* to resist tourism even when it is directly interrupting their livelihoods. However, there are a myriad of ways in which local people have responded to tourism development, showing that they are not victims of a burgeoning, unstoppable industry. This is also Ticknell's conclusion after conducting a postcolonial analysis of novels depicting independent travel:

> within the diverse set of practices which make up tourism we should be wary of reading the encounter between guest and host as one of inevitable victimage. In many cases, where tourism operates between the former 'First' and 'Third' worlds, poorer 'host' cultures show a resilient, hybridising response to the appearance of the international tourist. (Ticknell 2001: 52)

Parnwell (1998) asserts that the emergence of NGOs and advocacy groups within a number of developing country states has enhanced local power to resist or transform tourism. While the engagement of local people with tourism is not always positive, they are nevertheless active agents who may be able to adapt tourism processes to suit their own circumstances (Cheong and Miller 2000; Parnwell 1998). Arguing that tourism is 'a negotiated process', Pagdin (1995: 195) states that ' . . . locally-affected people are not shaped passively by outside forces but react as well, at times even changing the conditions of the larger system'.

Other authors question dependency theory logic which suggests that expansion of tourism necessarily undermines the economic and political sovereignty of developing countries. Thus Parnwell urges us not to assume that globalisation is an unstoppable, uncontrollable force because 'The way that global processes and forces are negotiated, regulated and inter-preted at the local level may be just as important as the nature and extent of globalisation itself' (Parnwell 1998: 214). Local actors and institutions can play key roles in influencing the nature of tourism development.

Community groups which act as watchdogs on tourism development can, for example, be very powerful advocates for appropriate local devel-opment, working to keep their local and national governments honest and to ensure that the interests of investors do not override the concerns of local residents. This is particularly evident in Goa, the former Portu-guese colony south of Mumbai in India. Local action groups in Goa have taken up a number of tourism-related causes from the 1980s through to the present, as seen in Table 3.3. These groups in Goa have had some suc-cess. This includes taking legal action against the construction of hotels and resorts within 500 metres of Goan beaches, stopping development on community land and ensuring that hotels do not erect fences which cut off the access of locals to the beach (Magic Lantern Foundation 1999). They have also networked with tourism lobby groups in other parts of the world and drawn international attention to their cause (Lea 1993; Singh and Singh 1999). The most well-known tourism protest group in Goa is Jagrut Goenkaranchi Fauz (JGF), or Vigilant Goan's Army. One campaign named 'Our homes—their holidays' focused on the need for strong local input into tourism planning to ensure that tourism does not undermine access of local residents to essential services and infrastruc-ture, including water and electricity. Another campaign targeted labour practices of the luxury hotels, attempting to ensure that workers gain the security of permanent jobs and wages rather than being exploited by being employed as 'trainees' whereby their only income is the tips they gain (Herald News Desk 1999).

In 2007, a Centre for Responsible Tourism was formed in Goa and it is working in an integrated way with various community and business groups, including a taxi owner association, shack owners (those selling food and beverages on the beach), and the small and medium guesthouse association, to ensure ethical practice in the industry (Solomon 2009). In addition to playing a watchdog role and conducting tourism impact assessments in different villages, the Centre for Responsible Tourism also supports community groups such as a group that opposed licensing of outside vendors in their village area, as this undermined local livelihood options (Solomon 2009: 20). One of the groups associated with the Centre for Responsible Tourism, the Shack Owners Welfare Society—Goa, has gained support from the government for a policy which protects traditional owners of beach shacks, prevents foreigners from owning beach shacks, and reduces the application fee for getting a licence to operate a beach shack (Solomon 2009: 42–49).

By examining the nature of protests against tourism, we can gain insights into the most critical concerns faced by local people. For example, Wilson (1997) cites a well-publicised case of Goan people throwing rotten fish and cow dung at tourist buses. Rather than an attack against all forms of tourism, he explains, this incident was instigated by small-scale local entrepreneurs who felt that charter-package tourism was putting them out of business by providing for all of the needs of tourists (accommodation, transport and food) in a single outlet. Wilson argues that in general, Goans welcome international backpackers and domestic tourists because they can easily service their needs, and this has resulted in a tourism industry characterised by ' . . . wide local ownership of resources and the broad distribution of benefits throughout the local community' (1997: 63).

Thus it is simplistic, if not erroneous, to cast developing country peoples as victims of globalising forces such as tourism:

> Tourism is part of the process of modernization, and globalization, but local actors are agents in this process, and not just the recipients of modernization processes. They attempt to develop strategies by which encounters with tourists can be beneficial to them. (Erb 2000: 710)

This section has suggested that we need to move beyond using tourism as a scapegoat for economic disparities, environmental degradation and social problems emerging in developing countries and develop a more nuanced understanding of the way in which tourism affects developing country states, peoples and their environments. It is problematic to see tourism development as being uniformly exploitative of local peoples and places. The critical views of an author like Britton (1982), for example, who wrote that tourism was linked to underdevelopment in small island states, largely failed to acknowledge the fact that where there are high levels of local ownership and strong economic linkages between tourism and other local industries, the benefits can be great (Milne 1997). Similarly, while larger hotels may be foreign-owned or managed, they may be preferable to smaller, locally owned accommodation in some cases because they help to attract more tourists to a location and they offer training, job security, better working conditions and higher rates of pay for employees.

Table 3.3   Reasons for Protests over Tourism in Goa

Source of protest	Examples
Behaviour of 'hippies'	Drug taking; immodest dress, including nudity on the beach; loud parties.
Undermining of local livelihoods	Toddy tappers denied access to coconut trees on lands leased for hotels; luxury hotels attempt to restrict access of fisherpeople to the foreshore, even though officially the coast of India is public property. Outsiders have come in and taken over tourism jobs previously held by local people, e.g. operating beach shacks.
Lack of amenities for locals and pressure on scarce resources	Tourist hotels use water for swimming pools while nearby villagers suffer from a shortage of drinking water; power shortages in local villages.
Bowing to demands of large Indian businesses and multinational corporations rather than local concerns and interests	Plans to develop large resorts, casinos (including floating casinos) and golf courses in the State to attract high-spending tourists, regardless of potential social and environmental consequences. Locals unduly pressured to sell coastal land.
Social breakdown	Rising inequality has fueled discontent and crime. There has been a noticeable increase in theft, and corruption occurs within the police force and the tourism department.
Undermining the dignity of the people	Locals gain work in hotels as cleaners, guards and waiters - they are at the beck and call of others as opposed to the past when they were self-employed. There are particular concerns about exploitation of female workers.
Damage to the physical environment	Coastal environment has been degraded. There have been many violations of the law that no construction is allowed within 500 metres of the beach - sometimes 'in the interest of tourism and profits' certain development is allowed up to 200 metres from the shoreline. Sewage from hotels often goes untreated.

Source: Magic Lantern Foundation (1999); Singh and Singh (1999); Solomon (2009)

CONCLUSION

In sum, criticisms of tourism as a development strategy came to the fore from the 1970s to the 1990s, fuelled by evidence of increasing economic disparities in countries with high levels of tourism and negative social and environmental impacts of tourism. It was clear that tourism *per se* did not provide the answer to overcoming the significant development challenges facing many countries. (Khan 1997)

This chapter has shown that there are certainly circumstances in which tourism has deepened the fissures separating rich and poor, and where it has impoverished people culturally, socially or environmentally, even when economic benefits have been real: 'While tourism can be an important income generator, on its own it cannot close the global gap between the Rich and Rest. Quite the contrary, neocolonialist tourism often perpetuates and even exacerbates the void between the Rich and the Rest' (Jaakson 2004: 179). In de Kadt's preface to his classic book *The Holidaymakers* over 30 years ago, he argued that:

> no development strategy can hope to be successful without restructuring of North-South economic relations . . . major institutional and structural adjustments will be needed in the industrialized countries if the poor nations are to achieve their development goals. (1979: xii–xiii)

This is an interesting challenge to the neoliberal stance which insists it is the developing country economies which need restructuring.

While there has been ample evidence of the potential negative impacts of tourism presented in this chapter, in line with what we would expect from advocates of dependency theory, it is interesting to see that a number of authors have taken a more post-development stance in recent times. They argue that an impacts approach to tourism research is not particularly helpful as it assumes that tourism is an external force which erodes local cultures and undermines local economies and societies (Picard 1993; Wood 1998). Rather than assuming that local peoples are victims of a burgeoning, unstoppable industry, writers are now showing there are a myriad of ways in which local people have responded to tourism development, sometimes resisting it—as in Goa—and other times adapting it to meet their own needs.

Thus while criticisms of the global tourism industry can play a valuable role in identifying power relations at national and international levels which can provide constraints to the implementation of effective PPT strategies, this does not suggest that we should get trapped down a narrow cul-de-sac by focusing on the negative impacts of tourism. Just as idealists need to be careful not to overstate the potential of tourism as a tool for poverty alleviation, critics need to be rigorous in their analysis of problems associated with tourism development without making generalisations or overlooking the potential of tourism. Marchand and Parpart (1995: 1) suggest that critiques of development which reject development strategies outright are little more than 'a "First World" preoccupation, if not indulgence, with little practical application for Third World . . . development problems'. It seems particularly inappropriate to reject all notions of tourism as a strategy for development when it has been identified by developing country governments and communities as a potential means of development and improving their well-being. Fundamentally, it seems that most communities that have tourism development *want* tourism development for both economic and other reasons. What they may seek, however, is more control over the industry and a greater share in its benefits. This suggests that tourism researchers, government officials and development agency staff should consider *how* there can be more local control over tourism and more equitable sharing of its benefits. Thus we should be listening to the voices of developing country peoples regarding both their concerns about tourism and what they hope to achieve through tourism, before carefully considering if there are appropriate means of pursuing tourism, and appropriate types of tourism, which will readily meet the needs and desires of local communities:

> It seems ironic that contemporary scholarly debates should clamour for a 'post-development' era, just when voices from the margins—so celebrated in discourses of difference and alternative culture—are demanding their rights to greater access to a more generous idea of development. (Rangan 1996: 222)

Chapters 5, 6 and 7 will take a more positive stance towards tourism as a tool for poverty alleviation.

4 Poverty Attracts Tourists

INTRODUCTION

Previous chapters have highlighted the complex relationship between tourism and poverty alleviation, with Chapter 3 explaining why a number of commentators are convinced that tourism often entrenches poverty. In this chapter, the contention is more audacious: poverty attracts tourists. At first this may seem nonsense: we know that the majority of the world's tourists travel to Europe and North America, not to the least developed countries of the world like Bangladesh and Burkina Faso. We also know that a great number of tourists seek relaxation in comfortable if not luxurious surroundings when they holiday. How could poverty possibly be appealing?

The attraction of poverty will be explored in Chapter 4 using two main angles. Drawing upon postcolonial and postmodern interpretations of developing country tourism, the first part of the chapter presents critiques of the ways in which images and representations of developing country peoples and places are utilised and manipulated by the tourism industry. Stereotypical images and narratives from travel media show how women and men are turned into the 'exotic other' for the consumption of tourists from wealthier places. The industry explicitly exploits 'difference' in its marketing efforts: rich tourists can now visit the poor via cultural tourism; those of us living in built-up urbanscapes filled with modern conveniences can experience first-hand a 'primitive' African village. This is what Mowforth and Munt (2009: 81) refer to as the 'ultimate aestheticism of reality . . . [through] which racism and class struggle actually seem to be enjoyed'. The poor, along with their 'authentic' traditions and their 'untouched' natural landscapes, are offered up for our consumption. Never mind that Maasai in Kenya living in *bomas* (homesteads) constructed specifically for tourists have unwritten rules which mean that residents should remove all signs of modernity when tourists visit (e.g. mobile phones, watches, sneakers). And if we are to believe the images of tourist brochures, poor children from remote locations around the globe will always be delighted to greet us: ' . . . the local population is . . . represented as a group of smiling, servile natives ready to respond to the bidding of predominantly White tourists' (Potter et al. 1999: 102–103). The question is, what do these people get in return? We should consider whether visiting the poor helps to improve their economic or social situation, or whether on balance it is harmful to them. More insidious is the concern that the attraction of poverty might provide a disincentive for enhancing the well-being of the poor.

Secondly, this chapter considers the way in which poverty also attracts tourists who wish to do charitable or volunteer work (sometimes known as 'voluntourists'), and those who take 'justice tours'. Voluntourism has grown enormously in recent years, with one survey showing that 11 percent of tourists wanted to make volunteer work at least part of their holiday experience (Atkinson 2007). I examine the motivations and impacts of volunteers who work in disaster zones, orphanages, health clinics and similar places throughout the developing world, before considering the situation of those on justice tours who seek to develop a better understanding of inequality in our world. The chapter concludes by discussing whether all tourists—conventional, mass tourists or voluntourists and justice tourists—seeking interactions with poorer peoples and places are simply 'voyeurs of poverty', or whether they might make significant contributions to development through their travel experiences.

THE ALLURE OF POVERTY

Every day, marketing images and messages are churned out in a bid to entice tourists to some of the world's poorest countries. Cappelli (2006: 325) clearly shows the ways in which a language of tourism has evolved, a language which ' . . . persuades, lures, woos, and seduces millions of human beings . . . ' to visit 'authentic', 'exotic', 'out of the way' locations—including poor places. As Echtner and Prasad (2003: 661) note with genuine alarm, 'the vast majority of Third World destination marketing is created and distributed by First World promoters who are economically motivated to sell a particular brand of fantasy to a First World market'. This is disturbing from an ethical perspective, as poorer countries seem to have little control over the images of their people and their environments which are presented to the rest of the world. Such marketing can then 'replicate colonial forms of discourse, emphasizing certain binaries between the First and Third Worlds and maintaining broader geopolitical power structures' (Echtner and Prasad 2003: 660).

Fundamentally, is such blatant marketing of poverty unfair to the poor, or is it to their benefit? Strong growth in tourism to developing countries, while generally encouraged by the governments of these countries, lending institutions and donors, can be of concern precisely because in going to developing countries for their holidays, many tourists are seeking the 'untouched' (read 'pristine environments') and/or the 'exotic' (read 'tribal peoples in ethnic dress'), both environments and peoples which are particularly vulnerable to exploitation (Albuquerque and McElroy 1995).

Urry's (1990) notion of the tourist gaze can help us to understand this curiosity we have about other peoples and places, which is part of our motivation for taking holidays. Thus we go to gaze upon new and interesting landscapes. The suggestion is that in seeking out 'exotic' or 'out of the way' destinations such as those in the developing countries, we are seeking encounters with 'the Other'. Thus the 'Otherness' of hill tribe peoples wearing ethnic dress in Thailand can be packaged and sold to tourists: 'For the vast majority of people, otherness makes the destination attractive for consumption by establishing its distinctiveness' (Hall 1998: 140). This 'exotic Other' is becoming much more accessible to tourists thanks to new technologies which result in time-space contraction. Thus, for example, West Africa need no longer be perceived as out of reach by city dwellers in Berlin; in fact it only takes six hours to fly to the Gambia, while it takes twice as long to reach Los Angeles.

In the following sections, a number of the forces that draw tourists towards 'poverty' are considered, from a desire to experience an 'unspoilt' location to the quest for 'authenticity' and 'adventure'.

'Unspoilt' Beauty and Uniqueness

The push by development agencies and governments for poor regions and countries to develop tourism is centred squarely on a combination of beautiful 'untouched' natural and cultural attractions: 'Tourism is promoted today as an industry that can turn poor countries' very poverty into a magnet for sorely needed foreign currency. For to be a poor society in the late twentieth century is to be "unspoilt"' (Enloe 1990: 31). In her critical discussion of ecotourism, Duffy notes how traditional communities come to be part of the package sold to tourists:

> The host societies are packaged and commodified for consumption by an external audience, promising the exotic, the unspoilt, the pristine and—even worse—the primitive. (Duffy 2002: xii)

Similarly, many tourists are drawn to travel by their yearning for authenticity (MacCannell 1989), and poor places have come to be associated with 'authentic' experiences of culture and nature:

> To the mystifying tourist gaze, "aesthetic poverty" represents values long lost in Western society. A distorted symbol of naturalness, simplicity and (paradoxically) life contentment, poverty has become an important signifier of the authentic (cross-) cultural travel experience. As much as villages can successfully 'showcase their real-ness'

through simple markers of 'backwardness', they can quickly lose their authentic appeal through obvious signs of development. (Schellhorn 2007: 189)

Desforges (2000: 190), discussing the rapid growth of tourism in Peru, also suggests that tourists associate authentic culture with a 'cheap' destination: 'In regions where tourism is central to the economy, such as in the Cusco area, the tourist imagination of an "authentic" Andean culture works against local producers, who are expected to sell products such as ethnic handicrafts at low prices' (Desforges 2000: 190).

If we are tourists seeking authentic experiences, our range of options may seem to be diminishing because 'Every niched packaging of adventurous or exotic place-experience has the effect of narrowing the scope of tourisms which are yet to be encountered' (Cloke 2000: 842). We are attracted by the exotic other yet the exotic other changes in response to contact with tourists. What is seen as 'authentic' in the minds of tourists can also change over time. What Thailand offered 20 years ago, Vietnam was selling 10 years ago, and Laos offers it today. Thus our tourist gaze shifts over time, reflecting cultural change. This has implications for developing countries wishing to sustain a certain level of tourism interest. Box 4.1 provides examples of countries specifically trying to trade on the 'natural', 'authentic' or 'unspoilt' themes in their tourism slogans.

Box 4.1   Tourism Advertising Slogans for Developing Countries

Those selling 'authenticity' or 'uniqueness'

Zambia – The Real Africa

Malaysia – Truly Asia

Sri Lanka – A Land Like No Other

Rwanda – Discover a New African Dawn

Those selling 'unspoilt' nature

Burundi – The Eden in the Heart of Africa

Botswana – Unspoiled Vision, Untamed Vitality

Tobago – The Capital of Paradise: Clean, Green, Serene

Source: Official government Internet sites for each country (February 2009)

Poverty = Picturesque?

Cater (1995) asserts that while language used in tourism advertising can be selective and as shown previously, visual images are especially superficial, failing to show the complexity of life in destination areas. The spread of these images has been facilitated enormously by the development of communications technology, such as satellite television and the Internet, which are ' . . . the means by which simplified, inaccurate or downright misleading images and representations can be propagated' (Potter et al. 1999: 101). A photograph taken at sunset of a fisherperson cleaning nets beside a small boat may look romantic when it appears in a glossy brochure beside images of the luxury resort accommodation visitors will be treated to during their tropical island vacation. Readers will have no inclination, however, of the realities of life for the poor fisherpeople of this area: perhaps they are battling yet another resort developer who wants access to 'their' stretch of beach; perhaps they have already been moved down to the far end of a beautiful strip of beach, leaving the most pristine white sands for the tourists—and also leaving behind the only source of fresh water in the vicinity and the best place for launching their boats; maybe untreated sewage from resorts pumped out to sea is threatening their livelihoods.

Similarly, Marshment (1997) notes that images of women in 'traditional' roles are often presented in tourist brochures for developing country destinations, such as fetching water in large urns or crushing grains manually: the hardship and drudgery of these roles is not what is presented, rather, ' . . . the poverty of the people is transformed into the picturesque' (Marshment 1997: 28). While en route to the Ngorogoro crater to observe wildlife, tourists may ask their minivan driver to stop so they can take photographs of Maasai people to intersperse with their other holiday snaps, focusing on the beauty of these 'native people' and their costumes while remaining blissfully unaware of the realities of their lives. These realities include a history of land loss as their cattle grazing lands have been designated as national parks or intruded upon by other tribal groups, lack of access to quality health facilities and schools, and poor infrastructure (Photo 4.1).

Of grave concern to this writer is that when poverty itself becomes a tourist attraction, there may be no incentive to assist people in moving beyond the difficult circumstances they face. For example, volunteers working on a sea turtle conservation project in Costa Rica were mainly concerned about the physical environment, so they said of the area, 'I wouldn't want to see it more civilised' (Gray and Campbell 2007: 477). A freeze on development may not, however, be in the interests of local communities. Similarly, on the island of Flores in Indonesia, Cole (2008: 118) explains how government officials and tourist guides feel that the presence of electricity poles in a cultural village spoils it, and guides specify which villages do not yet have electricity: ' . . . this implied celebration of pre-electricity has worked against other villages getting electricity'. Tourists to cultural villages in

Photo 4.1 While main roads to internationally renowned national parks in Tanzania are sealed, Maasai in adjacent lands have to make do with inferior infrastructure and poor transport services.
Source: Author

Flores have aestheticised poverty and indeed, they seek out poorer, more peripheral villages for this reason as 'tourists equate authenticity with poverty' (Cole 2008: 198). As one backpacker visiting a village near Gunung Rinjani National Park in Indonesia also commented,

> For foreigners who have come out of a society where everything is steel and cement and asphalt and plastic already, poverty is aesthetic; by

which I mean everything is made out of leaves and stone and mud and all these natural things so as soon as you are going to get some money here that sort of spoils it. (Marcel from France, Interview, August 2003—cited in Schellhorn 2007: 189)

Furthermore, tourism itself may not even offer those being gazed upon the option of an economic livelihood:

Attempts by the villagers to make money are viewed negatively by tourists. Villagers that sell tickets are 'touristy' and therefore less authentic. Although some tourists want to drink chilled bottled drinks, for many the sale of such drinks indicates modernity and therefore inauthenticity. While some tourists wanted to buy postcards, most saw villagers' attempts to make sales to tourists as signifiers of 'being spoilt'. In seeking a contrast with their own culture (Rojek, 1997), tourists have notions of how the villages should be: rural, poor, primitive, dirty and traditional in contrast with their urban, rich sophisticated, clean and modern lives. (Cole 2008: 157)

Poverty = A Cheap Destination

Combined with these unspoilt characteristics and the allure of the exotic, poor countries also typically feature poorly paid workers and other low cost 'inputs', thus providing a 'cheap' holiday option. This leads Plüss and Backes to conclude that, 'to some extent tourism always feeds off the poverty of host regions' (2002: 12).

Backpackers perhaps represent the ultimate attempt by tourists to travel medium- to long-term 'on the cheap'. Their form of travel has been the subject of stringent critique, with some suggesting they are self-indulgent, and that they should not take the moral high ground when comparing their travel experiences to those of conventional tourists (Mowforth and Munt 2009). Hutnyk (1996: 10) is particularly critical, suggesting that backpackers think they are involved in an ethical form of travel when they are exploiting the fact that exchange rates allow them to live 'like Rajas in Indian towns' (Figure 4.1):

Budget travellers can visit the 'Third World' because it is cheap; because there are developed systems of transnational transportation and communication; and because they have the ability—even, perhaps, the need—to leave their usual domestic circumstances in order to travel and "see the world." (Hutnyk 1996: 214)

Novels such as 'The Beach' (Garland 1997) and 'Are You Experienced?' (Sutcliffe 1999) also suggest that contemporary backpackers are engaging in a self-centered form of poverty-tourism, traveling around shrouded from

'THE BEACH'

Figure 4.1   Poverty attracts backpackers.
Source: http://www.polyp.org.uk/

the 'real Third World' by the backpacker ghettos which provide the major stepping stones along their well-trodden route.

The bargain destination which a backpacker gets excited about is likely to be a place where many people still live in extreme poverty. Thus, for example, Ghana came to be seen as a cheap destination by travellers after the structural adjustment measure of devaluing the currency, the cedi; however this made it difficult for local people to afford imported products such as medicine—something which most travellers would have been blatantly unaware of (Konadu-Agyemang 2001).

Backpackers have also been criticised for being excessively concerned with bargain hunting. Thus in order that their funds will last for the duration of their travels, bartering may turn into a game in which they ultimately exploit artisans and traders desperate for a sale (Bradt 1995; Goodwin et al. 1998; Riley 1988). All this so they can brag to their friends back at their pension or losmen 'What?! You paid $xxx for it?! You were ripped off, man. I scored a great deal on this sarong/necklace/fake Student ID'.

Poverty = Adventure

There has been an upsurge in tourists seeking 'adventure' in unusual places in recent years, including slums and shanty-towns. This is sometimes referred to as 'poorism'. In a novel by William Sutcliffe which parodies backpacker travel in India, the following observation is made by a journalist on a train: ' . . . it's not hippies on a spiritual mission who come here anymore, just morons on a poverty-tourism adventure holiday' (Sutcliffe 1998: 140). Mowforth and Munt criticise the way in which poverty has effectively been commodified—thus, for example, people living in slum areas have been 'aestheticised', turned into something ' . . . worth experiencing and enjoying' (Mowforth and Munt 1998: 78):

> a range of less savoury realities of some parts of the Third World today—inequality, poverty and political instability—are also there to be enjoyed as part of the tourism experience. They are called upon to both titillate and legitimate travel, to help distinguish these experiences from mere mass tourism and packaged tourists. (Mowforth and Munt 1998: 74)

Tourists who seek out destinations 'off the beaten track' can be a problem when they fail to understand, or simply choose not to respect, cultural norms regarding what is appropriate behaviour in these new locales (Bradt 1995; Noronha 1999). Scanty or excessively casual dress, even in places of worship, drug and alcohol abuse and casual sexual encounters can all cause insult to local residents (Mandalia 1999; Aziz 1999).

As noted in Chapter 3, postcolonial scholars have argued that tourism embodies power relations between 'the West' and 'the Rest', building on inequalities established through colonial relationships (Hall and Tucker 2004). Ticknell agrees, identifying ' . . . traces of colonial adventure in narratives of independent tourism' (2001: 39). Thus tourists' travel fantasies may be fuelled by images of dark-skinned porters, waiters, masseurs and other modern day service industry workers who will be at their beck and call. Munt (1994) discusses how this is evident in a particular brand of 'eco-friendly' holidays pursued by the middle classes. Citing the example of the growing popularity of colonial style luxury safaris, he suggests that such trips are based upon racism and class subordination and that they exude a 'neocolonial aura':

> This is symbolically reproduced by J & C Voyageurs. In the single black and white photograph offered in its brochure . . . a trail of porters (thirty-five, they tell us) are shown tramping through an eco-colonial landscape, carrying the supplies for the group of six, 'most of the comforts of home—iced drinks, spacious sleeping tents, loos and showers'. It is an image and ambience that is recreated by many new, independent tour operators, whether it be luxury safaris or treks and expeditions for the young and adventurous; an army of global porters trot behind or ahead . . . to ensure that these new ethical tourists are regularly refreshed. (Munt 1994: 55)

A Chance to Understand the Lives of the Poor

There is evidence that tour experiences which include interactions with the poor can increase the understanding of tourists, rather than providing a kind of freak show experience. Goudie et al. (1999), for example, suggest that to exclude places like townships or shanty-towns from a tour operator's schedule essentially isolates them further from a country's social and economic life, reinforcing inequalities of the past:

> In the light of the history of South Africa and current socio-economic/spatial inequalities, it is a serious weakness within the tourism industry that its potential as a tool for economic empowerment and social integration has not been fully realised. Black areas . . . have largely been terra incognito for the tourism industry and, consequently, black South Africans have been given little opportunity to participate as partners or leaders within this industry sector. (Goudie et al. 1999: 27–28)

Interestingly, since Goudie et al. wrote, township tours have become a popular, almost mainstream, travel activity in locations like Johannesburg and Capetown as well as Rio De Janeiro and Nairobi. There are mixed opinions on whether they aestheticise the poor, or whether they allow local people to take control over what is presented to outsiders (see Mowforth and Munt 2009: 286–287 for contrasting examples). An example of the former is a car wash worker from Kibera, Nairobi's most well-known slum, stating, 'They [tourists] see us like puppets, they want to come and take pictures, have a little walk, tell their friends they've been to the worst slum in Africa' (ibid: 287). What is most critical is whether these tours offer local people opportunities for economic empowerment and social integration.

A positive example is the Max's Maximum tour which this author took in 1998 in Soweto, South Africa. Max's tours were run by township residents and were highly informative and interactive. Max insisted that all participants disembarked from the mini-coach regularly and spoke with Soweto residents who gathered around.[1] The tour I was on involved entering one woman's very modest one room dwelling which she shared with her grandson, and hearing her story of how she had come to live in Soweto and what dreams she had for the future. Tour participants were invited to leave donations when they left her home. Max rotated his tours around different houses so as to spread the contributions the tourists were making. The tour ended at a shebeen (traditional drinking house) on the street where Max lived and here again, tourists literally rubbed shoulders with the locals. The general impression of other tourists on the mini-coach was that they had learned a great deal and had a better understanding of the diversity and complexity of life in a township.

While some may argue that such tours bring direct economic benefits to only a handful of township residents, in another way, safe and informative tours of townships help to overcome stereotypes of township life and people. They also provide opportunities for visitors to meet residents and find out a little about their lives, thus they are helping to overcome the legacy of social and economic exclusion which characterises township life.

Similar tours are conducted by Reality Tours & Travel in Dharavi, a squatter settlement with over 1 million residents in Mumbai, India. They try to limit the possibility of their tours offering a voyeuristic, intrusive experience by restricting the size of tour groups to five people, and not allowing photographs to be taken by the tourists. What they are trying to do, meanwhile, is to show that those living in Dharavi are working hard to earn a living, and that they are neither lazy nor criminals. As noted by a previously sceptical journalist after he had been taken on a tour of Dharavi, ' . . . the purpose of the tour was not to generate pity, but understanding' (Lancaster 2007). There are plans that when the company makes a profit it will donate 80 percent of its slum-tour profits to a charitable organisation that is based in the slum (Lancaster 2007).

Disaster Tourism

Poverty also attracts tourists in the wake of conflict, natural disasters, security threats or other issues which result in, firstly, a rapid decline in tourist numbers and, secondly, a rash of 'cheap deals' to attract tourists back to a destination. This has occurred, for example, in Fiji post-coups, in Bali post-bombings, and in Mexico in the wake of the A(H1N1) influenza outbreak in 2009. Martin Dunford, co-founder of Rough Guides, states that while it is generally insensitive to travel to a disaster zone in the immediate wake of the disaster when people are still grieving, after a period of time Rough Guides would encourage visitors to return in order to bolster the economy (Irvine 2007). Similar sentiments were expressed by a representative of the Samoan Hotel Association after the 2009 tsunami in that country.

Others travel to areas of disasters, whether natural (e.g. hurricane, earthquake or tsunami) or human-induced (e.g. genocide, war), not for a cheap holiday but for a different type of experience. Richburg (cited in McLaren 1998: 56), calls independent travellers who seek out sites of famine and human tragedy, 'voyeurs of misery'. He was particularly referring to the situation in Somalia in the late 1980s when numerous independent travellers tried to hitch rides on aid convoys so they could get a close-up, personal view of the famine. While some travellers may have been motivated by a desire, however misinformed, to 'lend a hand', others wished to exploit the situation, taking pictures of the dying to sell on their return home. Similarly, people flooded to southern Thailand and India after the Indian Ocean tsunami of 2004, keen to 'experience' and/or take photographs of the affected communities and environments—some, for their own interest, others, hoping to sell these images to news agencies.

Of those who genuinely wish to help in a disaster zone, unfortunately only a minority have dedicated technical skills and experience in the type of work that would actually be helpful. These people take up positions with well-established humanitarian agencies, while others become 'voluntourists' for groups like Help International Phi Phi, which did very good work on a devastated Thai Island after the 2004 tsunami (see upcoming section on voluntourism). A Times of India article was nevertheless rather scathing of the attempts of well-meaning volunteers after the tsunami:

> They come in hordes with truckloads of relief material and a newfound urge to serve, but their presence is doing more harm than good in many areas hit hard by the tsunami. As unseemly as it sounds, these well-meaning people have spawned a new industry—disaster tourism. The massive inflow of charitable organisations and aid volunteers . . . is now being seen as the second giant wave. And overzealous volunteers, obsessed with the need to "do good" are making things worse. (Times of India 2005)

Another form of tourism to a supposedly imminent disaster zone is occurring in Tuvalu. Recently this tiny Pacific Island state, home to around 12,000 residents and comprised of five main atolls, has come up with an innovative form of disaster tourism. As one of the first countries in the world predicted to be directly impacted by rising sea levels associated with climate change, Tuvalu has announced that it will celebrate with an annual King Tide Festival from 2010. King tides lead to inundation of garden plots and homes on the main island of Funafuti, and tourism officials feel that by having music, entertainment and games at this time people will get to see the impacts of sea level rise on the people of Tuvalu (eTurboNews 2009e).

As noted by Kendal (2007), people's curiosity about the impacts of a disaster is not amoral in itself: we are often glued to television or computer screens watching disasters unfold in real time before our eyes. However this can be seen as 'vulgar voyeurism' if the presence of curious outsiders impedes the work of those trying to aid in recovery from disasters, if it uses up resources (e.g. accommodation, water, electricity) which are scarce in the wake of a disaster, and if it any way exploits the vulnerability of those directly impacted by the disaster: 'If you hamper rescue/recovery operations or contribute further to the pain of the people whose space you are invading, then you have crossed that fine moral line' (Kendal 2007).

The first part of this chapter has discussed a range of ways in which poverty attracts tourists, from those seeking 'authenticity' and 'difference' to those wanting a cheap holiday or to experience first-hand a disaster zone. It finished by suggesting some tourists travel to poorer places in order to help others less fortunate than themselves: they are sometimes called voluntourists, and they form the subject of the second part of this chapter.

VOLUNTOURISM

Often now condensed into the single term 'voluntourism', volunteer tourism programmes ' . . . seek to combine the hedonism of tourism with the altruism of development work' (Simpson 2004: 681). Mustonen (2005) suggests that altruistic forms of tourism will continue to grow in future, likening volunteers to postmodern pilgrims with aspirations of goodness. Volunteer tourism is certainly a popular trend to the extent that short-term volunteer positions are now advertised on popular websites, are part of the regular repertoire of experiences offered by adventure travel companies, and are reflected upon regularly in the media by journalists who have unwittingly been lured to experience voluntourism first-hand. Travelocity, online travel specialists, conducted a survey in which 6 percent of respondents said they wanted volunteering to be incorporated in their travel plans for 2006. Twelve months later the same survey showed an almost doubling of interest, with 11 percent of respondents keen to be involved in volunteer tourism (Atkinson 2007: 70). More recent data suggests further growth in the popularity of volunteer tourism experiences, both due to interest from 'a new generation of travellers' who 'want to give back when going abroad', and due to job concerns in light of the global recession. Thus the company i-to-i, which offers volunteer tourism opportunities in 30 countries, saw a 28 percent increase in annual revenue in sales to March 2009 (eTurboNews 2009a). In an interesting development, the British government decided in 2009 to subsidise volunteer experiences overseas for hundreds of university-leavers who were unlikely to find employment immediately due to the effects of a global economic recession. Successful applicants to this scheme were to travel to countries such as India, Costa Rica and Indonesia to assist with projects which, for example, improved sanitation and education facilities (Sunday Star Times 2009: A13).

Simpson (2004) argues that it is important to distinguish between the types of experiences being marketed by commercial volunteer-sending organisation and development organisations. The latter tend to have a clearer focus on a two-way exchange of experiences, and put a great deal of effort into preparing volunteers for assignments requested by the communities concerned. By contrast, it was concern about the rise of profit-driven, unregulated voluntourism companies, coupled with the increasing popularity of voluntourism among the thousands of young Gap Year tourists who head overseas from the UK each year, that prompted British NGO, Tourism Concern, to publish The Ethical Volunteering Guide *(www.ethicalvolunteering.org)*. Tourism Concern examined over 70 companies in the UK that provide short-term volunteering opportunities, revealing that much hinges on:

- The nature of the organisations providing short-term volunteering experiences

Table 4.1   Examples of Travel Involving Voluntary Development Work

Company	Location	Activity	Duration	Cost $US
Calcutta Rescue	Calcutta, India	Calcutta Rescue is a charitable organisation offering free healthcare to those of low economic status; it is sometimes referred to as Dr Jack's after its founder, Jack Preger. Some volunteers are trained doctors and nurses, others assist with administration and more mundane work. Some Indian staff are also employed. Volunteers are mainly independent travellers.	Flexible – often several weeks to several months.	Volunteers meet all their own travel and living expenses.
Addventures	Cambodia	Includes seven days of holidaying and five days volunteering on a VSA (Volunteer Service Abroad – a New Zealand NGO) project in Takeo province where they work beside local community members. Past projects here have included building a reading shelter at a school, equipping a school library and assisting with English lessons.	12 days	$2418 not including flights – approximately $700 is a contribution to VSA two-year assignments
gapyear.com	Numerous countries	Not much emphasis on the skills of the volunteer – placements often involve coaching sports, conservation work, doing art work with children or teaching English. For example, in Zambia volunteers can teach English in a community school, assist with adult literacy classes, or help out in a medical clinic that deals with HIV/AIDS education. Duration and costs vary – those provided here are for a Zambian placement.	3 months	$3,193 not including flights or food

Continued

Table 4.1 Continued

Company	Location	Activity	Duration	Cost $US
Cross-Cultural Solutions	12 countries including Brazil, Costa Rica and Ghana	Small teams of volunteers work with local organizations with whom relationships have been established over a number of years, including hospitals, orphanages and community centres. Volunteer tasks could include: teaching English, caregiving, healthcare, and community development. Volunteers get some days off during their stay – see also Box 4.2.	2–12 weeks	$2,784–$6,843 not including flights
Learning from Ladakh project	Ladakh, Northwest India	Westerners provide voluntary help on farms during the summer harvest and through this gain insights into the links between the people, their culture and their ecosystem. This also helps to raise the profile of agriculture and farm life in an area characterised by urban drift of young people. Volunteers stay with a Ladakhi farming family for 28 days and have 5 days of group workshops about culture, sustainability and globalization. Volunteers are expected to discuss with Ladakhi people problems with western consumer culture, and to learn from the social harmony and environmental sustainability of the Ladakhi traditional lifestyle.	1 month (or more)	US$600 (approx. half is subsidized)

Source: www.calcuttarescue.org, www.vsa.org.nz/what-you-can-do/volunteer-overseas/adventure, www.gapyear.com, www.crossculturalsolutions.org, www.isec.org.uk/pages/ladakh.html

- How well they work in partnership with local organisations
- The sustainability/continuity of projects volunteers work on, and how well they educate their volunteers both prior to and during their travels.

Table 4.1 lists a number of different organisations, from charitable ones (such as Calcutta Rescue) to commercial enterprises (such as gapyear. com), offering voluntary development work to tourists. Some NGOs do not charge volunteers for their experience, but Addventures does do this and approximately one third of this is taken as a contribution to the wider work of Voluntary Service Abroad, which initiated Addventures. There are also differences in local engagement, with Learning from Ladakh, Addventures and Cross Cultural Solutions emphasising ongoing partnerships with local communities and local community organisations, which could make their programmes more sustainable.

On first examination of Table 4.1, it may appear that travel with a voluntary development work focus has much to recommend it. While this argument has some credence, it is important to recognise other perspectives as well. These fall along a continuum (Figure 4.2) which suggests that travel which involves voluntary development work can be understood in several different ways:

- As 'harmful': a new form of colonialism which entrenches inequitable relationships which see the West as having the answers to the developmental problems of the developing countries, while failing to acknowledge the place of the West in creating/entrenching such problems or the skills, resources and knowledge of developing country peoples.
- As 'egocentric': providing an outlet for the self-centred interests and desires of relatively affluent youths around the world to improve their CVs and/or have an adventurous experience.
- As 'harmless': giving vent to the altruistic tendencies of a small group of tourists, while neither making a major contribution nor impacting negatively on host communities.
- As 'helpful': offering constructive assistance to developing country peoples through transference of skills and resources.

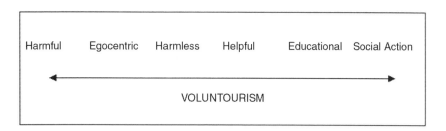

Figure 4.2   Continuum showing varied perspectives on voluntourism.
Source: Author

- As 'educational': providing for a richer cultural exchange and opportunities for cross-cultural understanding that would not be available on conventional trips.
- As 'social action': leading to greater involvement of volunteers in social movements in the long term.

Harmful

The view that voluntourists can be harmful is expressed by Hutnyk (1996) in his book titled *The Rumour of Calcutta*. Hutnyk is cynical about the place of international travellers engaging in 'charity tourism' here, whether for religious groups such as the Mother Theresa trust or for secular organisations such as Calcutta Rescue, informally known as 'Dr Jack's' (as was shown in Table 4.1). This organisation provides healthcare to 'street-dwelling destitutes and others of low economic status' (Hutnyk 1996: 44). Some of the volunteers who work at such clinics are qualified nurses or doctors, while others simply have a desire to help others. Most stay in Calcutta for at least a few weeks, with some remaining for over six months. Voluntary work is the primary reason that a number of these volunteers come to Calcutta, while for others, it provides a diversion from their backpacking sojourn through Asia:

> There is little doubt that most travellers who engage in volunteer work in Calcutta stumble into it with not much more than general notions of commitment and charity. Questions of cultural hegemony, international and class privilege, and the extent of relative economic advantage are, at best, understood in a vague, not an analytical, way. (Hutnyk 1996: 44)

Hutnyk suggests that those interrupting their travels to engage in charity work on the streets of Calcutta display a ' . . . nonchalant ambivalence' towards their work (1996: 59). They are also taking advantage of inequalities in the global politico-economic system which allow them to travel largely unimpeded around the world. Guidebooks reinforce the 'right' of those with money to travel wherever they wish around the world (Lisle 2008), oblivious to the fact that most people from poorer countries face real difficulties in terms of getting visas to travel to the western world, in particular, even if they have the economic means to do so. As Simpson notes: 'The processes that allow young westerners to access the financial resources, and moral imperatives, necessary to travel and volunteer in a "third world country", are the same as the ones that make the reverse process almost impossible' (2004: 690).

While Hutnyk was discussing how independent travellers may decide to do charitable work as part of their travels, it is through commercial companies that most contemporary voluntourists book their experiences. Unlike the medical specialists who volunteer at Dr Jack's, often this new breed of voluntourists has no specific development skills. This leads Simpson to suggest that the commercial volunteer sector

> legitimizes the validity of young unskilled international labour as a development "solution" . . . the very legitimacy of such programmes is rooted in a concept of a "third world", where there is "need", and where European young people have the ability, and right, to meet this need. (Simpson 2004: 682)

The gapyear.com company is an example of such a company which perpetuates negative stereotypes of 'poor people' while suggesting young travellers can help to solve their complex problems. They advertise on their website that volunteering overseas is ' . . . a great way to soak yourself in another culture; you may find yourself working with people who know only poverty, disease, hunger and monotony' (cited in Simpson 2004: 686).

Egocentric

The egocentric interpretation of volunteer tourism is that voluntourists are interested in going to somewhere 'exotic' and 'adventurous' in order to develop skills which may look good on their CVs, to impress their friends who have chosen 'tamer' Gap Year options, or to pursue a personal quest for adventure. They are thus more motivated by the opportunity for a 'Survivor Africa' experience (such as some of the disaster or adventure tourists referred to earlier in the chapter) than the chance to learn about the lives and experiences of others, or to assist those they visit. This is what Devereux (2008: 358) refers to when he argues, 'At its worst, international volunteering can be imperialist, paternalistic charity, volunteer tourism, or a self-serving quest for career and personal development on the part of well-off westerners'. While such tourists may be somewhat transformed by their experience, it is not likely that they will make a significant difference to the well-being of the poor or raise awareness among others of global inequalities on their return home.

Harmless

Voluntourists may not be delighted to hear that they can be seen as 'harmless', as this also means they are actually making little difference to the communities they visit. This can be a reality when the volunteer experiences are not well planned, such as when a commercial volunteer-sending organisation is interested only in placing paying volunteers into preconceived projects such as 'helping the disabled' or painting a classroom.

Luh's (2006) research on Singaporean voluntourists found that local Cambodian organisations lacked power in influencing when volunteers would come, and for which projects. In such cases local organisations may ask the volunteers to repeat work already completed by previous volunteers, or to carry out work which has not been agreed to by local communities. This power imbalance points to a serious flaw in the way volunteer tourism is organised by some agencies. In terms of good practice guidelines, communities should themselves nominate projects they would like assistance with before volunteers are recruited, and this is easier to do when the outside agency organising the volunteers has a long-term relationship with the host community. Furthermore, after each group of volunteers have visited, communities should be asked for feedback to ensure that their goals and aspirations are being met by the volunteer scheme.

Helpful

The view that voluntourism is 'helpful' is based on the notion that many of the individuals from western countries paying to come to the developing country to assist with development work are motivated by a desire to help to overcome poverty, rather than seeking a pleasure-filled, self-indulgent holiday. Research has shown that voluntourists show greater altruistic tendencies than other types of tourists (Coghlan 2006; Wearing 2001):

> the main motivation for undertaking the volunteer project was not primarily related to sightseeing but to volunteering, to work, 'not just be tourists', 'to give' and 'to experience a service project.' (McIntosh and Zahra 2007: 546)

McIntosh and Zahra (2007: 554) thus conclude that due to the altruistic motives of volunteers 'the host-volunteer encounter has the potential to be authentic, mutually beneficial and more sustainable than traditional cultural tourism consumption'.

Voluntourism is also 'helpful' in that the money they spend on local accommodation and food can contribute directly to poverty alleviation in areas which would not attract conventional tourists. Volunteers working on sea turtle conservation in with Asociación ANAI in Costa Rica, for example, were found to provide good economic returns to the host families (cabineros) who provide them with room and board for $14 per night. Volunteer ecotourism is now the main economic activity in the Gandoca area. As one cabinero commented, ' . . . many people live on the money volunteers bring in' (cited in Gray and Campbell 2007: 471).

Educational

Another view of volunteer tourism is that this can be educational, particularly when volunteer-sending organisations specifically seek to open the eyes of affluent westerners to global problems. In McGehee and Santos'

(2005: 771) research with participants from three US organisations, for example, they found that, 'An overwhelming majority of participants reported a heightened awareness of global issues as a result of the volunteer tourism trip itself. Many reported that it changed their previously myopic and self-centred views of the world'. The cross-cultural interaction that occurs can thus contribute to 'development', in a broader sense and it 'can be a rich source of narrative, learning, appreciation, inspiration, cultural respect, solidarity and equality in the search for sustainable models of tourism' (McIntosh and Zahra 2007: 543). For example, the Learning from Ladakh Project (Table 4.1) is focused on building relationships between people from different parts of the globe so while some transference of skills may occur, their main motivation is to promote cross-cultural understanding. Thus tourism can encourage contact between otherwise distant 'others', allowing at its best opportunities for learning, a two-way exchange, and a sense of our 'common humanity' (Butcher 2003: 94).

However, warns Raymond and Hall (2008: 530), cross-cultural understanding will develop only if volunteer-sending agencies plan carefully for this in terms of preparation of volunteers, support in-country, and follow up: ' . . . development of cross-cultural understanding should be perceived as a goal of volunteer tourism rather than a natural result of sending volunteers overseas'. In some cases, volunteers are expected to prepare for their experience by reading briefing notes provided by the organisation and to come with a positive attitude, whereas in other cases they are asked put considerable thought into what they are doing before they embark on their travels. Learning from Ladakh volunteers, for example, prepare for their placement by reading the book *Ancient Futures: Learning from Ladakh* (1991), which is Helena Norberg-Hodge's account of the value of traditional culture and lifestyles in Ladakh. This is so they can reflect critically on western consumer culture in their conversations with Ladakhi people (Acott et al. 1998).

This confirms Wearing's (2001) finding in his landmark book on volunteer tourism, that relationships between tourists and hosts are *not* necessarily characterised by neocolonial power relationships. Rather, these relationships can be meaningful for both hosts and the volunteer tourists. Clearly, it is the approach of the tour operators or volunteer-sending agency and the attitudes of the tourists themselves to poverty which is critical. This was evident in the clean-up and reconstruction process in Honduras after Hurricane Mitch devastated large parts of Central America in November 1998. There was a clear difference between those voluntary organisations that did rebuilding *independently* of local communities, and those who rebuilt *alongside* local communities (Jeffrey 1999). A large number of work teams organised outside of the country came to assist with the reconstruction effort. Often dressed in uniform t-shirts, they came with their own agendas and provided most of their own resources and equipment. There was very little community involvement. This type of approach engenders dependency and fails to establish relationships of mutual trust and understanding. By contrast, Don Tatlock, the coordinator of a group that worked alongside local communities, explained their purpose in bringing volunteers:

> If all we were interested in was throwing up homes as quickly as possible, we would ask these folks to send us the money they spend on their airline tickets. What's more important than how many cement blocks they can lay in a week or two are the relationships they can build with the poor during those days, what they can learn about why people are poor, and the impact their presence has on the Hondurans. By giving their time and spending their money to come so far to sweat in the sun with the victims of Mitch, they're conveying a sense of love and caring that pays off in increased self-esteem and encouragement among villagers. (Jeffrey 1999: 4)

These volunteers learned how hard-working and industrious local people were and that building relationships with them was more important than constructing houses. Local people responded well to this approach, as seen in the following comment from Teófilo López, a Honduran farmer: 'We don't understand a lot of their jokes, but we understand their solidarity and their sacrifice' (cited in Jeffrey 1999).

An emphasis on building relationships is also evident in the work of Cross-Cultural Solutions, which focuses its programmes in 12 countries where they seek to maintain sustainable, long-term programmes. Thus when one group of volunteers leaves, another group replaces them. Their philosophy emphasises working side by side with locals and empowering, not pitying, local people (see Table 4.1 and Box 4.2).

Box 4.2   Cross-Cultural Solutions: Vision, Mission and Values

Our Vision is a world where people value cultures different from their own, are aware of global issues, and are empowered to effect positive change.

Our Mission is to operate volunteer programs around the world in partnership with sustainable community initiatives, bringing people together to work side-by-side while sharing perspectives and fostering cultural understanding. We are an international not-for-profit organization with no political or religious affiliations.

Our Values are:

Shared Humanity
– When people of different cultures have an opportunity to connect, there comes an understanding of our shared humanity.

Continued

Box 4.2   Continued

Respect
– We accept, appreciate and respect that people know and understand what is appropriate for their own communities.

Integrity
– We commit to ensuring the safety, flexibility, professionalism, transparency and excellence of our programs.

Source: Cross Cultural Solutions (2009)

Social Action

At the far right of the continuum presented in Figure 4.1, we can find organisations that go a step further than 'helping' or providing educational experiences. Rather, they attempt, sometimes idealistically and other times based on a sound platform of knowledge about the political, cultural and economic context, to make the volunteers part of the solution to global problems. Their work supports the vision that, when planned carefully,

> volunteering can raise awareness of, and a commitment to, combating existing unequal power relations and deep-seated causes of poverty, injustice, and unsustainable development [and it] . . . has the potential to challenge the economic and technical focus of globalisation in favour of people connecting and relating with each other on a global scale. (Devereux 2008: 358)

For example, in Thailand an agency called Life Travel Service was established with the assistance of academics and development workers to build solidarity among people from different parts of the world. It did this by showing visitors evidence of inequalities between western and developing countries and encouraging their support for Thai people's efforts to overcome injustice (Pleumarom 1994).

Similarly, McGehee's research with Earthwatch volunteers, who are involved in short (10–14 day) expeditions which have a research focus such as assessing the health of a coral reef or examining the maternal mortality of women in West Africa, also revealed that this voluntary work has a very positive effect on the involvement of the volunteers in social movements:

> Although not overtly political, an Earthwatch expedition, through its unique emphasis on the type of participation most likely to predict or promote further activism, may reasonably be expected to draw together like-minded individuals from far-flung geographical areas, enabling the establishment of network ties and idea exchange. (McGehee 2002: 128–129)

A follow-up study by McGehee and Santos (2005: 760), which examined three different US-based organisations which utilised volunteer tourism, confirmed the previous findings about the importance of network ties, and showed that 'participation in volunteer tourism had a positive effect on both intended post-trip social movement activities and support for activism'.

This section of Chapter 4 has clearly shown that there are a variety of types of organisations offering opportunities for people to have voluntourism experiences in poorer countries. Some such organisations are simply capitalising on the demand from Gap Year tourists to have an adventure, while others are seriously committed to assisting the poor, enhancing the understanding of the voluntourists about class, ethnic, political, and economic inequalities which lead to poverty in our world, and in building solidarity between the voluntourists and those they visit.

JUSTICE TOURISM

Closely related to the voluntourism organisations promoting education and social action, is a form of tourism sometimes termed 'justice tourism'. This is an alternative approach to tourism which does not involve volunteer work, but which, ' . . . seeks to achieve mutual understanding, solidarity and equality amongst participants' (Holden 1984: 15). This is one of the 'alternative' forms of tourism referred to in Chapter 2 that emerged in the 1970s and 1980s in response to criticisms of the negative impacts of mainstream tourism and the desire to show solidarity with social justice issues in other parts of the world. 'Work brigades' to Cuba, for example, are a classic, early example of justice tourism.

Wenham and Wenham (1984), who in the 1980s were operators of a tour agency in Australia called 'Just Travel', suggested what justice in travel means to both travellers and those in the communities they visit. As Box 4.3 indicates, travellers can be part of a liberation process, they should have the opportunity to build relationships with local people, and for the local community, economic benefits and pride in their own culture should be maximised through engaging with tourism.

In sum, ideally justice tourism means tourism which is both ethical and equitable. It has the following attributes:

- Builds solidarity between visitors and those visited.
- Promotes mutual understanding and relationships based on equality, sharing and respect.
- Supports self-sufficiency and self-determination of local communities.
- Builds pride of community members and maximises local economic, cultural and social benefits.

Box 4.3   What is Justice in Tourism?

From the point of view of the traveller:

- The knowledge that s/he is not an agent of oppression but is attempting to participate in the liberation process.
- That a travel experience will offer genuine possibilities of forming meaningful relationships with people of different cultures.
- That there is opportunity to experience first-hand what other people are doing to create new life possibilities for themselves and others.
- That they will receive adequate preparation for their travel.

From the point of view of the people in tourist-receiving communities:

- Travellers will be seen as people who are coming to share and not to dominate their lives.
- Local accommodation and infrastructure will be used. As far as possible the services of foreign-owned or operated companies will be avoided.
- Tourist sites and shows which degrade or debase the culture will be avoided. Opportunity will be given to local people to develop a real presentation of their culture with pride and dignity.
- Travellers will be required to observe standards of decency and will not be tolerated if their presence is offensive to local people.

Source: Extracted from Wenham and Wenham (1984)

Justice tourism can be applied to tours of poverty-stricken areas where education and understanding, not horror, is the outcome. It was thus argued earlier in this chapter that tours of slums, shanty towns, favelas and townships are not necessarily voyeuristic. This is only the case, however, if tourists are given the opportunity to develop a deeper understanding of the injustice underlying poverty.

Justice tourism can also include cases whereby historically oppressed communities have the opportunity to share with visitors their experiences of past wrongs, thus re-writing the history books in one sense. Their people may have experienced enslavement, civil war initiated by the state, or a legal system—such as apartheid in South Africa—that denies the oppressed group the same rights as other citizens. In the last few decades, legal changes, independence and democratic elections have removed a number of oppressive regimes from power and the countries which they ruled over have in some cases become popular tourism destinations. One way in which formerly oppressed peoples are engaging with the tourism sector is to offer heritage tours. Such tours can promote visitors' understanding of human rights and justice issues. Such heritage tourism does not romanticise, simplify or glorify the past: it simply tells the story of what an oppressed population went through from their own perspective, and reflects on the implications this has had for their lives today. In the Caribbean, for example, there were plans to put together an educational tour package focusing on the sites of the trans-Atlantic slave trade (Boyd 1999). Similarly, community-controlled 'Black heritage tourism' has been encouraged in South Africa (Bartis 1998). This is tourism which brings visitors to sites of significance to the anti-apartheid movement, such as the house where Steve Biko resided, or the primary school attended by Nelson Mandela. The significance of such tours should not be underestimated in a country for which 'heritage' for so long meant 'white heritage':

> South Africa's cultural infrastructure, such as monuments and muse-
> ums, reflects the needs and interests of the white minority, focusing
> on aspects of colonial heritage rather than offering a more diverse and
> sensitive portrayal of South African history. By 1991, for instance, it
> was estimated that little more than 2% of all national monuments had
> been explicitly dedicated to black culture and history. (Goudie et al.
> 1999: 24)

On a positive note, some efforts have been made to redress this obvious bias under the new regime in South Africa. Examples include museums now displaying scenes of townships and working life for black people and providing information on the work of black organisations and trade unions under apartheid, and monuments erected in the memory of people who died during uprisings against apartheid. Tours of the Robben Island Museum, for many years home to South Africa's most famous political prisoner, Nelson Mandela, attracts over 2,000 visitors a day and a number of former prisoners are employed as guides (Goudie et al. 1999; Phaswana-Mafuya and Haydam 2005).

Other tours are more concerned with an accurate portrayal of current issues and events. Rethinking Tourism Project, which for the first time was offering an 'alternative' tour to Temixco, Mexico, in conjunction with local NGO the International Center for Cultural and Language Studies, claimed that tourists would:

> Learn about global tourism and free trade's impacts on Indigenous Peo-
> ples of the region, as well as alternative development projects implemented
> by communities to help retain their culture and heritage, empower local
> people, create microenterprises, and curb youth migration. (Rethinking
> Tourism Project, electronic discussion list, 22 February 2000)

A good example of a hotbed of revolutionary tourism is the Chiapas area of Mexico, where the indigenous people have been in conflict with the state since the Zapatista rebellion of 1994. It is claimed that the 'tourists of conscience' who come here contribute significantly to the local economy, make purchasing decisions based on support for cooperatives which are linked to the Zapatista cause, and they have a commitment to the cause that continues after they return home: 'People go back home, look at their photos, talk about their experiences, and participate in the solidarity movement', according to Ernesto Ladesma, who manages a local accommodation outlet (Ross 1999: 5). Some tourists pay $1000 for an eight-day 'Reality Tours' trip to Chiapas with the social justice organisation Global Exchange, which is based in San Francisco. Global Exchange is a non-profit organisation which offers tours as a means of promoting cross-cultural understanding between people in the West and developing countries, and educating western travellers. Wrelton's thesis (2006), which examined a Reality Tour to Chiapas, found that Global Exchange demonstrated a high level of social responsibility and that those participating in the tours often became involved in forms of activism upon return home. Global Exchange offers similar tours to countries such as Afghanistan, India and South Africa, aiming to put their clients in contact with local people, including community leaders, families and activists, who can inform them about the history and contemporary situation of their country.

CONCLUSION

The first part of this chapter discussed how words, images and ideas are being used to 'sell' poor countries and their peoples to the tourists of the world. While it is right that we should be concerned about this, particularly where erroneous, stereotypical and/or neocolonial views are being promoted, it is also true that people from poor regions and countries generally *want* tourists (and the money they bring) to come to their areas. *How* this occurs it of utmost relevance. It is not enough that tourism operators, organisations or individuals focus on a *subject,* such as poverty. Tourism to sites of poverty should not be about the rights of western travellers to explore 'untouched', exotic places and peoples, and nor should it simply be about providing an outlet for the altruistic tendencies of some tourists through voluntary work. Rather, it should be about enhancing the wellbeing of those visited, building understanding between tourists and those visited, and if 'assistance' is given, providing this on terms set by local peoples.

The second part of this chapter considered the growth in voluntourism and what this means for the voluntourists and their 'hosts'. Voluntourism, like other 'new' forms of tourism, should not automatically be seen as ethically and morally superior to mass, conventional tourism. There are still plenty of tour operators who are just pleased to be able to exploit the interests of a segment of tourists in 'helping the poor', rather than having any commitment to raising tourists' awareness of injustice, making a difference to a community's development over the long term, and building relationships between tourists and local people as part of the experience. Others, however, have development of cross-cultural understanding as a central aim, something which Devereux sees as holding considerable potential:

> If we want the meaningful change in North-South relationships and structures required for enabling equitable development in our complex, interdependent, and globalised world, international volunteers who return home may in fact be a crucial complementary element. (Devereux 2008: 368)

In the case of justice tours, discussed in the final part of this chapter, there is ample evidence of development agencies and tour operators which are building solidarity between distant peoples and raising westerners' understanding of poverty and justice issues through their work.

I hope readers were somewhat disturbed by the title of this chapter, 'Poverty Attracts Tourists', even if they understood the unsavoury truth embedded in this statement. What is of importance now is to consider ways in which tourism might help people to move out of a situation of poverty, such that they are empowered, have access to resources, and are able to build more sustainable livelihoods. One thing this chapter has shown is that where people are living in poverty, it is unrealistic to expect that on their own they will necessarily be able to harness any opportunities that tourism brings:

> I think wherever you get poverty you get people who are least able to develop commercial enterprise that will relieve tourists of their money. It tends to be the educated ones in the community that are the most enterprising that will scoop the money . . . and . . . the poor people become the inhabitants of a traditional village and become the subjects of tourism, or objects rather . . . Poverty in its own way can actually almost become a tourist attraction . . . and you get the "Kepala Desas" [village head] and the losmen owners on the periphery of poverty that are making all the money and very little may get handed down to the people that . . . are needing the benefits of tourism. (Interview with project staff, August 2002—Schellhorn 2007: 263)

The following three chapters will thus explore the strategies adopted by private sector businesses, governments and development agencies which support the notion that the poor should have opportunities to be more involved in and claim greater benefits from tourism.

5 Tourism Reduces Poverty
Tourism Industry Approaches

INTRODUCTION

One of the most potent claims of PPT advocates is that the tourism industry can play a significant role in ensuring that the poor gain greater benefits from tourism. This is not an assertion that can be made lightly. This claim goes against the grain of much academic writing on tourism in developing countries, as shown in Chapter 3, which is most likely to suggest that the private sector is exploitative of poorer peoples and their environments. With PPT, however, things have changed. We are told that PPT aims to 'unlock opportunities for the poor within tourism, at all levels and scales of operation' (PPT Partnership 2005b: 1). Proponents of PPT want to ' . . . "mainstream" pro-poor tourism so that it is a business approach across the industry, rather than a niche market' (Ashley and Ashton 2006: 3). In fact, PPT proponents suggest that to achieve poverty alleviation, it is more constructive to work through large-scale, mainstream tourism businesses than small-scale, alternative operations with all of their stated good intentions.[1] While the numbers of alternative tour operators on the market have escalated since the late 1980s, the changes they are implementing will mean little overall if the mainstream tourism industry fails to reassess its operations: 'Despite moves by the smaller 'alternative tour operators', tourism is still a mass event and the operations of large, transnational companies (TNCs) have come to dominate and control most areas of tourism development' (Sobania 1999: 81).

The claim that the private sector offers the greatest hope for PPT runs contrary to the fact that major players in the tourism industry, as in any industry, are centrally concerned with profit maximisation (Ashley and Haysom 2006; Zhao and Ritchie 2007). We cannot, therefore, assume that they might have an ethical commitment to ensuring their businesses contribute to poverty alleviation. Recent years have seen consolidation of the power of the largest tourism-related organisations through mergers and growth, rather than a dismantling of their power. Thus transformation of the *modus operandi* of the mainstream tourism industry, including large companies operating in a multitude of different countries and with a high degree of vertical integration, is a 'big ask'. As Table 5.1 suggests, of all

Table 5.1   Priorities of Different Tourism Stakeholders

Stakeholder	Community Development	Conservation	Industry Development
Local residents	* *	*	
Development NGOs	* *	*	
Conservationists	*	* *	
Government officials	* *	*	* *
Donors	* *	* *	*
Tourism industry		*	* *

Source: Adapted from Ashley and Roe (1998: 10)

stakeholders in tourism, the interests of the tourism industry are least likely to align with concern for community development (which can be a proxy in this case for the interests of the poor).

However, as noted in Chapter 2, advocates of tourism who draw on liberal and neoliberal logic have provided strong support for tourism and its potential to bring development to the poor. Christie and Sharma (2008: 428) discuss links between the private sector and tourism, noting that there are many '. . . profitable opportunities in unlikely places'. While this is undoubtedly true, it is a much bigger conceptual jump to then assert that there is an automatic link between growth of tourism and achievement of the MDGs.

Mitchell and Ashley (2007a) note that to appreciate the potential benefits of tourism we need to realise that there can be both direct and indirect impacts of tourism on the poor. They suggest three 'pathways' by which tourism affects the poor:

1. Direct effects from tourism to the poor: e.g. employment, small enterprises, lease monies paid to communities.
2. Secondary effects from tourism to the poor: e.g. indirect earnings from related sectors that supply goods and services to tourism (such as fruit and vegetables).
3. Dynamic effects on the economy: e.g. impacts on entrepreneurialism, skills, opportunities to interact with 'outsiders' and gain access to markets, improvement of infrastructure (e.g. roads and water supply) or the natural environment.

Most of these benefits are also highlighted in the UNWTO's list of ways in which tourism can contribute to economic development (Box 5.1).

In Chapter 5, therefore, we return to a question posed in Chapter 1 of this book, that is, can an industry driven by profits ever be expected to prioritise

Box 5.1   UNWTO's Reasons that Tourism is an Especially Suitable Economic
Development Sector for LDCs

1. Tourism is consumed at the point of production; the tourist has to go to
   the destination and spend his/her money there, opening an opportunity
   for local businesses of all sorts, and allowing local communities to benefit
   through the informal economy, by selling goods and services directly to
   visitors.
2. Most LDCs have a comparative advantage in tourism over developed countries. They have assets of enormous value to the tourism industry—culture,
   art, music, natural landscapes, wildlife and climate, including World Heritage Sites. Visits by tourists to such sites can generate employment and
   income for communities as well as help in the conservation of cultural and
   natural assets.
3. Tourism is a more diverse industry than many others. It has the potential
   to support other economic activities, both through providing flexible, part-
   time jobs that can complement other livelihood options, and through creating income throughout a complex supply chain of goods and services.
4. Tourism is labour-intensive, which is particularly important in tackling
   poverty. It also provides a wide range of different employment opportunities especially for women and young people—from the highly skilled to the
   unskilled—and generally it requires relatively little training.
5. It creates opportunities for many small and micro-entrepreneurs, either in
   the formal or informal economy; it is an industry in which start-up costs
   and barriers to entry are generally low or can be lowered.
6. Tourism provides not only material benefits for the poor but also cultural
   pride. It creates greater awareness of the natural environment and its economic value, a sense of ownership and reduced vulnerability through diver-
   sification of income sources.
7. The infrastructure required by tourism, such as transport and communications, water supply and sanitation, public security, and health services, can
   also benefit poor communities.

Source: UNWTO (2005: 1–2)

the interests of the poor? The focus will be, firstly, on considering recent
shifts towards greater social responsibility in the tourism industry. Secondly,
the main part of this chapter will outline progress to date by discussing the
variety of ways in which tourism industry players are now engaging in forms
of PPT or showing support for tourism as a tool for poverty alleviation. This
will include the roles played by tourism industry bodies such as PATA, as
well as accommodation providers, travel companies, airlines and so forth.
Rather than looking broadly at the ways in which the private sector may
unintentionally have benefits for the poor while still maintaining their drive
for profit maximization (e.g. a resort provides jobs for 230 workers), the

focus in this chapter will thus be largely on the *direct efforts* of the private sector to engage in poverty alleviation through tourism (e.g. a resort trains local residents from poorer villages so they have the skills to be employed in a range of jobs in their resort). Thirdly, Chapter 5 will consider ways in which governments will need to engage with tourism industry stakeholders if PPT is to have any chance of working: this includes considering the policy frameworks they have in place, the regulations they enforce, and the incentives they provide for private sector interests to act in ways which may seem contrary to their primary focus on profit making. The final section of the chapter will reflect on constraints to Corporate Social Responsibility (CSR) in tourism. In particular, it questions whether business motives for PPT can be just as effective as development-driven motives for PPT, or whether there are limits to what we can expect from the private sector.

IS THE TOURISM INDUSTRY BECOMING MORE SOCIALLY RESPONSIBLE?

The PPT Partnership assert a number of reasons that poverty should be of concern to tourism companies, and provide a detailed 'to do' list of action points (Roe et al. 2002). A win-win argument is proposed whereby pro-poor activities will both save businesses costs and be good for their publicity. This logic aligns well with the industry's commitment to CSR and triple bottom-line sustainability:

> Steps can be taken to increasingly involve the private sector in sustainable tourism development, tapping their expertise and interest in enhancing their own reputation as drivers for preservation of the culture, environmental and social sustainability and contribution to poverty reduction. (Epler Wood and Leray 2005: 4)

In recent years there has been a determined and rapid shift to support CSR in the tourism industry:

> In the mid-1990s . . . its [the tourism industry's] focus on issues of business ethics, social development and human rights was seen as rather radical and ill-focussed. Less than six years later, the same issues could be discussed comfortably in most Board rooms. (Corporate Social Responsibility Forum 2002, cited in Mowforth and Munt 2009: 199)

This undeniable shift in the tourism industry is reflected in industry conferences focusing on sustainable tourism, responsible tourism and ethical tourism—in addition to tourism for poverty alleviation. Thus, for example, at the 2008 World Travel Market in London there were regular pleas to use tourism as a means for generating peace and alleviating poverty in the world, and there were discussions on climate change and water scarcity, leading one commentator to note that 'The word responsible has taken over this year's World Travel Market. Wherever you turn, "responsible" seems to be the buzzword' (Alcantara 2008). However, this does not necessarily suggest that the motivations for this shift are altruistic. Rather, the tourism industry could be, quite naturally, motivated by a 'Tourism First' approach, which seeks expansion of the sector and sanctions globalisation and the needs of the tourism industry, as opposed to a 'Development First' approach, which is more concerned with sustainable development of tourism and the needs of local people (Burns 2004: 26).

The tourism industry, in one sense, has *had* to change because of changing tourist demand. Tourists are increasingly showing the industry through their spending decisions that they have a social and/or environmental conscience, and sales of ethical tourism products have escalated, as shown in Chapter 4's discussion of 'voluntourism'. Adapting to this changing consumer demand has been essential for the survival of some tourism operators, while enabling others to expand in new directions.

While the initial impetus for CSR in tourism emerged from concern for the environment, it has since broadened to include social and economic dimensions (Holcomb et al. 2007). An examination of 136 tourism practices which had received awards from the tourism industry revealed that it was increasingly common for CSR practices in developing countries to have social programmes, and these often included health or education themes and youth development (Levy and Hawkins 2008).

Due to such changes in the tourism industry, a number of tourism scholars are now suggesting that we need a more balanced understanding of the roles of private sector tourism organizations in contributing to development. Telfer and Sharpley, for example, argue that rather than automatically criticizing multinational corporations for investing in tourism, we should consider that ' . . . these corporations also bring investment funds, know-how, expertise, managerial competence, market penetration and control, and opportunities for local entrepreneurs' (2008: 88). They make a good point here, but it is also important that we recognize that the contributions to economic development that Telfer and Sharpley highlight are not necessarily synonymous with poverty alleviation.

PPT INITIATIVES BY THE PRIVATE SECTOR

Private sector agencies involved in tourism have developed a number of strategies that support poverty reduction. A private sector business supporting PPT need not be limited to giving donations to the poor. Rather, the changes a business can be far more wide-ranging:

Boosting pro poor impact is about how to use the 'core competencies' of tourism business—their marketing and procurement power, and their influence on tourist behaviour—not just donations. (Ashley and Ashton 2006: 3)

These other initiatives, which will be considered in more detail in sections to follow, can also include training and capacity building, support for labour rights, and education of tourists. Interesting initiatives have emerged from both in small-scale family ventures and large-scale resorts. Following on from the discussion in Chapter 1 on transforming mainstream tourism, Weaver (2001), in fact, suggests that it is possible to promote sustainable mass tourism (SMT) and that large tourism businesses are in the best place to contribute to this:

> the same corporations that control the mega-resorts are probably in the best position to effect the transition towards sustainability, relative to their smaller counterparts. This is owing to the critical mass that allows them to allocate significant resources specifically for environmental and social purposes. In addition, they generate enough waste to justify sophisticated recycling and waste disposal systems, and they can exert a positive influence on suppliers to act in a similar manner. (Weaver 2001: 167)

Table 5.2 provides an overview of the main types of private sector actors involved in the tourism sector and PPT initiatives which they may support. It does not, therefore, involve the full 'value chain' of associated industries: it includes hotels and resorts and reflects on their procurement practices, but it does not separately discuss businesses which provide fresh produce to resorts, cleaning products, furnishings and so forth. The upcoming discussion elaborates on the types of PPT strategies used by tourism businesses and provides a number of examples, finishing with a focus on the concept of 'fair trade in tourism'.

Tourism Industry Bodies

Private sector tourism industry associations range in scale from the local through to the global. An example of the latter is the influential World Travel and Tourism Council (WTTC) which is comprised of the CEOs, chairs and presidents of 100 of the world's 'foremost' tourism-related companies. Its mission is 'to raise awareness of the full economic impact of the world's largest generator of wealth and jobs' (Roe et al. 2004: 9). In light of the global economic recession the current Chair of WTTC asserted that part of their mission was also 'to persuade governments that they have it in their power to unlock the industry's potential to generate employment

Table 5.2   Types of Private Sector Stakeholders and Their PPT Strategies

Business or tourism associations	• Mentoring schemes • Facilitate linkages between mainstream and alternative tourism businesses • Adopt a code of ethics or code of conduct guiding practices of members • Give awards for ethical practice • Provide networking opportunities • Assist members to run viable businesses by linking them with training and credit opportunities
Tour operators	• Adopt ethical codes of conduct • Incorporate small-scale, locally owned enterprises into the itinerary • Make donations to schools and charities • Use local guides • Provide clients with information on how to behave/dress in a culturally and environmentally sensitive manner • Inform tourists about ways in which they can contribute to local development e.g. through their spending choices • Provide accurate information on local history, culture and nature
Hotels/resorts/lodges	• Employ local staff under fair employment conditions and practices, considering addition of health insurance and pension schemes • Human resources policy which provides security of employment, training and progression opportunities • Employ a 'social equity manager' or similar • Establish a community development fund (which guests can contribute to) • Develop joint ventures with community groups • Partner with local suppliers of produce, crafts or tours • Procurement of a wide range of local services (e.g. laundry, security) and goods (e.g. furnishings, art and crafts, soaps, linen and produce) • Assist and mentor microenterprises, e.g. advice and support for guides, craftspeople and entertainers • Encourage guests to spend more locally by providing information on entertainment options, tours, taxis and local charities. • Share resources with nearby residents (e.g. food scraps for fertiliser, glass and paper to local recycling companies, allowing them to use resort phones or transport in emergencies)

Source: Based on ideas from Ashley and Ashton (2006), Karammel and Lengefeld (2006) and Meyer (2007).

and increase prosperity' (Geoffrey Kent, cited in WTTC 2010: 3). Clearly, WTTC is very pro-tourism, but is it also pro-poor?

WTTC keeps its members up to date with regular statistics on the industry, including jobs created and contribution to GDP, and provides forecasts which can guide the marketing of tourism. They also administer annual 'Tourism for Tomorrow' awards, a scheme which rewards best practice examples of sustainable tourism within the industry. Other activities include organisation of a summit which gives opportunities for members to work together on promoting sustainable tourism, and WTTC is a member of the Tourism Emergency Response Network, which helps to provide an industry response to crises, such as health scares, through coordinated communications among members (WTTC 2010). In 2009 WTTC embarked on a partnership with a Millennium Foundation project named MASSIVEGOOD, through which travellers booking flights, reserving a hotel room or a rental car, will be asked if they would like to contribute an extra $2 towards fighting TB, malaria and HIV/AIDS and to improving maternal child health in poorer countries (WTTC 2010: 16–17). Undoubtedly a lot of money could be raised for a good cause in this way. From another perspective, however, this could be seen as a means of encouraging people to fly more, but to feel ok about their travel choice as their $2 is going to a good cause. This aligns with Chok et al.'s analysis of WTTC which is that the Council supports conservative reform of the sector, while continuing to espouse growth in the long term (2007: 43).

National level associations have also been active in espousing initiatives which may be beneficial for the poor. In the case of the Federated Hospitality Association of South Africa, they decided to develop an incentive for tourism businesses to act in a socially and economically responsible manner; thus in 2002 they repackaged their environmental award and made it a responsible tourism award instead (Spenceley and Goodwin 2007: 259). This sends a signal to the tourism industry about what approaches and initiatives are valued as 'best practice'. Also operating at the national level but representing small tourism businesses only is the Association of Small Scale Enterprises in Tourism (ASSET) in the Gambia. ASSET has 80 members, including tour guides, craft vendors and taxi drivers, whom it assists with grant development and with training in product development and customer service (Levy and Hawkins 2008). They also play a critical role in helping micro-enterprises access tourism opportunities (Mitchell and Faal 2007).

Finally, the Sengiggi Business Association provides an example of a tourism association which has been active at the local level. Formed in the wake of riots in Lombok, Indonesia, the Sengiggi Business Association involved over 100 small and larger businesses working together to clean up the area and encourage tourists to return. There was also emphasis on training for local people so they would be able to access employment opportunities when the economy was revived (Fallon 2001).

Tour Operators and Travel Agents

Some tour operators are involved in innovative schemes to bring tangible benefits to local communities, although this occurs more in alternative forms of tourism than mainstream tourism. Lew's (1998) research on eco-tour operators found that almost half of them provided a percentage of tour profits to local organisations. Meanwhile research by Tearfund (2001) showed that small operators were more ethical than large operators in practice, 'paying a higher proportion of profits to charity, offering more training to local operators and developing more local partnerships' (2001: 25, cited in Mowforth and Munt 2009: 199). The challenge of transforming larger, mainstream tourism providers thus remains and is particularly important as these agencies cater for the vast majority of the tourist market.

Some interesting initiatives by mainstream travel industry groups have nevertheless emerged in recent years, particularly in the UK and Europe, perhaps spurred on by the presence of advocates of responsible tourism and PPT in this part of the world. Certainly the NGO Tourism Concern has tried to work closely with travel industry groups in the UK, introducing them to the concepts of CSR and fair trade in tourism, developing a tool they can use to audit their social impacts, and more (see Chapter 7). They also launched a campaign in 2004 to urge tour operators to take some responsibility for the labour practices in tourism businesses they worked with internationally. This led to some UK tour operators embedding labour conditions in their policies, and labour conditions are also included in a checklist for hotels promoted by the Federation of Tour Operators (Barnett 2008: 1001). In addition, the Tour Operators Initiative (TOI) is a non-profit initiative established in 2000 with the support of UNEP, UNWTO and UNESCO. It promotes sustainable tourism practices including cooperation with destinations and supply chain management (Telfer and Sharpley 2008: 53). TOI has published the following toolbooks on its website: 'Supply chain engagement for tour operators—3 steps towards sustainability' and 'A practical guide to good practice: managing environmental and social issues in the accommodation sector'.

TUI Tourism and First Choice Holidays PLC merged in 2007 to form TUI Travel PLC, which is the largest tour operator in the world in terms of people moved, estimated at 30 million annually. TUI had a good environmental programme, and First Choice had a good social programme, so they tried to marry the two in the new company. What they are doing is significant because they cater for mainstream tourists. The UK and Ireland branch serves over 7.5 million customers each year and has more than 83 aircraft, which makes it the UK's third largest airline. First Choice did research which revealed that 30 percent of tourists are 'concerned' about how their holiday may impact on the destination (Ashley and Ashton 2006). However, it was questions asked by their *investors* about improving practice that led to some interesting changes. For example, 87 percent of TUI businesses now support charitable programmes. Two objectives for their destinations demonstrate their commitment to social responsibility and spreading the economic benefits from tourism: 'Implement the principles of the Child-Protection Code across TUI Travel businesses', and 'Support destination initiatives to stimulate increased local involvement in the tourism supply chain'.[2]

A critical question we could ask of tour operators involved in seemingly altruistic activities is whether they are actually handing any control over tourism to local stakeholders. Mann (2000) gives the label 'responsible tours' simply when a commercial tour operator provides direct benefits to local communities through avenues such as donations to community projects and training local people to be tour guides. What is also needed is adequate education of travel agency staff so that they are aware of the range of alternative tourism options and can advise their clients on ways of supporting local communities through choices they make, such as where they eat and what tours they take: 'Undoubtedly "good travel agents" will help promote and influence "good tourism"' (Wood and House 1991: 64).

Chapter 2 raised the question of whether tourism development contributed to improvements in human rights, noting that the realisation of human rights often underpins poverty alleviation. It is interesting to note that a number of organisations within the tourism industry have chosen to take a stand on specific ethical issues, such as supporting campaigns to deter travellers from entering countries where human rights abuses abound, despite the implications this may have for their profit margins. An interesting situation developed, for example, when East Timorese people voted overwhelmingly for independence from Indonesia during a referendum in August 1999, sparking a violent backlash from Indonesian troops and their supporters in the territory. A number of human rights groups advocated boycotting tourism to Indonesia and they were supported by large travel agencies such as Flight Centre, operating in New Zealand and Australia, which refused to service clients wishing to travel to Indonesian destinations such as Bali during this time. Similarly, the East Timor conflict provided the catalyst for the British Guild of Travel Writers to take their first ever ethical stance on travel to a particular destination: they issued a press release urging tour operators and tourists to boycott Indonesia until there was peace in East Timor. The Guild's Vice-Chairman, Peter Lilley, provided the following explanation for their action:

> It is quite unacceptable that foreign holidaymakers should continue to visit Bali and Lombok after the appalling catalogue of atrocities in East Timor—carried out with the tacit approval of the Indonesian authorities . . . Individual tourists and tour operators offering holiday packages to Bali and Lombok have got to examine their consciences. It is all too easy to stand by and convince oneself that the matter does

not concern you or that there is nothing you can do. (cited in Wheat 1999a: 5)

While the British Guild of Travel Writers are openly supportive of travel boycotts for ethical reasons, this is not the case with one of the major guide book publishers, Lonely Planet. Some NGOs have urged tourists to stay away from Burma[3] because of the direct links between the development of tourism and human rights abuses in this country (Parnwell 1998). Specifically, millions of Burmese were forced to provide labour on the military regime's projects, including infrastructure and tourism development. In addition, income generated through tourism supports the military government. The Burma Campaign UK and Tourism Concern called for a boycott of Lonely Planet publications, because they published a new edition of their guide to Burma in January 2000. Their actions were in direct contradiction to the wishes of the country's pro-democracy leader, Aung San Suu Kyi, as quoted here:

> 'Guide book writers should listen to their consciences and be honest about their motivations. Profit is clearly their agenda. It's not good enough to suggest that by visiting Burma tourists will understand more. If tourists really want to find out what's happening in Burma— it's better if they stay at home and read some of the many human rights reports there are'. (Tourism Concern 2002)

In 2007 Tourism Concern, one of the NGOs discussed in Chapter 6, decided to revive their Burma campaign after the violent repression of thousands of peaceful pro-democracy demonstrators in September and October 2007, which led to a number of deaths and numerous arrests.[4] Tourism Concern asserts that leisure travel to a country where the basic human rights of citizens are not upheld is simply unethical. Lonely Planet, which was bought by BBC Worldwide Ltd in 2007, has responded to criticisms by including a chapter in their Myanmar guidebook entitled 'Should you go?' in which they assert that all tourists should weigh up the information available and make this decision for themselves. Nevertheless their stance is largely positive, arguing that tourism offers economic opportunities to local people, that careful choices about spending will ensure that most tourist money does not end up in government coffers, and that the very presence of foreigners reduces the likelihood of human rights abuses occurring (Reid et al. 2009: 13–26).

Accommodation Providers and Restaurants

Accommodation and food providers can contribute actively to poverty reduction by, for example, implementing procurement practices which prioritize locally produced goods and services, or by encouraging the philanthropy of guests, providing in-house training to people from poorer backgrounds, and establishing a community development fund in conjunction with local actors. The following discussion expands on these points.

Procurement

In many contexts one of the most effective means of bringing more benefits from tourism to the poor would be for there to be greater procurement of local goods and services by food and accommodation providers. This can offer important economic opportunities for poorer members of communities, in particular, who do not have the capital to establish their own enterprises or the skills to find formal sector employment (Ashley and Roe 1998). Thus in Fiji, when Uprising resort was being constructed the owner spent FJD$20,000 on thatch, which directly benefited three local villages, in addition to purchasing locally made furniture, table mats, sun loungers and timber for the main buildings (Author's fieldwork: June 2009). Local communities can also benefit on an ongoing basis by, for example, selling food (fresh or processed), crafts or guiding services. This option is already boosting the incomes of farmers, traders and service providers in locations like Barabarani village in Tanzania, where ' . . . almost all food consumed in hotels, campsites, and restaurants is sourced from the local market . . . and the suppliers to this market are overwhelmingly local small-holder farmers' (Michael 2009: 177). However, in many other locations around the world those who could provide relevant goods and services to the tourism sector lack market access. Through developing economic linkages with tourism outlets and agents such as souvenir shops and hotels, such access can be facilitated.

In the example of the tourism value chain in Luang Prabang in Box 5.2, it was found that the poor rates of pay and use of family labour in the accommodation sector meant that this sector did not offer great pro-poor potential; however, there were a number of possibilities for the poor to benefit from selling fresh produce to restaurants, producing raw materials for handicraft production, and developing new products to sell to tourists visiting villages. It is thus important to appreciate how potential benefits to the poor will differ from one context to another. Photo 5.2 shows the range of high-quality fresh produce available at a town market in neighbouring Vietnam.

Adama Bah is founder of the 'Gambia is Good' project, which encourages hotels to purchase their produce from local farmers rather than relying heavily on imported foods. It is now estimated that 11 percent of the tourist spend on food and drink in the Gambia has a 'pro-poor impact'. Bah sees far more potential for delivering benefits to the poor in developing these sorts of linkages between mainstream tourism businesses and other sectors of the economy than in pursuing alternative tourism (Brazier 2008: 16). Some industry players have been accommodating and have found that

Photo 5.1   Main reception building at Uprising Resort, Fiji, showing extensive use of local building materials.
Source: Uprising Resort

Photo 5.2   High-quality fresh produce for sale in Hoi An Market, Vietnam.
Source: Author

supporting local producers and service providers can be mutually beneficial. A good example of this is the 'Adopt a farmer' scheme which was
initiated in the 1990s by the St Lucia Hotel and Tourism Association. This
scheme matched chefs with one or more local farmers, and assisted farmers
to diversify their crops and improve the quality of their produce (Tourism
Concern 1999). This approach was also piloted in Tobago with The Hilton
Tobago and the Mount St Georges Farmers' Association, which led to seven
farmers supplying TT$80,000 worth of produce in the first year (Ashley et
al. 2006: 3). Too often, however, such linkages have been shunned by members of the tourism industry, because of perceptions of unreliable supplies
or low quality products. In general, the more upscale the hotel, the more
they are likely *not* to buy local.

Nevertheless there have been some very positive large-scale initiatives
to increase local procurement as well. While hotel chains may have cen-
tralized procurement procedures for certain products such as computer
equipment and crockery, most do actually allow managers to source other
inputs from wherever they choose: this offers considerable scope for building better linkages between tourism and other sectors within a particular
country (UNCTAD 2007: 113). An impressive example was the collaboration between foreign hotels, central banks and the International Finance
Corporation of the World Bank in Berimbau resort in Brazil. This involved
support to local businesses including agriculture and fishing cooperatives, a
recycling factory, a cultural group and a textile cooperative, and resulted in
1,300 jobs as well as a ten-fold increase in the earnings of artisans (Barrowclough 2007: 634; UNCTAD 2007: 114–115). Another positive local procurement initiative by a global hotel chain is that of the Accor group, which
operates almost 4,000 hotels in 90 countries. Accor has partnered with the
International Trade Centre of UNCTAD to raise rates of local procurement
in two Accor hotels in Dakar, Senegal. The role of the International Trade
Centre is to identify local producers who, with appropriate support, will
be able to improve their range and quality of products and provide for the
needs of these hotels on an ongoing basis (Pro-Poor Tourism Partnership
2007: 3). In the Dakar hotels there are particular opportunities for enhancing local purchases of fruit, vegetables, meat and furniture.

South Africa hotel Spier Leisure has adopted a comprehensive approach
to reviewing its procurement strategies in order to find ways of bringing
more local benefits, and staff attitudes have shifted considerably due to this
initiative. They started by surveying all existing suppliers in order to collect
data on local, black and sustainable sourcing, and from this they developed
a staged programme to source more supplies locally, from liquid petroleum
gas through to laundry services and guest welcome cards:

> Spier Leisure's total procurement in 2003 was R44.2 million. Its man-
> agement are well aware that if they are able to shift ten per cent of that
> procurement to local small and medium suppliers, the annual spend

---

Box 5.2   Value Chain Analysis in Luang Prabang, Laos

There have been few detailed research studies on the economic impacts of tour-ism on the poor in local destinations. One exception is Caroline Ashley's (2006) study of Luang Prabang town and surrounds in Laos which attract both western backpackers and up-market tourists from Asia and abroad, who come to view the temples, the culture and way of life. Tourism to the area has grown rap-idly, with numbers doubling between 2000 and 2005, when they had 133,569 international arrivals. Ashley examined ' . . . where tourist expenditure goes, and where poor and poorish people are earning incomes from tourism' (2006: vi). Her Value Chain Analysis[5] showed that 27 percent of tourist expenditure reached the poor (Ashley 2006).

The use of 'poorish' is interesting here, and reflects the view long expressed by the PPT Partnership team that it can be difficult to ensure that the very poor receive direct benefits from tourism as they may be lacking in both skills and capital, meaning others are not keen to employ them and they have no basis upon which to start their own small enterprise. Thus Ashley chose to focus on what benefits tourism has brought to semi-skilled and unskilled people.

Interestingly, the accommodation sector did not offer very large benefits to the poor. Only 6 percent of the $8.7 million spent by tourists on accommodation in Luang Prabang reached the poor, due to low wages in the sector and use of family labour. However, up to 50 percent of the $7 million tourist spent on food and drink reached the poor, along with 40 percent of the $4.4 million spent on crafts and curios.

Ashley thus identified three areas where there was potential for tourism to bring greater benefits to the poor:
• increasing the amount of Lao-grown fruit and vegetables used by restaurants
• increasing the amount of Lao cotton and silk used for handicraft production
• improving the range of products offered in villages and increasing the time tourists spend in rural areas

---

into the local economy of over R4 million will—simply in cash flow terms—far outweigh their philanthropic spend . . . (Ashley and Hay-som 2006: 273)

To enhance local procurement, it is essential to stimulate attitude change—of chefs, purchasing officers, managers, etc.—towards small-scale local entre-preneurs and communities. Those making decisions about purchasing inputs, whether they are about food, crafts goods, furniture or services, often make assumptions that they will not be able to get the quality of products or continuous availability that they require. Tourism and business associations could get more creative with their initiatives to help shift attitudes, for example, by bringing in a celebrity chef to work with chefs from large restaurants and hotels, showing them how they could incorporate more local produce in their meals.

Joint ventures

While community-based tourism ventures in which members of local communities have a high degree of control over the activities taking place may seem like an ideal, in practice many communities lack the skills, resources, experience or networks to successfully engage in tourism in such ways and they may prefer to work in partnership with other stakeholders. Joint ventures provide such an example of partnership. They can involve community resources being used for tourism in exchange for profit-sharing, jobs, a share of ownership of the venture, and other material benefits from a private sector partner. Such ventures ideally allow communities to gain skills and confidence in dealing with tourists but without having ultimate responsibility for the effective running of the business immediately, while simultaneously earning some revenue.

In practice joint ventures vary considerably, however, in terms of the degree of control accorded to local communities. Perhaps the most significant way in which private sector interests can contribute to poverty alleviation is by sharing ownership and control over a tourism venture with local people, as shown in the following example from Ecuador. Rainforest Expeditions is a private operator which developed a partnership with the village of Infierno. The local community owns the lodge, which is co-managed by Rainforest Expeditions, who also train community members in all matters related to the operation and management of the lodge. The profits are split with 40 percent going to the company and 60 percent to the community. After a 20-year period—by 2016—the ownership of the venture will pass into community hands (Stronza 1999).

In another interesting example, the Community Lodge concept launched in Namibia provides for a joint venture between a donor-funded conservancy (an area of communal land set aside to conserve and utilise wildlife in a sustainable manner) and a private company. What makes this joint venture arrangement unique is that the private company is required to mentor and train local community members so that when the company's contract expires, they will be able to operate the lodge independently. There is a also a strong emphasis on developing linkages between the local community and the tourism value chain, such that the community can provide goods and services for tourists and the lodge (Novelli and Gebhardt 2007: 469). Thus one community initiated a conservation system in the rocky desert landscape, the Torra Conservancy, and in 1996 joined together with a South African business, Wilderness Safaris, to establish an upmarket campsite named Damaraland Camp. The camp offers ten luxury walk-in tents with en-suite. Ten percent of the average $200 occupancy rate per night is paid to the Torra Conservancy. The aim is ultimately to give the local community full control and ownership. Meanwhile 13 members of the local community are employed at the camp and can develop appropriate skills and knowledge regarding the management of this successful tourism enterprise (Koro 1999).[6]

Direct economic and social benefits

Not all tourism businesses are willing to develop joint ventures such as those described; however, they can still be involved in good initiatives to deliver direct economic and social benefits to communities. In Samoa, owners of beach *fale* (basic beach huts) make a conscious attempt to support the wider community by hiring youth groups, church groups and the like to perform at their weekly *fiafia* cultural nights (Scheyvens 2005). This support helps to strengthen such community institutions. Similarly, a Fijian resort contracts hat weavers, allows local people to set up a craft market at the resort, hires people to perform *rukukuleve* (fire walking) for guests, contracts a local band to entertain guests, and employs a local church choir to sing at weddings (Author's fieldwork, June and December 2009). Provision of these services leads to a welcome cash inflow to nearby villages.

Others encourage guests to donate funds which contribute to community development projects. Phinda wildlife reserve in South Africa is operated by the largest private company in South Africa involved in wildlife tourism, Conservation Corporation Africa (CCA).[7] Phinda includes five luxury lodge complexes and tourists have the choice of a range of activities including game viewing, canoeing, fishing and bird watching. With almost 30,000 economically disadvantaged people living around the reserve, community participation is seen as vital to ensure support for Phinda's conservation efforts (Carlisle 1997). They have thus established a development fund to benefit these communities (the Rural Investment Fund, or RIF). CCA guests, who are taken on tours of local communities at their own request, provide most of the funding for the RIF. This money has been used to build 20 schoolrooms and a clinic, to purchase a computer and generator for one school, and to provide training for members of development committees and community leaders. CCA's contribution to the RIF is their management and administration of the fund, which they estimate costs them R500,000 per year. It has been suggested that the RIF provides a good example of how 'a private company can act as a catalyst in mobilising funding for community projects' (Wells 1996: 44).

Phinda has also directly contributed to economic livelihoods of local people in several ways. Firstly, employment has been provided. The land that CCA bought to establish the Phinda reserve was formerly used for raising cattle, game and pineapple. Ecotourism at Phinda, however, is more labour-intensive than any of these former uses, employing 350 people in 1998,[8] compared to 64 people employed by the previous land-owners. It is estimated that with very low employment rates in this area, the average wage earner supports ten family members (Les Carlisle, CCA: Author's fieldwork, May 1998). All employees who have worked at Phinda for over six months are involved in training programmes, some of which cover basic skills such as literacy and numeracy. Secondly, Phinda has supported local entrepreneurs, helping one to establish a brick-making business which originally sold bricks for the first lodge at Phinda, and allowing another to set up a charcoal-making business in the reserve using wood which needed to be cleared. The charcoal business employs seven people. Thirdly, Phinda allows sustainable harvesting of certain plants from the reserve, including medicinal plants, wood and thatch (Cherry 1993).

Fallon's (2001) research in Lombok, Indonesia, provides an interesting contrast to those who suggest that local people are overall not happy with the impacts that resort development has on their lives. She documents how a model of co-operative power was initiated between the management of the Holiday Inn near Senggigi and the local Sasak community, and that the community was approached with respect and consideration at all stages of resort development. This included careful consultation at the construction phase of the resort to ensure villagers retained access to the beach and their fishing boats, and invitations to senior people from the community to discuss with the general manager various employment options that would be open to their people. Once the resort was operational, management continued with careful rostering of staff to respect their religious beliefs (there is a mix of Muslim, Hindu and a few Christian staff), efforts to purchase inputs locally, and provision of medical assistance to villagers using resort medical staff and supplies. This led to a very positive relationship developing such that when riots broke out in Lombok in January 2000 and Christian and Chinese homes and businesses were specifically targeted for attack, the local Sasak community's loyalty resulted in them acting to protect hotel property. Unprompted, they also guarded the home of a Holiday Inn manager when he was evacuated from the hotel (Fallon 2001).

Are resorts 'the last resort' for PPT?

For an example of a resort which has recreated itself and now supports many of the initiatives previously discussed, from local procurement through to good employment conditions for staff, see Box 5.3.

It is now recognised that resorts can offer significant potential for promoting PPT in some circumstances. Research conducted by the author in

---

Box 5.3 'Alien' No Longer?

Chapter 3 discussed how resorts, particularly those that are foreign-owned and/ or all-inclusive, have long been slammed by tourism researchers. This chapter cited a calypso song named 'Alien' which won a Carnival Competition in St Lucia in 1994; however, what I did not point out was that the song referred specifically to Sandals resort as an example of a resort which put up barricades to keep local people away and operated 'like a state within a state' (see Pattullo 1996: 80–81).

It is interesting, in this regard, to see the remaking of Sandals resorts in various countries in the Caribbean. Sentiments expressed in 'Alien' may have provided impetus for resorts like Sandals to recreate themselves, realising that it was counter-productive to try to create an enclave of paradise within a sea of poverty and discontent. In Negril, Jamaica, Sandals operates a local elementary school, provides scholarships for local students, provides seeds and technical support for local farmers, and purchases their produce at guaranteed market-value prices (Kingsbury 2006). Sandals in Negril also incorporates local community-based organizations in the corporation's decision-making. In addition, Sandals encourages its guests to establish off-property contacts with local people, hires local entertainers and guides for a variety of cultural and educational programs, and provides space on its property for local craftworkers to display their wares.

Sandals looks after its employees very well, too. When the German bilateral donor GTZ conducted research on Sandals in Negril, Jamaica, they found that: the resort provided a secure work environment, with half of the employees working there for 3 to 12 years; most employees were locals; career options were provided, including language training abroad; staff development options open to all staff included training on environmental awareness, customer service and HIV prevention; employee benefits included health insurance, life insurance and a pension scheme (Karammel and Lengefeld 2006: 5).

Furthermore, over half of fruit and vegetables purchased by Sandals in Jamaica and St Lucia are from local suppliers – this draws upon Sandals Small Farmers' Programme cooperatives (Karammel and Lengefeld 2006: 5). In Jamaica the Farmer's Programme began in 1996, involving ten farmers providing produce for two hotels, but by 2004 hotels all over the island were being supplied by 80 farmers. Some of the key ingredients to the success of this initiative are that farmers visit hotels to see how their produce is used and why they need to meet certain specifications, and farmers get visits from both extension officers and hotel managers and chefs. The chefs then make local foods a feature of their menus. One result is that farmers' sales increased from $60,000 to $3.3 million just three years later (Ashley et al. 2006).

Fiji in 2009, where most resorts are on land leased from communal landowners, shows that resorts can bring significant social and economic benefits to local communities. Benefits to landowning communities and others living near to resorts can come from the following:

- Lease money which may provide dividends to landowners and/or be used to improve infrastructure (such as water supply systems, footpaths and community halls), and to provide school supplies and scholarships
- Fees from village tours or school tours run by resorts whereby a set fee per head (usually $5) is paid to the Village Development Committee (which plans for projects such as education and village hall construction)
- Projects by visiting corporate groups e.g. to build and equip a village kindergarten or to provide rainwater tanks
- Ad hoc support from resorts themselves, e.g. scholarships, sports gear for a local rugby or volleyball team, donations for churches and schools
- Resort contributions to environmental causes (such as mangrove rehabilitation and Marine Protected Areas) which benefit all people living along and deriving seafood from a section of coastline
- Resort assistance to communities during and after natural disasters— e.g. after severe flooding in Fiji in January 2009, chefs from one resort cooked food for people in the evacuation centres for almost 3 weeks, and the resort's parent company contributed $1 million to help repair the district school
- Mentoring and support from resorts for the development of businesses owned by indigenous people (see Box 5.4)

Thus beyond economic benefits, there are also social and cultural benefits to communities such as the support of community institutions, including the churches, schools and sports clubs previously mentioned.

Employment conditions

It is not just access to a job and wages, but overall employment conditions and opportunities for training that determine whether tourism employment can be seen as pro-poor. Table 5.3 provides an interesting contrast between employment conditions in small-scale and large tourism resorts in Fiji. While it may be assumed that smaller businesses are better at looking after their staff, it appears this is not always the case. In fact, larger resorts are more likely to pay their workers better, abide by labour laws and offer training and opportunities for progression. Nevertheless, job security is often not guaranteed even in large resorts.

Mentoring

Going a step further than philanthropy or charity, tourism businesses can mentor fledgling community enterprises, helping them to get established or to find strategies to tackle constraints to business success. This has occurred in the case of two Fijian resorts (Box 5.4). It is essential that good business

Table 5.3   Comparison of Employment Conditions in Small- and Large-Scale Tourism Resorts in Fiji

	Small, indigenous-owned budget resorts	4-5 star foreign-owned resort on land leased from indigenous owners
Employment conditions		
Job security	Many employees are members of the extended family and have no contracts; employees brought in from outside the area likely to be on monthly contracts.	Employers abide by labour laws. Staff have contracts but most are on temporary monthly contracts; less than a quarter of staff likely to be on permanent contracts (i.e. one year or more).
Wages	Usually paid the minimum wage, but sometimes less, for a 40 hour week, even though they may work 60–70 hours.	Usually start at the minimum wage but above this if they have qualifications and experience. Some places pay overtime, others expect employees to work extra hours without pay.
Training	Usually not provided, apart from some on the job training specific to their role.	On the job training provided as well as support for staff to do courses offered by external providers. May provide 'cross training' to expose employees to jobs in other areas of the resort.
Opportunities for progression	Employees are often given work without needing any formal qualifications, but there are limited opportunities for progression once on board.	Employees require at least sixth form education, and some resorts offer good opportunities for progression and/or provide progression planning for all employees. Foreign staff still dominate a number of management and supervisory positions. Exposure trips may be provided to visit tourist attractions and/ or other resorts.
Leave	Staff often work seven days a week and do not get time off until they fall ill.	Abide by labour laws re the minimum leave requirements for staff.
Other worker benefits		
Meals	Often pay a small fee for meals.	Often pay a small fee for meals.

Continued

Table 5.3 Continued

Transport	Charged for water taxis.	Staff transport available for free or low cost but only at certain times of the day and after hours.
Medical benefits	No – but employer likely to help with specific requests (e.g. if a close family member is sick)	Subsidised benefits might be available for all staff or only senior supervisors and managers

Source: Author's fieldwork, December 2009

mentoring is provided to the indigenous owners so that they can eventually manage their own enterprise effectively. A paternalistic approach will not ensure that the 'partner' develops the necessary business and management skills. This was a limitation of the approach taken by Richard Evanson, who owns the exclusive Turtle Island resort, also in Fiji. After residents of nearby islands occupied Turtle Island and expressed their frustration at a lack of access to local marine resources and annoyance that a foreigner was reaping big rewards from tourism while local people missed out, Evanson decided to assist local enterprises. In particular, he provided large, interest-free loans and much needed business advice so that two families could establish modest accommodation ventures, also assisting with quality control, marketing and administration (Harrison 1999). Not so ideal, however, was the situation with at least one of these businesses which, up until 2009, was still very dependent on services provided by the luxury resort, for which they had to pay commercial rates. For example, bookings were made via Turtle Island resort, which took a 30 percent commission, and they were charged $200 per day for 'their share' of a travel desk run by

---

Box 5.4 **The Value of Partnerships between Existing Tourism Enterprises and Novice Indigenous Enterprises**

Two businesses owned by indigenous Fijian groups were supported greatly by nearby resorts.

Assistance offered by Sonaisali resort was instrumental in the establishment of a taxi venture by the landowning unit at the resort's taxi base. This assistance extended throughout the initial setting up period, including the formation of pricing structures, and the GM personally helped to negotiate the vehicle lease deal (GM, Sonaisali: December 2009; Manager, Taxi Company: February 2010). Naisali taxis is now a successful enterprise that employs ten people (six drivers and four other staff members), and depending on occupancy rates at the resort will

Continued

Box 5.4   Continued

generate between F$2000 and F$4000 weekly. Two drivers and the manager were interviewed, and all talked with pride of the achievements of the enterprise. They spoke of the benefits of gaining new experience and the knowledge and confidence to operate a business, and the increased morale and self-esteem which has resulted for the landowning *mataqali*. One driver said he is proud to 'help build up a Fijian business' (Villager: February 2010), with another commenting that his work has allowed him to 'mingle with tourists, open up new opportunities for future friendships and new opportunities for [my] village' (Landowner: February 2010). The manager said that the success of the business had shown ' . . . that Fijians can excel in business, like our Indian counterparts'.

Meanwhile Uprising resort helped the people of Wainiyabia village to establish a business named Jungle Trek by training guides and providing equipment and uniforms, as well as doing marketing on their behalf and taking bookings. Importantly, this included securing a contract with Fiji Adventure, a tour service for backpackers, which ensures custom for Jungle Trek three days a week. It was noted by Uprising's operations and project manager, who oversaw the creation of the Jungle Trek, that it would have been much easier for management to simply hire guides as employees of Uprising. Rather, the decision was made to assist the local community in the initial phases, with the understanding that once the business was viable it would be handed over to the village (Operations Manager, Uprising: December 2009).

Empowerment is reflected by the sense of ownership and pride expressed by both the Jungle Trek guides and the staff and drivers at the landowner's taxi company in regard to their respective ventures. The Jungle Trek coordinator, himself a member of the village, says there has been a 'change in mentality' among the young men employed as guides in the business (Interview: December 2009). All six were previously unemployed, and none had completed their high school education. They are paid F$45 a week for three days work, and a proportion of the money generated goes to the village committee. Most also contribute between 50 and 100 percent of their wages to their immediate family. Each of the guides said it was better working for a company owned by the village than one owned by an outsider:

'We've been able to develop the village and learn business skills. We've learnt to be independent, self-sustainable, use our resources. We do our own village development plan and do financial planning' (Guide, 18 years old – March 2010).

Although Jungle Trek had only been operating for a few months, at the time of fieldwork, revenue had already been utilized for village beautification, with further plans to set up an education fund (Jungle Trek Guide: March 2010).

Source: Author's fieldwork

Turtle Island resort at Nadi airport (Author's fieldwork, December 2009; personal communication with Richard Evanson, July 2010).

Fair Trade in Tourism

Tourism which supports sustainable livelihoods and aims to minimise negative effects and maximise positive effects for local people has also been referred to as 'fair trade in tourism' (Shah and Gupta 2000). The Fair Trade in Tourism movement offers an opportunity for tourism enterprises to be accredited for ethical business practices which deliver genuine benefits to the poor. This approach holds much promise: it is multi-dimensional, considering social and cultural benefits as well as economic ones, and is different from other approaches in that it seeks to change the awareness and practices of western consumers:

> Fair trade tourism policies seek to create social, cultural and economic benefits for local people at the destination end and minimize leakages. Such policies adhere to national laws; establish strong First World and Third World consultation structures; are transparent; involve open trading operations (such as social accounting); are ecologically sustainable; and respect human rights. The key focus is on changing consumption patterns in the First World. (Mowforth and Munt 2009: 99)

The Fair Trade in Tourism movement is not just an economic movement; rather, it is based upon recognition of the uneven economic playing field on which developing countries must try to compete, and the need to overcome political and social factors which often lead to exploitation of poorer players in the tourism equation. It can include the following components:

- Fair trade partnerships between tourism and hospitality investors and local communities
- Fair share of benefits for local stakeholders
- Fair Trade between tourists and local people
- Fair and sustainable use of natural resources
- Fair wages and working conditions (see Figure 5.1)

(Tourism Concern 2008)

FTTSA (Fair Trade in Tourism South Africa) is perhaps the most active national movement to support fair trade in tourism (see www.fairtourismsa.org.za). FTTSA embraces ideas of participation, equity and empowerment. As noted by a Volunteer Service Abroad volunteer working with FTTSA in 2007,

> FTTSA is about contributing to the transformation of the South African tourism industry and integrating the small, locally owned businesses alongside the more established white-owned companies . . . It's about spreading benefits around a community and making sure the tourism

'TOURIST PRICES'

Figure 5.1   The struggle for fair remuneration for tourism workers.
Source: http://www.polyp.org.uk/

experience is beneficial for locals and visitors alike—environmentally, socially and economically. (cited in Jennings 2007: 24)

FTTSA certifies enterprises also, under the world's first fair trade in tourism certification programme, and thus provides a guarantee for consumers regarding a business's ethics. This provides assurance to clients that these tourism enterprises contribute substantially to the well-being of local communities, and that the business is socially and environmentally responsible. As of April 2009, there were 46 certified fair trade tourism businesses in South Africa, including community-based endeavours, adventure tours, mainstream accommodation providers (e.g. four Mecure hotels) and exclusive private lodges. This includes, for example, Singita Sabi Sand, known as the world's best place to view leopards in the wild. The Singita company owns a number of lodges in South Africa and elsewhere, and has a stated commitment 'to our local communities and to assist in generating prosperity and social upliftment' (www.singita.com). Another enterprise with fair trade certification is Bulungula Lodge, which was established by a South African entrepreneur, with the Nqileni community having a 40 percent share in the endeavour. The Nqileni people use the Lodge somewhat as a community centre and often congregate there to mingle with the tourists. In addition to providing direct jobs accommodating visitors, the Lodge has helped provide an income for over 30 families through associated activities including horseriding, woodcarving, cooking and guiding. Tourists who use local transport to get to the Lodge, rather than a tourist bus, receive free accommodation for one night (Jennings 2007).

LIMITS TO CORPORATE SOCIAL RESPONSIBILITY IN TOURISM IN PRACTICE

Most of the chapter thus far has discussed initiatives by the private sector that align with pro-poor tourism. Undoubtedly there have been major changes to the ways in which some businesses are operating, and this is resulting in more benefits for the poor. It is important, however, to put these changes in a broader perspective, and to consider views of dissenting commentators, that is, people who are sceptical about the tourism industry's commitment to self-regulation and reform (see Mowforth and Munt 2009, Chapter 7). In particular, there are concerns that CSR may be used as a smokescreen to hide more serious concerns:

> The fact that Corporate Responsibility is so popular today is an indication that big business is feeling the heat. But the solutions they advocate and pursue—voluntary unenforced codes of conduct, piecemeal eco-improvements, token philanthropic donations, endless rounds of meaningless 'engagement' with 'stakeholders' who might otherwise be publicly criticising them, dubious but lucrative techno-fixes—are actually dangerous diversions. (Worth 2007: 7, cited in Mowforth and Munt 2009: 199)

Thus while the rhetoric of CSR has entered the boardroom and international travel fairs—ITB Berlin in 2009 had a Corporate Social Responsibility Day with the slogan 'From nice-to-have, to need-to-have'—and some genuine changes have taken place which are resulting in benefits for the poor, there are still great strides to be made if the tourism industry as a whole wants to be identified as exemplifying CSR and if this is to result in widespread benefits for the poor. Some of the limitations to CSR in tourism are expanded upon next.

Often CSR is Limited to Environmental Initiatives

Utting (2007) suggests that most CSR initiatives are limited to environmental or social protection. In practice, it is far easier to be green than to support PPT if you're in the tourism industry. Thus most of the industry representatives at the broadly named Responsible Travel and Tourism Forum (RTTF) conference in 2008 in Toronto, Canada, spoke about *environmental* responsibility. For example, Adam Stewart, CEO of Sandals Resorts International, showed in his keynote presentation how he would ensure their newest resort in the Bahamas was 80 percent self-sustainable in terms of power.[9] It is much easier to 'sell' these initiatives to shareholders because of reduced costs of being environmentally friendly. It is no surprise then that a general finding from Tearfund's research into the business practices of 65 UK-based tourism operators has been that they have made good strides in addressing environmental issues, but were not as determined as other industries at addressing social and economic issues (Mowforth and Munt 2009: 199).

Lack of Respect for Labour Rights

CSR initiatives lag behind in areas of empowerment and human rights, as is particularly evident when examining labour rights (Utting 2007). As noted by the director of Tourism Concern, ' . . . there is almost no integration of workers' rights and conditions in the CSR framework' (Barnett 2008: 1000). This is of grave concern considering the treatment many tourism sector workers receive as outlined in Chapter 3 and also raised in this chapter (Box 5.5 and Table 5.3). A report into labour standards in the tourism industry which was commissioned by Tourism Concern found that a number of problems plagued the tourism sector in the developing world, particularly low wages, long hours, unremunerated overtime, lack of secure contracts and few opportunities for promotion (Beddoe 2004). This does not impress Chok et al., who argue that ' . . . *any* industry or commercial activity that condones exploitative labour conditions and income instability cannot be considered pro-poor' (2007: 50).

The Tour Operator Initiative for Sustainable Development suggests tourism businesses should pay more respect to the human rights of their employees, in the following ways:

- Provide a fair living wage and benefits to all employees
- Sign formal contracts with all employees (less than 50 percent of tourism employees are permanent or full-time)
- Ensure that working hours, rest periods and remuneration comply with local legislation and practice, as well as with collective agreements where they exist

- Train destination nationals for management positions and support career/personal development and employability across all employment categories
- Encourage women and ethnic minorities to pursue careers (approximately 70 percent of tourism employees are women, but their numbers drop at management levels)
- Have a fair and legal child employment policy (NB this needs to recognise that child labour may be essential to the operations of small, family-based businesses)
- Respect freely elected workers' representatives and provide them with relevant information (rates of unionisation in the tourism industry are less than 10 percent globally) (Meyer 2007: 567–568)

Some of these strategies would be much easier to implement in large businesses, while small enterprises would find them a real challenge.

Tokenistic Efforts

Many tourism enterprises have engaged in what could be seen as token efforts to assist the poor, such as setting up a community development fund using voluntary donations from guests, while otherwise carrying on as usual. Being able to donate a few thousand dollars to a local school is not particularly inspiring, however, if the same business has exploitative labour practices and purchases most of its produce from abroad, even though there are options for buying locally produced fruit and vegetables.

However, introducing wide-ranging changes to the industry is a major challenge. Thus, for example, when the South African resort of Sun City took part in the PPT Pilot Programme, through which it received assistance to implement pro-poor approaches, its major initiative was to support development of two small enterprises from which it could procure products, one producing glasses from recycled bottles, the other manufacturing greeting cards. As noted by Ashley and Haysom (2006: 274), 'The scale of these enterprises is tiny compared to Sun City's budget'. However, these authors are hopeful that the different approach which has now been established in terms of procurement of these products will spread to other aspects of procurement in the business. Reflection on the PPT Pilot Programme led to the conclusion that while happy to engage in philanthropy, such as asking for donations from guests for a community development fund, few companies were willing to make more enduring changes to their business strategies and practices (Ashley and Haysom 2006).

Moving beyond tokenistic efforts can be particularly difficult for small- to medium-sized enterprises, which make up 90 percent of all tourism businesses. While larger businesses might be able to afford to devote a proportion of their funds to CSR goals (e.g. Sun City's CSR department

;eives 1.5 percent of pre-tax profits—Ashley and Haysom 2006), smaller
Jsinesses cannot easily reorient their activities to meet the interests of the
ioor because their margins are slim. Such businesses have lost power and
autonomy in recent years in the face of the consolidation of power of large
travel companies. Smaller enterprises often work in an extremely competitive environment where daily efforts to keep afloat are the reality.

Weak Commitment to Gender Equity

Despite the assurances of PPT advocates that tourism can bring substantial
benefits to women, because '. . . it can be labour-intensive, inclusive of women
and the informal sector' (Ashley and Roe 2002: 61), in practice many tourism
businesses still confine women to the most subservient, poorly paid and low-
skilled work such as housekeeping (Enloe 1990; Kinnaird et al. 1994). The
cultural positioning of women in different societies also affects their options
in terms of tourism employment. Thus in the Philippines and in Indonesia
women often receive front-line jobs in tourism because they are considered
to be more servile and compliant than men and more physically attractive
to tourists (Kindon 2001). Similarly, in the Caribbean, women's alleged car-
ing, mothering nature sees them directed into jobs as chambermaids, landla-
dies or receptionists (Momsen 1994). The way in which the tourism industry
relies upon women's subservient, poorly paid labour, based on expectations of
women's 'natural' roles and behaviour, is one of the factors which leads Enloe
(1990: 41) to comment that 'The very structure of international tourism *needs*
patriarchy to survive'. Female employees in service sector roles tend to face
particular problems with sexual harassment (Phillimore 1998): 'Women are
routinely propositioned and harassed in the context of their waitress, cham-
bermaid and other tourist occupations' (Richter 1995: 78–79).

   In addition, other work opportunities in tourism are not readily available to women.[10] Some of the reasons for an employer's reluctance to hire
female staff for positions in rural southern Africa are suggested by a tour
operator working in Zambia, in Box 5.5.

   It is important to note, however, that where women *do* have access to jobs
in tourism which pay them a fair wage and are not degrading or exploitative,
they report numerous benefits. For example, Morais et al.'s (2005) gender
analysis of ethnic tourism in Yunnan Province, China, revealed that women
appreciated both how tourism had both positive economic effects (increased
income, more diverse sources of income, ability to buy more goods), and
cultural effects (contact with the outside world, increase in knowledge, protection of their culture, more educational opportunities and sharing of the
economic burden between husbands and wives).

Problems with Self-regulation

With continuing growth in tourism internationally, regulation will be abso-
lutely critical in the future to ensure the protection of the resources and

Box 5.5 A Tour Operator's Reluctance to Employ Local Women in Zambia

In the 1990s in the area of the Chiawa communal lands which border the Zambezi River, the Chieftainess granted up to twenty tourism operators, mainly expatriates, the rights to lease land along the river bank and bordering the Lower Zambezi National Park. Her decision was based on the hope that this would bring much wanted investment and jobs to the region. While a small number of jobs were made available to local men, women were completely overlooked. One tour operator from the area cited several reasons that her company did not employ women:

• Staff needed to be mobile, as they were often expected to move between the three camps the company owned along the river.
• Having women in the camps would encourage infidelity.
• Pregnancy/parental leave would be inconvenient.
• The company would have to provide accommodation for families, rather than individuals, as women would not want to leave all of their children to come to work (camps are often quite isolated and there is no public transport service in the Chiawa area).
• The presence of children and babies could annoy guests.

Source: Author's fieldwork, July 1998

interests of poorer people in destination areas. To the tourism industry, government regulation is often seen as an unnecessary interference and hindrance to their operations. Instead, tourism industry players generally proffer strong support for self-regulation (Garrod and Fyall 1998; Milne 1998). However, industry support for self-regulation can be more cosmetic than genuine, serving the purpose of good publicity. Essentially many private sector businesses feel that promotion of sustainable tourism is not their responsibility—it is that of host governments. This was clear in a survey of British tour operators:

> Not one commercial operator interviewed saw ultimate responsibility for action as lying with themselves. This . . . casts great doubt on the effectiveness of current self-regulatory measures, and suggests that many of these may indeed be superficial or seeking to achieve good public relations rather than long-term change. (Forsyth 1995: 226)

Some tourism industry players have a stated commitment to ethical issues, including self-imposed codes of ethical conduct which provide rules by which members of an association should abide. Others support the UNWTO's Global Code of Ethics for Tourism (see Chapter 7). However most of the statements in industry codes favour environmental and social issues while ignoring economic impacts and benefits, which could be very important to the poor (Malloy and Fennell 1998). In addition, codes of conduct are weak in regulatory terms. There are no universal standards which guide the construction of codes of conduct in the tourism industry (Lew 1998), leaving it open to individual operators to devise a list which suits their interests, may not be based on consultation with affected communities, and may require little effective change in the way in which they operate (Forsyth 1995). They also typically cannot be enforced because they do not include measurable criteria; they also do not require independent verification—thus they hold limited weight. Thus self-regulation is a rather weak mechanism which allows for continued growth of tourism, regardless of whether this is sustainable or equitable:

> self-regulation led by bodies such as the WTTC and the UNWTO, whose stated aims are the promotion of the tourism industry rather than its restraint, is likely to lead to policies which further the pursuit of profits in a business world where profit maximization and capital accumulation form the logic of economic organization. (Mowforth and Munt 2009: 197)

Thus, for example, while it is commendable that Green Hotelier came out with recommendations of strategies the travel industry could adopt to address the Millennium Development Goals, these may be quite ineffective in practice. The mechanisms include recommending that businesses and their suppliers do not use child labour (to address the MDG on universal primary education), and also to 'support climate change initiatives', 'support women's NGOs and community health services' or 'support NGO or community-led projects'. Mowforth and Munt thus argue that, 'the effectiveness of these initiatives can be disputed, not least because they are highly generalised and do not address the issue of enforcement mechanisms' (2009: 339).

Furthermore, Hall and Brown suggest that codes of conduct may ask more of clients and employees than of the managers of a business:

> the compilation of codes of practice and conduct in tourism may sometimes appear to be a means whereby company management can deflect responsibility away from itself towards its employees, or . . . to its tourist clients. (Hall and Brown 2008: 1028)

While certification schemes should provide a more rigorous option than other means of self-regulation, many schemes still do not require input from an independent body. With the industry's most prominent certification scheme, Green Globe 21, for example, companies were awarded a logo as soon as they committed to undertake the certification programme. The logo for achieving certification is only slightly different from the original logo (WWF 2000).

Furthermore, the corporate sector is often 'a step removed' from taking the blame when things go wrong. If a village of fisherpeople is moved inland so a company can build a resort, the company can say the government was responsible for this. And if the presence of too many tourists in an area degrades the environment, both the government and the tourists themselves can be blamed:

> The chaos brought about by industrial scale tourism is shrugged off by the travel industry which blames it on consumers or governments. Excuses offered by the travel industry such as 'it's what the consumer wants' or 'these local governments don't have proper planning regulations' . . . don't stand up when seen in the light of other businesses. (Burns 1999a: 5)

Radical change of the corporate sector may be hard to achieve in light of the attitudes of many industry players. And even when businesses have ethical intentions, the practicalities of running a successful business may sometimes stand in the way of ethics:

> . . . the pathology of many tourism firms stems from the perishable nature of their services and the inability to store the product and sell it at a later date: a hotel bed or an airline seat that is not sold today is lost forever . . . [thus] the tourism producers may be tempted to undercut their rivals (Papatheudorou 2006:6)

Thus, for example, package holiday prices are driven so low by competition that those hotels or resorts included as part of the package cannot possibly guarantee labour rights, sustainability, or a long-term commitment to resident communities in the host country.

THE NEED FOR A MORE CONSIDERED SHIFT IN APPROACH

The preceding section on limitations to CSR showed clearly that despite some very good PPT initiatives by tourism businesses, to date most organisations have only dabbled a little in CSR while otherwise continuing on with business as usual (Ashley and Haysom 2006). A more considered shift in approach is needed if businesses are to comprehensively contribute to poverty alleviation through tourism.

Table 5.4 provides examples of the types of approaches to CSR being applied by tourism businesses. At the first two levels donations are popular with businesses, which is not surprising as through donations tourism businesses can: a) satisfy their guests' desire to 'do good' while they are on holiday; b) provide good public relations value as they are visible; c) help to satisfy members of local communities including people who do not otherwise benefit from tourism. Donations are also straightforward to administer for the business (Ashley and Haysom 2006). Problems with these approaches, however, are that they embody a paternalistic approach and can create dependency, and that the one-off nature of donations means more enduring programmes are not supported.

Most companies have not, unfortunately, moved beyond a minimalist or philanthropic approach whereby they are likely to be interested in local community development for pragmatic reasons rather than having a philosophical commitment to equity and justice. In a WTTC report from 2002, only 3 of the 17 CSR initiatives implemented by its members went beyond support to local social projects by actually adapting their business practice (Ashley and Haysom 2006: 268). Similarly, owners of private wildlife reserves that incorporate community development in their work typically take a minimalist or philanthropic approach:

> The private reserves, where investors are primarily concerned with wildlife as a business, probably become involved in CWM [community wildlife management] because it makes for good publicity, limits land claims and may limit the negative activities of unsupportive communities adjacent to their property. (Mander and Steytler 1997: 7)

Ashley and Haysom (2006) recommend that more tourism businesses should consider adapting their businesses practices, which would align more closely with the 'encompassing' approach in Table 5.4. Van der Duim and Caalders (2008: 123) concur, suggesting that changes be made to one or more aspects of a business, while retaining the business function, so that there may be more positive social, environmental or economic impacts. Such authors do not advocate specifically that businesses take on a 'social activist' role. Benefits of adapting business practice are the longer-term impacts on a community, with more opportunities for multiplier effects. There can also be greater recognition of the business's approach by others in the sector, and this may lead to enhanced market appeal as well as support from the government and access to finance—the latter because some finance organisations, such as the International Finance Corporation, specifically support businesses with strong social investment.

More progressive strategies could include working in partnership with local communities by supporting social projects over the long term and providing mentoring around businesses set up by people from these communities. Hotels and resorts could also implement broad policies that support labour rights and employee well-being (including training, health and retirement schemes), going beyond what is required by law. They could also review all of their purchases to support greater local procurement, as seen in the example of Spier Leisure earlier in this chapter. If we cannot expect such wide-ranging changes as a result of a PPT approach, then it can only hope to benefit a minority of people.

While there are bound to be very few businesses willing to go a step further in terms of taking a 'social activist' role, this could occur with some fair trade in tourism initiatives. It has also occurred in special cases

Table 5.4   Different Approaches to CSR in Tourism

Approach to CSR	Examples in the tourism sector
Minimalist	Tokenistic support to stakeholders, e.g. donations of used equipment to neighbouring communities.
Philanthropic	Support for conservation and development projects (e.g. donations to local environmental groups, schools and health clinics). Encourage guests to donate to specific environmental and/or social development initiatives.
Encompassing	Company management style and values reflect a desire to run a more socially responsible business. Works more in partnership with local communities over the long term to ensure the business is not undermining social or environmental well-being and provides ongoing support for local development initiatives and for local businesses (rather than ad hoc donations).
Social activist	Strong philosophical approach which is not based on profit maximisation. Motivation is to catalyze change.

Source: Structure based on Locke (2003, cited in Ashley and Haysom 2006)

where a business owner is not directed primarily by profits, for example, Uprising resort in Fiji. This resort, mentioned earlier in this chapter due to its high level of local procurement and support for a nearby village-owned business, Jungle Trek, was established because the owner wanted to provide jobs for unemployed youths and re-establish pride in the local area (Author's fieldwork, 2009).

CONCLUSION

Chapter 5 has also shown that a number of private tourism stakeholders are responding positively to pressure from various domains to display greater social responsibility, including efforts to reduce poverty. A commitment to employee well-being and up-skilling, efforts to procure goods and services within the local economy, working in partnership with nearby communities to enhance their development—all of these initiatives can bring meaningful change to the lives of the poor. Further examples in this chapter have shown that the private sector can support 'fair trade in tourism', that tour operators are utilising tools to conduct social audits of their activities, and that some resorts have seriously re-thought their way of operating, resulting in significant spin-offs for their employees and others from local communities. These changes should not be taken for granted in an industry characterised by extreme competition and where the short-term need to make profits could easily stand in the way of long-term strategies to make ethical improvements to business practice (Forsyth 1995). This is especially apparent at times of economic crisis, such as the 2008/9 global economic recession, or when political instability, health issues or natural disasters strike, all of which can lead to the collapse of tourism businesses. Efforts of smaller tourism businesses that have never heard of CSR are also often laudable, because they tend to operate in ways that have direct benefits for the poor. Those offering homestay accommodation, for example, are often closely embedded both socially and economically in their communities, thus they assist community groups when asked and utilise local goods and services to a much larger extent than many larger, foreign-owned businesses.

However, as noted in the introduction to this chapter, private sector tourism players are, by definition, focused on profits, not altruism or social justice. Logically, therefore, most will show an interest in PPT only if there is something in it for them. This 'something' is often good publicity, the ability to market their operation as offering a niche product, or, quite simply, cost savings. If you buy locally produced produce, chances are this will be cheaper than that brought from distant markets, plus your resort can claim in its promotional literature to be supporting local farmers.

When one examines what real changes PPT has brought about in the practice of the tourism industry, many examples appear tokenistic rather than transformational. It will be a major challenge for the industry to move beyond this. This leads Higgins-Desbiolles (2006: 1201) to claim that PPT is merely, 'a program of minor reforms for a marketised tourism sector to deflect criticisms and prevent unwanted regulation'. It is vital, therefore, that developing country governments create an environment which promotes ethical business practice and also seeks to control the nature of tourism development in order to minimise potential harm and maximise local and national level benefits. It is, after all, the role of the state, not private companies, to advance the well-being of citizens:

> Companies should not be expected to take over governments' responsibility for social policy—the state should set the rules and regulate in the interests of all groups equitable and efficiently. (Standing 2007: 2)

Chapter 6 will thus pay due attention to the roles of governments in promoting PPT, including a discussion on ways in which they might encourage private sector actors to work in a pro-poor manner. It will also consider ways in which development agencies have collaborated with the private sector so that the interests of the poor are considered.

6 Tourism Reduces Poverty
Government Approaches

INTRODUCTION

The mantle of poverty alleviation has been taken up by developing country governments. Governments of most developing countries have prepared Poverty Reduction Strategies, many of which cite tourism as a sector with significant growth potential. It is claimed that the World Bank's renewed investment in tourism is ' . . . driven by strong country demand' (Hawkins and Mann 2007: 348). Despite this the power of the state has not been adequately appreciated in research on tourism to date (Coles and Church 2007). Sofield laments that so often tourism literature 'glosses over the role of government' (2003: 23). He urges us to think beyond tourism as a private industry: 'While tourism as an industry is generally regarded as a private sector activity where market forces predominate, in fact the embrace of the state is comprehensive' (2003: 23–24). Mowforth and Munt agree, noting 'It is governments that have a pivotal role and possess the potential power to control, plan and direct the growth and development of tourism' (2009: 293). Friedmann, whose work on empowerment was considered in Chapter 2, argues that the state should play a key role in directing development:

> an alternative development requires a strong state to implement its policies. A strong state, however, is not top heavy with an arrogant and cumbersome bureaucracy; it is, rather an agile and responsive state, accountable to its citizens. (Friedmann 1992: 35)

The state's approach, therefore, is critical. As shown in Table 6.1, there have been major changes in the ways in which governments have approached tourism over time. There have been periods when the industry has been left to operate free of both support and regulations, and when it has been targeted as a tool for economic growth. In the past 30 years, however, growing concerns over the potential negative social, economic and environmental impacts of the industry have led to calls for greater government control over tourism. Such views regularly conflict, however, with the growth ethos still espoused under the neoliberal rationale which is directing many governments.

Local empowerment alone is not sufficient to corner the benefits of tourism and ensure that this industry benefits the poor (Sofield 2003: 346). Rather, it is up to governments to set the ground rules, or regulations, within which tourism takes place. And it is governments that have the power to establish policies which can determine whether a country follows a path of tourism development dictated primarily by overseas interests and capital, or a path which seeks to achieve economic gains for a wide range of local people and the state while preserving the integrity of social, cultural and environmental features of their country. Finding a balance in terms of the state providing direction and control while also being responsive to citizens and to the private sector is the critical challenge facing states that wish to promote PPT.

Table 6.1 Public Sector Approaches to Planning for Tourism

Era	Tourism planning stage
1950s	Virtually no public sector tourism planning
1960s	Candy-floss image of tourism at official levels, reluctance to consider tourism as equal to other economic sectors; government priority focused on investment incentives and operation; little or no critical analysis of sector; minimal attention given to practicalities of implementation; spread of the blueprint approach to master planning.
1970s	Tourism planning approaching its apex; focus on luxury resort tourism; ideology of 'planners know best'; continuing lack of political will in shaping tourism development to the destination's own needs and aspirations; recognition in mainstream planning of community involvement; corporations follow international strategies.
1980s	Acknowledgement of economic, socio-cultural, and environmental impacts of tourism giving rise to recognition of the need for comprehensive and coordinated goal-setting framework; recognition in North America of need for community involvement.
1990s	Recognition that if not fully planned, tourism fails to deliver the economic benefits expected by Third World nations; total destination management seen as the way forward with sociologists, anthropologists, environmental scientists and human resources specialists joining physical planners.
2000+	Much greater awareness of the need for government regulation of the environmental impacts of tourism and the benefits of community involvement in decision-making. However, many governments are still preoccupied with a growth agenda and make unrealistic and unsustainable projections for growth of tourist numbers and revenue.

Source: Adapted from Table 1 in Burns (1999b: 331–332)

This chapter begins by discussing inherent weaknesses in a government approach that focuses narrowly on increasing tourist arrivals and achieving economic growth. The main part of the chapter, to follow, then considers the wide range of roles governments can play to control development of tourism, uphold the rights of their citizens, and to create an environment which encourages other tourism stakeholders to ensure that tourism is pro-poor.

THE LIMITATIONS OF GROWTH-ORIENTED APPROACHES

Too often developing country governments focus narrowly on earning more tourism revenues and increasing tourist arrivals, rather than being concerned with the impacts of tourism, socially, environmentally and economically (Harrison 2003: 17). Thus, for example, the structure and policies of the Egyptian state led to massive growth in the tourism sector in the 1990s and enabled foreign investors and local elites to earn huge revenues from the tourism sector (Richter and Steiner 2008), yet it has not attempted to target benefits towards the poor. Photo 6.1 shows a billboard promoting further development of tourism in coastal Vietnam, in an area already struggling to meet basic standards of waste management. Ideally, suggests Friedmann, states should not ' . . . make a fetish out of economic growth' but they should search ' . . . for an "appropriate" path that includes growth efficiency as one of several objectives that must be brought into harmony' (1992: 34). Thus for example, while Siddique and Ghosh (2003) suggest that the role of governments is to promote tourism, provide appropriate infrastructure, research the market, and provide financial incentives for investors, I would argue that governments need to play a stronger regulatory role and to develop strategies to direct benefits of tourism to the poor if sustainable, equity-enhancing tourism is to emerge.

Yet still we find authors such as Raguraman (1998: 534), who complains that tourism in India has shown a 'dismal performance' because their share of world tourist arrivals and world tourism receipts declined between 1981 and 1995. For this same period, however, tourist arrivals and tourism receipts in India both actually showed a steady increase. Any further increase in tourism in India may have been at the expense of social and environmental well-being, especially if issues such as the distribution of tourists were not considered. This is an issue which seems to have been clearly understood by, interestingly, the tourism department in the state of Himachal Pradesh, India. Rather than just planning for accelerated tourism development, they supported the dispersal of tourism to ensure both that there was not undue pressure at one site and that the benefits tourism brought were spread more widely than established popular sites (Shah and Gupta 2000).

Photo 6.1   Billboard depicting further tourism development near Lang Co, Vietnam, where the existing water and waste management systems cannot meet current needs.
Source: Author

Governments have scrambled to do the bidding of outside organisations even when this would clearly compromise the well-being of some of their citizens: 'In the past, states have all too often abdicated their responsibility to help the people in their efforts to help themselves' (Potter 1993: 113). It is evident that in some countries which have taken a neoliberal path, the poor have seen few benefits from the growth of tourism. For example, in Peru, neoliberal policies adopted under Fujimori from 1990 onwards contributed to a three-fold increase in tourist arrivals between 1992 and 1996. While this did result in some macroeconomic benefits, poverty has been entrenched and the agricultural sector has decreased in size (Desforges 2000). Similarly in Ghana, which has been hailed as a structural adjustment success story for Africa, tourist arrivals increased from around 85,000 in 1985 to over 286,000 in 1995, and tourist receipts increased from $20m to $233 over the same period. However, spatial disparities have become entrenched, the quality of life of many Ghanaians has declined and increasing rates of foreign ownership of tourism infrastructure are leading to higher leakages. Devaluation of the cedi enabled travellers to see Ghana as a 'cheap destination', while making it difficult for locals to afford imported products such as medicine (Konadu-Agyemang 2001: 194).

Arguing that 'externally-oriented, growth-maximising' paths to development have resulted in increasing levels of inequality among local populations in many Eastern Caribbean states (1993: 103), Potter goes against dominant neoliberal discourse and instead asserts that 'the needs of the poor should be met *in priority* to externally-oriented growth imperatives' (1993: 97—emphasis added). For this to happen, governments must play a strong role. Interestingly, some governments have sought to prioritise local interests above those of outsider investors via tourism planning processes. Thus when Milne (1997: 289) examined the national development plans of Tonga, Vanuatu, Kiribati and Cook Islands, he found that in each case the government stressed that tourism development should not progress at the expense of local culture and values.

It is important to recognise, however, that states may be constrained in their actions due to pressure from national and transnational forces (Carbone 2005: 562; Williams and Shaw 1998). In the 1980s and 1990s, actions of states were often heavily influenced by the neoliberal agendas of multilateral institutions to whom they were indebted, thus ' . . . developing countries had no option but to choose profit maximisation over social and environmental concerns' (Carbone 2005: 561). While the neoliberal doctrine has been tempered somewhat due to criticisms of the negative social and environmental impacts of growth-oriented development, there is still a danger in that governments of developing countries feel that they must show those offering them development loans that they will be able to grow their economies in future. This has led to some wildly exaggerated and unsustainable projections for tourism growth. Thus, for example, in 2007 the Fijian government's Tourism Development Plan stated that one aim was to reach the 1 million arrivals mark by 2015, which would entail a doubling of tourist numbers in just 8 years. This desire for rapid growth of tourism was also expressed by trade diplomats from a number of Africa's poorest countries when attending an UNCTAD meeting: they wanted to double, triple or quadruple tourist arrivals within a very short time period (Personal communication, Tricia Barnett, Tourism Concern: September 2008). Thus some very poor countries are aiming for huge tourism growth—seeing it as a panacea, but with no solid groundwork to back up if this is logistically feasible (with respect to infrastructural, human resource and capital requirements), nor if there is a demand from tourists, and nor if this could adversely impact on local people and environments. It is likely under such circumstances whereby growth is simplistically equated with poverty alleviation that governments will do whatever is necessary to secure investment in the sector. It is less likely, meanwhile, that they would wish to regulate the activities of foreign investors, or present them with performance standards.[1]

Even more startling was the announcement in 2005 by International Council of Tourism Partners, variously described as 'a non-profit organisation' and 'a travel industry group', which purports to promote a social conscience within the tourism sector, that it wanted 'to help Africa *sustainably triple* its tourism export income by 2015' (Travel Wire News 2005—emphasis added). This is the same group that launched a 'Make Poverty History' initiative at the world's largest travel mart in Berlin in 2005. There is clearly a neoliberal agenda here: continued growth of tourism is being justified under a poverty alleviation banner. It is particularly alarming that ICTP suggests such growth could be done *sustainably*.

It is not sufficient for governments to simply put more money into promoting tourism, as has happened in a number of countries in the wake of the global economic recession. For example, the Thai prime minister announced in mid-2009 that up to 55 percent of the new stimulus package established to help his country through the global recession would be directed at the tourism sector (eTurboNews 2009b). Along similar lines, the Fijian government almost doubled its tourism budget from F$12 million in 2008 to $23.5 million for 2009. This led to criticism from people in other industries who feel the government is subsidising the tourism sector. Other commentators have urged that if governments are going to provide such revenue to the tourism sector, they should insist that the industry purchases more local products, including food and furnishings, and that fair wages are paid to those working in the tourism sector (Fr Kevin Barr, ECREA, June 2009: personal communication).

EFFECTIVE ROLES FOR GOVERNMENTS

A number of researchers argue that governments in developing countries need to play a more central and comprehensive role in the development of tourism than seen in other countries where resources are more readily available and there is a strong private sector (Potter 1993; Richter 1983; Wilkinson 1989). Having identified limitations to a growth-oriented approach in the previous section, it is clear that governments will need to play a guiding role if PPT is to offer more than simply another way of expanding tourism with benefits for the major players in this sector.

This role for government stretches well beyond simple promotion of the sector. Firstly, the onus is on the governments of developing countries to step forward and develop appropriate policies and plans for tourism development if the needs of the poor are to receive priority. Secondly, governments should coordinate development across sectors to ensure coherence and support for appropriate tourism development with other sectors such as infrastructure development, agriculture, fisheries, and training. Thirdly, they need to regulate development of tourism to minimise negative social, cultural and environmental impacts. This involves establishing legislation, monitoring impacts, and prosecuting perpetrators. Fourthly, governments should find effective ways of stimulating and supporting growth of tourism businesses, including small-, medium- and large-scale enterprises, and engage in marketing initiatives. Fifthly, they need to do research on the sector and collect statistics, so their tourism plans, policies and strategies can be well informed.

In the UNWTO's (2006a) compilation of good examples of tourism for poverty alleviation, it was noted that many of the successful pro-poor tourism enterprises had received direct financial and technical assistance from public institutions, from local authorities through to national-level institutions, so the government does indeed play an important role in developing a supportive environment for PPT. A summary of the different instruments which governments can use to facilitate progress towards PPT, ranging widely from providing incentives to encourage PPT initiatives to punishing those who break regulations, is provided in Table 6.2. Examples of the implementation of some of these instruments are provided throughout this Chapter.

Tourism Planning and Policy

One very important role for government is to mainstream poverty reduction into tourism policies, plans and programmes, thus building an overarching policy framework for sustainable, pro-poor tourism development. The background note prepared by the UNCTAD secretariat for the High Level Meeting on Tourism and Development in the LDCs states that countries that have been unsuccessful in integrating tourism as a tool for economic development have usually had inadequate or non-existent poverty-led tourism policy frameworks (Benavides and Pérez-Ducy 2001). Tourism policy

Table 6.2   Instruments That Governments Can Use to Facilitate the Development of Pro-Poor Tourism

Instruments	Examples
Measurement	Identification of limits; Sustainability indicators and monitoring
Command and control	Legislation and regulation; LicensingLand-use planning; Development control
Economic	Pricing; Taxation (e.g. no goods & services tax on basic foods); Property rights; Financial incentives (seed funding for entrepreneurs; tax breaks for businesses with strong linkages into the local economy);Voluntary contributions
Voluntary	Guidelines; Codes of conduct; Reporting and auditing; Voluntary certification
Supporting	Infrastructure provision and management (e.g. establish visitor information centres; develop good water and sanitation systems; support farmers to establish marketing cooperatives so they can sell to resorts); Capacity-building (e.g. training to tourism sector employees; advisory services on small-business development); Marketing and information services

Source: Based on ESCAP (2007: 11)

must address the needs of all tourism stakeholders in pro-poor tourism, for example protecting local communities engaged in public-private partnerships, but also potentially offering incentives to hotels and resorts to engage in comprehensive pro-poor tourism practices (as discussed in Chapter 5)—note that this is different from just offering investment incentives with no links to PPT objectives.

For tourism policy to be effective it must be coordinated with the policies of all relevant government departments and ministries whose work intersects with the tourism sector. This could include, for example, agriculture, public works, conservation and parks, communications, transport, economic development and education. It may also be necessary to build capacity of government officials so they have the skills to effectively manage PPT programmes:

> LDC governments, at the highest political level, need to understand well the potential of tourism . . . to generate entrepreneurial and employment opportunities even in the most remote places and suitable for everyone. They need to provide a high-powered political framework for this potential to develop, committing the involvement of all senior ministries, and not assuming that the tourism authority alone will be sufficient to generate all the conditions for that development to take place. (UNWTO 2005b: 7)

Thus, for example, the government of Lao PDR has shown strong commitment to policy and planning for pro-poor tourism in both the National Tourism Strategy and Action Plan (2006–2015) and the National Ecotourism Strategy. Enhanced benefits for the poor are now central to tourism policy and planning. Associated changes in legislation make it possible for rural communities to set up small inbound tour agencies, whereas previously this was illegal (Schipani and Oula 2006).

A step above this, the government of Vietnam drew upon advice from Netherlands donor SNV to develop a Tourism Law in 2005.[2] The law provides opportunities for poor people to benefit from growth in tourism and encourages community participation in tourism. For example, Article 7(2) states that:

> Local communities shall be provided with conditions to invest in tourism development, restoration and promotion of various traditional cultures, folklore arts, crafts, and production of local goods in service of tourists, contributing to raising the material and spiritual life of local inhabitants. (Socialist Republic of Vietnam 2005: 10)

Poverty is only mentioned explicitly, however, in Article 2(g) where it is noted that the State will provide incentives and preferential policies regarding land, credit and finance for those investing in,

Development of tourism in remote and isolated areas and in areas with socio-economic difficulties where there are tourism potentials so as to make use of the labor force, goods and services in the spot, contributing to raising the people's intellectual level and to hunger elimination and poverty reduction. (Socialist Republic of Vietnam 2005: 9)

In 80 percent of Poverty Reduction Strategies developed at the national level, tourism is identified as an important economic sector (Mann 2005: iv); however, as of 2006 only eight country assistance strategies deriving from these strategies provide earmarked funding for tourism (Hawkins and Mann 2007). Ministers of tourism may need to lobby donors more strongly to ensure that tourism is adequately incorporated into Poverty Reduction Strategies where relevant, and that resources are directed towards PPT-related programmes.

Facilitating Better Linkages with the Local Economy

Reducing leakages and maximizing multiplier effects should perhaps be a major goal of governments of developing countries with a significant tourism sector.[3] To do this it is thus important that they ensure that national development plans highlight linkages between tourism and other economic sectors such as agriculture, fisheries and transportation, in order to maximise local multiplier effects (Ashe 2005). This is easier said than done, however. The literature on PPT emphasises how problematic it is to establish backward linkages in developing economies. A DFID (1999: 3) report notes that, 'Linkages are frequently discussed, rarely seen and particularly important but difficult to develop'. The report goes on to suggest that '
. . . there are few successful examples of action to stimulate linkages—this probably indicates that it is difficult, but also that concerted long-term effort has rarely been made' (ibid). These problems are related to the fact that fostering linkages is a resource-intensive and time-intensive undertaking, which is often conducted by under-resourced governments.

Linkages between agriculture and tourism are potentially great. However, inconsistency of a high-quality local supply is the most important factor leading tourism businesses in many places to rely primarily on imports. Reasons for this inconsistency in Fiji are provided in Box 6.1, and these can be seen more generally in many other developing countries where farmers are impeded by a lack of available credit, shortage of technical assistance, and inappropriate technology (Torres and Momsen 2004).

Torres' research of tourism-agriculture linkages in Cancun, Mexico revealed that the hotels procured only 4.5 percent of their fresh fruit and 3.4 percent of their vegetables from Quintana Roo growers, and only 9 percent of their poultry and 1 percent of other meat was purchased locally (Torres and Momsen 2004). There had actually been a number of initiatives to improve the use of produce by hotels here, ranging from irrigation schemes to post-harvest handling, and establishing a state-owned wholesaler to purchase products from farmers and on-sell to hotels and supplier. Such schemes were implemented in a piecemeal fashion in isolation from one another, however, and many did not succeed. An additional constraint was the geographical isolation of farmers and the class and ethnic differences which separated them from suppliers, chefs and hotel purchasing staff. The farmers in the area worked largely as individuals and lacked their own trucks; thus they were relatively powerless to negotiate when suppliers came to their gate to buy produce (Torres and Momsen 2004). This leads these researchers to conclude that,

> Only through an integrated approach that considers all aspects of production, producer organization, post-harvest handling infrastructure and marketing, and that is fortified by strong strategic alliances, is it possible to create sustainable linkages between tourism and agriculture. (Torres and Momsen 2004: 313)

While building better linkages clearly involves private sector actors, governments are in the best position to coordinate such an integrated approach.

Box 6.1   Impediments to the Supply of Quality Local Fruit and Vegetables to the Tourism Sector in Fiji

- Low levels of modernisation and commercialisation on subsistence farms, which is compounded by high-levels of out-migration from rural areas, leading to a lack of skilled labour.
- Very little start-up credit is available to small farmers outside the sugar industry, primarily due to the high transaction costs involved and little collateral available from farmers. Micro-credit remains poorly established in Fiji.
- Uncertainties in market conditions related to produce, and farmers being ill-informed about crop prices, thus leaving them vulnerable to exploitation by wholesalers.
- Lack of support for producers in terms of marketing and training, steady markets to supply to, and poor transportation for getting produce to markets.
- Lack of range of products available in quantities required, meaning hoteliers prefer the security of wholesalers (who often import produce) rather than establishing several contracts to secure their produce.
- The current land lease system – which limits a lease to a maximum of 30 years and maximum lease payments equivalent to a return of 6 percent per year of the unimproved capital value of the property – provides little incentive to renew leases for productive use.

Source: Scheyvens and Russell (2010), drawing on Berno (2006), Fleming (2007), Mahadevan (2009), Veit (2007 and 2009)

Using Revenue to Bring Tangible Benefits to Communities

Governments typically earn very good tax revenue from tourism.[4] For example in the Gambia, there is a 15 percent tourism-related sales tax. This raised $1.45 million in 2004 (Sharpley 2007). From a PPT perspective, however, the *use* of such revenue is of utmost importance. Governments can, in their policies, choose to use sales tax revenue to bring benefits to the poor. It is also reasonable to expect that some should be reinvested in tourism, such as upgrading infrastructure, including footpaths and street lighting, otherwise the sales tax is only a burden on the sector and undermines the profitability of those investing in tourism. However, such taxes can also be used to benefit the poor. What happens in practice in the Gambia is that 60 percent of tax revenue goes into general government expenditure with none specifically targeted at the poor, with 40 percent reserved for tourism (Sharpley 2007).

On a more positive note, governments can take practical steps to reduce poverty by ensuring that when costly infrastructural projects are undertaken to support growth in tourism, the needs of the poor are not overlooked (Ashe 2005; ESCAP 2003; MacNaulty 2002). For example, if new roads or water systems are to be built, the former should provide local access to markets as well as tourist access to resorts and the latter should be connected to villages as well as to hotels. For example, a pilot project to develop mountain tourism in the High Atlas, Morocco, which involved collaboration between the government, donors and NGOs, ensured that local people benefited considerably from construction of roads, provision of water, gas and electricity, and establishment of telecommunications infrastructure (UNWTO 2006a: 101–103).

Getting Regulation Right

Regulation and monitoring of tourism are important in order to minimise negative social, environmental and economic impacts of this industry. In Samoa, the government led the development of Sustainable Tourism Indicators, which provide a comprehensive way of measuring social and cultural, economic and environmental impacts of tourism (Twining-Ward and Butler 2002). This is a more positive approach than that taken elsewhere, where over-regulation threatens to force poorer people out of business. For example, Frew's (2005) study of tourism on the island of Ovalau in Fiji showed that approvals for business start-ups were an unnecessarily cumbersome process which deterred both local and international tourism operators. Another government regulation could involve the tightening up of visa requirements. When this occurred in Indonesia in 2003, it made it more difficult for long-term travellers like backpackers to explore the country (Cole 2008: 104).

Similarly, the Indonesian government's formalization of the tourism economy is thwarting opportunities for many to be involved in tourism:

'Licence and registration requirements generally reduce the entry of small entrepreneurs into the tourism sector, another factor in the stagnation of the local labour market' (Schellhorn 2007: 175). Poorer peoples tend to be congregated in the informal sector, where they may work as beach vendors, guides or porters, without any need for formal qualifications or a licence to operate. Kirsten and Rogerson (2002: 32) note that ' . . . informal enterprises are often either neglected by governments in tourism planning, or viewed as a "nuisance" and subject to official harassment'— the other option is for governments to attempt to regulate informal business, which can also undermine the livelihoods of the poor. If one must be qualified in safe food handling practices to be a beach vendor, or pass a test and pay a fee to be recognised as a qualified guide, or attend health and safety training to be a porter, many will miss out. Inventive solutions are possible, however, which ensure both safe and good-quality experiences for tourists while supporting small businesspeople. For example, in Vietnam they introduced the category of 'narrator guide' to allow people without a formal qualification to offer guiding services to tourists (ESCAP 2007: 12).

Similarly, government regulations may include high standards for the tourist accommodation facilities. Thus in the Solomon Islands, building codes based upon western standards made it very difficult for small tourism ventures to be developed. Using traditional construction methods and materials, local artisans could not meet the requirements of the building code. It was estimated that if building regulations were adhered to, a small-scale tourism venture would cost around $100,000, even though comfortable, village-style accommodation could be constructed mainly out of locally available resources for a fraction of this cost (Sofield 1993: 737). In Namibia in the past the government also had regulations for the registration of tourism accommodation facilities to ensure minimum standards, which effectively impeded the involvement of communities in this sector. There was no provision for tourists to stay in simple rondavels with access to basic ablutions; rather, the lowest category of accommodation had to provide 5 bedrooms and modern plumbing (Ashley and Roe 1998).

Supporting Small-scale Entrepreneurs

Governments can also develop what can be seen in Table 6.1 as 'supporting instruments' to provide basic infrastructure to help small-scale entrepreneurs and build their capacity. Hampton's (2005) research in Indonesia thus suggests that tourism departments and local authorities should provide more support for communities living in the vicinity of tourist attraction through providing business training, and ensuring local people have access to capital. To provide an urban tourism example, a tourism official in Bangkok noted opportunities for them to employ more poor people in city festivals and events:

Actually when we organize festivals and big events there can be a lot of opportunities for the poor, but no one gives any consideration to it, for example . . . we can organize to allocate special places near the river for poor vendors selling flowers and candles so that they can get a good business, but we never organize like that, so the big shop keepers always take the prime areas . . . (Officer, Tourism Division, Bangkok Metropolitan Area—cited in Mandke 2007: 237)

Another strategy for city and district councils could be to develop effective market places so that craftspeople or local farmers producing quality produce have a regular, attractive place from which to sell their goods, whether to local households, businesses, expatriates, hotels or the tourism industry directly (Strategic Management Solutions 2004).

Recognising Citizens' Rights

It was noted in Chapter 2 that tourism can be understood as a fundamental human right, and the state has a key role to play in assisting people to claim their rights: ' . . . the discourse of tourism as a "human right" demands the involvement of communities and governments in ensuring a just distribution of its bounties (as well as its ill effects)' (Higgins-Desbiolles 2006: 1199). Governments are now being encouraged to ensure that fair distribution of the benefits of tourism occurs (Hall and Brown 2006).

Most governments have made moves to protect the labour rights of employees in tourism and other sectors, in line with these recommendations from ESCAP:

Governments need to ensure that people engaged in tourism are remunerated fairly and receive adequate social protection in areas such as the minimum wage, policies on equal opportunities, holiday entitlement and security of employment. (ESCAP 2007: 12)

Governments can also uphold the rights of works by ensuring there are good health and safety provisions in tourism workplaces. In practice, however, they often do not invest a lot of energy in monitoring tourism businesses to ensure they are abiding by labour laws or health and safety regulations. Those governments that do invest in monitoring tend to focus on large tourism enterprises, particularly four- and five-star resorts and hotels, which leads the managers of these businesses to feel somewhat disgruntled:

Large organizations seem to be used as targets and test cases for OSH [occupational safety and health] issues. There are rules for big business which don't apply to others. We in Fiji are faced generally with over-legislation and under-enforcement. (Owner of a four-star resort, Fiji: June 2009)

Meanwhile it is in the informal sector and in small-scale enterprises that labour rights and the health and safety of workers are least likely to be respected. Readers can refer back to Table 5.3, which compares employment conditions in small and large tourist enterprises in Fiji, showing, for example, that employees in small-scale enterprises are often expected to work seven days per week and are never paid for working overtime.

Where some governments have recognised the rights of their citizens to good effect is in the area of customary rights to marine areas, land or wildlife. This allows these communities to view natural resources as an asset which they can use to benefit their people. This is evident, for example, in the case of the Makuleke community in post-apartheid South Africa. This group of around 14,000 people were the first group to win back their land under new land restitution laws passed in 1996. They agreed as part of this deal to continue to keep the 22,000 hectares of land within the Kruger National Park as a conservation estate for at least 50 years, and they manage this together with SANParks, the National Parks Authority. By having their rights over land restored, this community has been able to develop effective tourism ventures in partnership with private operators, with the latter establishing lodges and running them for an agreed time period after which they will be owned by the Makuleke people.[5] Lodges pay a concession fee (9 percent of turnover) to the community, which has been used to improve their irrigation system and build new classrooms. The Makuleke people have also benefited from jobs in the lodges, capacity building of local people, and development of small businesses connected to the tourism industry, such as a textile factory which produces uniforms for lodge staff and rangers (UNWTO 2006a: 131–137).

In a contrary example, Ying and Zhou (2007) explain how there is a fundamental weakness with the Chinese model of tourism development—despite some of the positive aspects of this as discussed in earlier sections—as it does *not* guarantee people's *right* to develop tourism in their own village: this is at the whim of government. Thus in the case of Hongcun village, even though the community owned the traditional structures in the World Heritage Listed cultural village, the government insisted that the right to development of tourism there (including establishment of commercial enterprises) belonged with government. When a community tourism business failed in 1998, the government transferred the operational right to an external company who gained control over Hongcun's tourism business for a 30-year period. Along with replacing local tour guides with outsiders, the company provided only 1 percent of ticket income to the community in 1999. Due to community protests, this was increased to 8 percent in 2002, still meaning that all residents received only $37 at the end of that year (Ying and Zhou 2007: 101). Ying and Zhou (2007) thus argue that communities which own a resource, like historical houses, that attracts tourists should be guaranteed a legal right to control tourism development in their area. Without such a right, disputes between the government, the host community and providers of capital are bound to occur.

Examples of Governments Using Tourism to Enhance Local Well-being

A number of effective strategies which governments can adopt to support PPT have been discussed, from integrating tourism and poverty alleviation in plans and policies through to building linkages between the tourism industry and related sectors. I now turn to examine how several countries have specifically chosen to adopt tourism policies which prioritise the interests of local people and seek to ensure that tourism development does not impinge on local well-being (Milne 1997). Thus in Samoa, effective, budget-style tourism enterprises have been established on communal lands, allowing communities to retain control over tourism and ensuring a wide range of multiplier effects (Scheyvens 2005). The tourism industry is largely made up of small to medium-sized enterprises that are locally owned and operated. Thus neoliberal imperatives have not guided the development of tourism in Samoa, yet tourism still earns more foreign exchange than any other sector, it provides numerous formal and informal sector jobs, and it has effectively rejuvenated a number of rural villages (ibid). Similarly, Bonaire's tourism policy clearly tries to balance the needs of tourists with the interests of local communities and protection of the environment. In support of locally owned food establishments, in one place it states that no permits will be given for 'American style fast-food restaurants' (MacNaulty 2002: 41).

A good example of government policy specifically targeting disadvantaged sectors of the population is South Africa's Black Economic Empowerment (BEE) programme, which has led to far more economic opportunities for those people designated as 'black' who were systematically disadvantaged during the apartheid era (Box 6.2). In another South African example, the national Department of Environmental Affairs and Tourism has a Poverty Relief Fund—in itself this point is of significance. One example of a proposed project it was to fund was the redevelopment of an arts and crafts market in Alexandra, a black township which is still home to many impoverished people (Rogerson 2002: 185).

Two other examples from Bhutan and Cuba will be used to show how a 'strong state' may be advantageous when promoting sustainable development of tourism. Over 80 percent of people living in the Himalayan country of Bhutan live in rural areas with many engaging in subsistence agriculture, and the two main economic sectors are agriculture and hydropower. The country is rich in natural resources, with over 70 percent of its area covered in forests (Gurung and Seeland 2008). Tourism is of increasing importance to the economy and society in light of a number of challenges the country is facing, including rural-urban migration, the need to diversify its economic

---

Box 6.2　Black Economic Empowerment and Poverty Alleviation in South Africa

Black Economic Empowerment (BEE) represents an effort by the South African government at supporting and encouraging equitable practices in business, including tourism, rather than taking an enforcement approach to this (Rivett-Carnac 2006). While some BEE initiatives have been criticised for benefiting only a small number of black people at the elite level due to an emphasis on black ownership, a BEE Charter and Scorecard that were launched by the South African tourism industry in 2005 definitely go beyond this. The Scorecard, used to rate the performance of tourism businesses, also considers issues such as working conditions of poor employees and involvement of small suppliers. Seven areas are specifically considered:

- The percentage of ownership of the business by black people
- Black representation at the board and senior director levels
- Equitable employment practices
- Procurement from black businesses
- Support of enterprise development
- Investment in skills development
- Investment in social development, including community tourism (Rivett-Carnac 2006)

PPT has been integrated into BEE initiatives which seek to support enterprise development and preferential procurement deals (Ashley and Haysom 2006). Thus, for example, when the first hotel linked to an international chain was to be built in Soweto, Holiday Inn Soweto Freedom Square, 80 percent of the construction workforce derived from small to medium-sized Soweto-based enterprises. As a result US$1 million was paid to labourers and contractors from the local area. Furthermore 40 permanent jobs were provided to people from Soweto and a good training scheme for young people wanting hospitality sector skills was implemented (Hjemdahl 2008).

---

options, and providing jobs for a rapidly growing population with an increasingly educated cohort of young people (Brunet et al. 2001). Until elections held in 2008, Bhutan was a constitutional monarchy, with a king who chose to take a unique 'middle path' approach to development, balancing the preservation of environment and culture with equitable economic development. This is perhaps best highlighted in the country's guiding concept of GNH (Gross National Happiness) (Brunet et al. 2001; Gurung and Seeland 2008). 'Happiness' is defined in both a material and spiritual sense; thus the focus is not a move towards a more individualistic, consumer-oriented, commodity-focused world—rather, there is strong recognition of the value of Bhutanese culture (Brunet et al. 2001: 257). Figure 6.1 shows that the goals of the 'middle path' approach are focused on holistic development and well-being, as compared with other countries whose focus is more squarely on maximizing export revenue or economic growth.

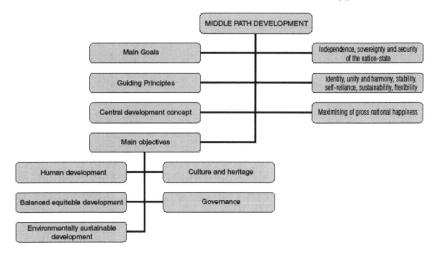

Figure 6.1   Bhutan's 'middle path development' approach.
Source: Brunet et al. (2001: 255)

Annual tourist arrivals in Bhutan were restricted to 2,000 up until 1985 and after that the government continued with a cautious approach, controlling tourism by requiring tourists to book through a registered Bhutanese tour operator and hire a guide, and to have a minimum spend of $200/day. This deterred independent and budget travellers. The impacts of tourism were carefully monitored by government officials and religious leaders so that concerns over social or environmental degradation could be quickly addressed. This led to the closure of some temples and monasteries to tourists in 1988 after religious leaders complained that the spiritual integrity of these sites was being undermined by tourism.

There are a number of performance requirements for foreign investors in the tourism sector in Bhutan, including transfer of technology, training and development of Bhutanese nationals to enhance their skills, and foreign investors can hold only up to 70 percent of equity in the venture (UNCTAD 2007: 117).

While strong state control over tourism has ultimately been to Bhutan's advantage in terms of ensuring that the industry has not overwhelmed this small country nor undermined its cultural values, a remaining challenge for the government is to find ways of promoting forms of tourism that help to alleviate rural poverty. So even though tourist numbers have been allowed to climb in recent years after earlier restrictions, such that by 2008 there were 27,636 foreign tourists compared with only 6,262 in 2003, the growth in numbers and associated revenue has not made a significant difference to the well-being of the poor.[6] Tourist itineraries are quite restricted due to lack of tourist infrastructure outside of urban areas in the west of the country; thus to date, 'Almost no economic benefits from tourism . . . go to rural Bhutanese communities' (Gurung and Seeland 2008: 490–491).

Another case in point is Cuba, where the socialist state saw a boom in tourism from 326,000 in 1989 to over 2 million in 2007 (Wilkinson 2008). Some authors argue that this rapid expansion of tourism has been largely beneficial because of considered planning and tight control exerted by a centralised state (Colantonio and Potter 2006): 'the success of tourism in Cuba is a result of one of the so-called evils of the socialist system, i.e. central planning and control' (Wilkinson 2008: 980). The tourism promotion strategy after 1989 was based: on a) environmental and economic reforms; b) institutional capacity building of both government departments and tourism training schools; c) setting up of tour operators and state holding companies; and d) the establishment of 67 tourism zones or poles across the country (Colantonio and Potter 2006). This integrated approach resulted in strong multiplier effects beyond the tourism sector: thus for every 100 jobs created in tourism, there are 53 manufacturing jobs, 36 construction jobs, 29 transportation jobs, 14 agriculture and forestry jobs, 3 urban service jobs and 3 communications jobs created (Figueras 2003, cited in Colantonio and Potter 2006: 29).

Tight state control in Cuba has allowed the state to direct profits from the sale of products in the hard currency stores for tourists, straight to the provision of 1 litre of milk or yoghurt per day for persons under seven or over 65 years of age. Similarly the well-respected medical system markets its services to tourists, and revenues from this are then channelled towards paying for medical treatments for Cuban citizens (Wilkinson 2008: 983). In addition, to retain more profits in-country, there are strict controls whereby foreign investors can come into Cuba only under joint venture arrangements.

In China, researchers appear to agree that a government-led tourism development strategy is entirely appropriate (Deng 2000; Ying and Zhou 2007). An example of this is the government's specific communal approach to rural cultural tourism development, which includes several components:

- A rural community or village is 'sold' to tourists as a single tourist destination.
- A specific corporation is formed to control the business of cultural tourism in the community.
- Revenue from ticket sales is shared by the community through both cash payments and an improved community welfare system; specific payments are made to households opening to tourists.
- Individual residents can also run their own small tourism enterprises, as coordinated by the corporation (Ying and Zhou 2007: 102).

Similarly, Dombroski's (2006) research on the governance of mass tourism and how it impacted the ethnic Tibetans indigenous to the Jiuzhaigou Biosphere Reserve found that there were good opportunities for this group to have influence over management of the Reserve as well as significant economic benefits to receive. In addition to job opportunities related to park management and tourism, the ethnic minority were given a 49 percent share in a purpose-built restaurant facility that provides meals for up to 4,000 visitors a day.

Aspects of this approach taken by the Chinese government align nicely with PPT: for example, the government coordinates activities to ensure outside entrepreneurs do not usually dominate, and communal and individual benefits are built into the model. However, this model is not being applied in all cases, as provincial governments in China can choose to approach the development of tourism in different ways and consequently their impacts on the poor vary enormously. Box 6.3 shows how in Yunnan province, rapid growth of tourism has not significantly assisted the poor. However, in the latter example in Guizhou, the deliberate strategy of developing tourism in poorer areas of the province and then linking small tourist attractions to popular tourist sites really helped to ensure there were direct benefits for the poor.

Box 6.3 Contrasting Examples of How Provincial Government Tourism Strategies Are Critical in Determining Whether the Poor Will Benefit

Donaldson provides a fascinating contrast between the ways in which the governments of Yunnan and Guizhou province in China structure tourism, and explains this is a major determinant of whether the poor see any of the benefits of tourism.

In Yunnan, the growth of tourism has resulted in rapid economic growth; however, it had a relatively small impact on rates of rural poverty. When the vice-premier visited the province in May 1992, he advised provincial leaders to concentrate on tourist destinations that were already advanced, expanding the scale of tourism by investing in large-scale infrastructure development and attracting foreign investment to these areas. Consequently most of Yunnan's well-known tourist sites are in rural areas designated as 'non-poor'. Local governments have tended to use revenues from tourism to invest in urban development of large centres, not in rural areas. Thus despite steady growth of tourism and receiving well over 1 million tourists annually, tourism in Yunnan has not contributed effectively to poverty reduction.

However, in Guizhou, although the industry is mostly small-scale, it has had a direct, positive impact on the lives of the rural poor, as the government targeted development of tourism in poor areas, and ensured that poor people could have direct participation in tourism by developing tourism in ethnic minority villages. An indication of Guizhou's commitment to poverty alleviation through tourism is that in 1992, well before the term 'pro-poor tourism' was coined, the slogan of the tourism industry here was: '... the tourism industry promotes openness to the outside; use tourism to promote poverty reduction' (cited in Donaldson 2007: 342).

Continued

Box 6.3   Continued

Thus, for example, in the 1990s the tourism administration of the province established two tourist routes that took visitors to established tourist sites but also tagged on some of China's poorest areas where new tourist sites were being established in ethnic minority villages. This strategy of linking smaller-scale attractions to popular tourism sites such as the Huangguashu waterfall has reaped big rewards for the poor in these areas.

Source: Donaldson (2007)

Similar examples of governments facilitating networks between tourism providers can be seen in Honduras and Mongolia. The Association of Colosuca municipalities developed the Colosuca Tourism Circuit Project in Lempira, the poorest department in Honduras. Rather than supporting small entrepreneurs to develop products or services for tourism in a piecemeal fashion, they took an integrated approach and developed a route which tourists could follow. Major initiatives included: building capacity of municipal staff and local tourism committees to manage tourism themselves; designing and developing tourism products (with the expectation that around 30 micro-enterprises would be improved or created through the project); establishing three tourism information offices to promote the area; and financing basic infrastructure including water and sanitation (UNWTO 2006a: 65–68). In Mongolia, rather than leaving nomadic communities to develop individual tourism enterprises whereby alternative tourists would stay a night or two in their *ger,* authorities facilitated the establishment of *ger-to-ger* tourism. After talking with and training families interested in taking part, they established 12 community routes over 3 provinces, allowing tourists to utilise a network of *gers.* In addition, the local people have greater control over this type of tourism as after cooperating to set up the venture, they no longer had to compete with tour operators. Fifty-five percent of the price of the trail passes goes directly to families while 10 percent is diverted to an environment fund (ESCAP 2007: 14).

This section has provided a wide range of examples of ways in which government agencies, at various levels, have developed policies and schemes to promote pro-poor benefits from tourism. The state can indeed have a very strong influence, in a positive way, on sustainable tourism development. In the following section I look specifically at how governments can encourage pro-poor actions by private tourism businesses.

GOVERNMENT–PRIVATE SECTOR COLLABORATION

Chapter 5's examples of business efforts to achieve PPT were useful in terms of demonstrating the wide range of ways in which private tourism enterprises can show a commitment to alleviating poverty. It is important, however, to note that they are not working alone. How they operate and whether they choose to be influenced by ethical issues, human rights, or philanthropy (in addition to profits) may be at least partly determined by the environment set by the governments of countries in which they operate. Governments establish the parameters within which the private sector operates, and it is possible for them to find ways of encouraging the private sector to consider social goals, such as poverty alleviation, as part of their mandate.

It should not be assumed that private sector businesses are against government intervention in tourism. Interestingly in Cambodia, managers of large hotels who were interviewed as part of a World Bank study examining CSR in the tourism sector requested 'strong directives from government', and 'better communication' if the government wanted corporates to show more support for CSR. A general conclusion of this study was that,

> The Royal Government of Cambodia is missing an opportunity to [capitalise on] the private sector's willingness to help ensure that tourism sector growth is environmentally and socially sustainable and optimally contributing to development and poverty reduction in the country. (Epler Wood and Leray 2005: 20)

Government Controls, Planning and Incentives

As noted in Chapter 2, under the New Poverty Agenda which emerged in the 1990s, governments are no longer letting markets rule unimpeded. Rather, they are making greater efforts to engage with the private sector and to create an enabling environment which could contribute more directly to poverty alleviation both through ensuring appropriate regulation (e.g. to ensure carrying capacities are not exceeded), and facilitating linkages between governments, the private sector, and communities (Sofield 2003). ESCAP (2003: 39) suggests a particularly useful strategy can be for governments to identify tourism zones sited in poor areas of a country, where public and private sector investment in tourism is encouraged to alleviate poverty. These are likely to be areas where there is opportunity to develop better linkages between tourism and other sectors as well.

Governments can also introduce initiatives which encourage private sector actors to support poverty reduction goals. Standing (2007) suggests that governments should develop national award schemes to highlight and reward the socially and environmentally responsible practices of tourism businesses: this might include businesses implementing good labour rights policies or local procurement programmes. Another option is for government to provide tax breaks to tour operators, hoteliers or other industry players that are actively working to direct more of their benefits to the poor. Given a supportive taxation regime, private sector actors might be willing to use a share of their profits to improve community well-being by funding a new well, irrigation system, or sewage treatment plant (Ashe 2005). In some cases governments have provided 100 percent tax relief schemes for families who wish to upgrade their bed-and-breakfast style accommodation, and a 50 percent subsidy for training costs (MacNaulty 2002: 35). Given the big incentives many governments provide to large investors in their tourism industry, which means foregone tax revenue for the state, there should be no philosophical reason that such support to small and medium enterprises would be opposed.

Ensuring that the country's banking system provides fair terms to borrowers is another area which the government can work on. Lack of access to credit can make investments in tourism by local entrepreneurs virtually impossible, while foreign investors may simultaneously be provided with very attractive incentives to invest. In the Gambia, for example, Sharpley (2007: 56) cites the bank lending rate of 31 percent as a major deterrent to local investment.

Partnerships

There are some very good examples of partnerships between government and private sector agencies too. An interesting urban tourism example comes from Medan in Sumatra, Indonesia. Here the city government and Ministry of Culture and Tourism collaborated with a private organisation, PT Star Indonesia Indah, to establish a food court in a central city street which is closed to traffic in the evenings. PT Star organised and implemented the project. This street had previously been a focus for high levels of crime and was a hangout for disenfranchised youth. Now space has been created and food carts provided for 120 food stalls, and the area has been transformed into a popular evening venue and a tourist attraction in its own right. Cultural performances take place on occasion and some stalls sell souvenirs as well as food. The city government has assisted the development of this initiative by providing lighting, a water supply and parking, and maintaining security and cleanliness. Those who were previously unemployed and involved in petty crime were recruited as parking personnel, while others found work as cleaners and waiters. Almost 1,000 direct jobs have emerged from this initiative, including work for those who prepare food for the market in their own homes (UNWTO 2006a: 73–75).

Similarly, in Baguio, in the Philippines, the city government collaborated with the Department of Tourism, local NGOs and several local tourism business associations under the structure of the Baguio Tourism Council. Some of their goals focused specifically on improving the well-being of the poor and underprivileged. Thus, for example, they provided unemployed youths and those without formal education with training in tour guiding and tourist reception (ESCAP 2003: 65).

STRATEGIES FOR GOVERNMENTS TO PROMOTE PPT

The preceding sections explained some ways in which governments can adopt pro-poor tourism practices or encourage others to do so. These ideas, and others, have been incorporated into Table 6.3, which provides a comprehensive list of policies and strategies which could be adopted by a government that specifically wants to direct more benefits of tourism to the poor. The strategies refer to tourism planning, marketing, development of infrastructure, training, community empowerment, provision of credit and working with the private sector. These strategies could also involve a variety of other stakeholders, including local communities, private sector groups, NGOs and bilateral donors.

CONCLUSION

For many decades governments of developing countries have pursued growth in their tourism sectors in the belief that this would create jobs and be an engine for development of their countries. The evidence presented in this chapter has shown that growth of tourism does not always lead to equitable distribution of benefits. Rather, 'a proactive interventionist approach is needed' whereby governments target the poor and establish legislation to back up affirmative action strategies (Sofield 2003: 351; Briedenhann and Wickens 2004). Governments need to ensure that local people are empowered with appropriate knowledge and skills and access to networks, so they are not sidelined from active involvement in tourism. This chapter explained, for example, how economic opportunities for small farmers are being lost because of inadequate linkages between them, agricultural extension officers and hoteliers. Strategic planning by governments committed to pro-poor tourism can make a real difference. Earlier in this chapter the contrasting examples of tourism in Yunnan and Guizhou provinces of China were discussed. Research here led Donaldson to conclude that:

> the effect of tourism depends upon whether the tourist industry is designed in such a way as to include or exclude the participation of the poor. To understand this, we must analyse not only the volume, but also the distribution and structure of tourism. (Donaldson 2007: 335)

It is governments that are ultimately responsible for the structure of tourism. While the role of governments is thus vital to implementing effective PPT policies and strategies, we must recognise that past policies have in many cases undermined the capacity and perceived legitimacy of government institutions, making it difficult for them to implement pro-poor policies: 'The neoliberal practices of the past two decades may also have had

Table 6.3 Policies and Strategies for Governments to Support Pro-Poor Tourism

Government tourism policy, and tourism planning	• Mainstream poverty reduction into tourism policy, planning and strategies. It should also be raised in policies of related sectors, e.g. agriculture, telecommunications, public works.
	• Include community involvement and benefits as key criteria in government planning decisions regarding approval for new tourism investment and initiatives.
	• Take a comprehensive approach to tourism development, thus explore and support if appropriate the potential of domestic tourism, regional tourism, urban tourism and budget tourism.
	• Ensure that local institutions have legal powers to enter contracts.
	• Seek effective ways of working with the private sector.
	• Plan for tourism to provide both collective benefits (e.g. funds for school books, improved water supply or roading), and individual benefits (e.g. paid employment, opportunities for micro-enterprises such as guiding or craft sales).
Understanding local populations in tourism growth areas	• Ensure adequate time and resources are devoted to social profiling of communities in order to identify: a) who are the poor; b) issues relating to customary tenure; and c) concerns deriving from religious/ethnic/gender/class inequalities (e.g. role of elites).
	• Target poorer people to ensure they benefit from growth of tourism.
Tourism regulations/ standards	• Establish regulations to protect environmental, social and cultural resources. Implement monitoring and evaluation procedures for all tourism projects and programmes, ensuring that both qualitative and quantitative indicators concerning changes to the lives of poor people are measured on an annual basis.
	• Revise complex regulations that provide a barrier to the establishment of small-scale enterprises, e.g. ensure that the accommodation grading system allows for 'simple' accommodation such as campsites and homestays to be promoted.
	• Ensure that complying with regulations does not require access to the capital city, large sums of money or complicated forms.
	• Remove discriminatory taxes, e.g. tax breaks to encourage investment may work against pro-poor tourism if they make it cheaper for hoteliers to import foods tax free than to source local supplies. Rank tourist establishments/reward them according to how well integrated they are in the local economy (e.g. sourcing of goods and services) and employment conditions for their workers.
	• Develop and implement fair labour laws, and health and safety laws.

Continued

Table 6.3 Continued

Tourism marketing	• The national tourism marketing body should market a wide range of tourism enterprises (e.g. small-scale enterprises, not just wildlife, beaches or luxury resorts) to a wide range of potential customers (e.g. domestic, regional and diaspora tourists, not just international vacationers). • Provide community tourism enterprises with access to external markets via the Internet.
Land-use planning	• Ensure land-use planning incorporates community views, recognises tourism as a land-use and supports multiple land-uses.
Development of infrastructure	• Invest in infrastructure that will benefit local residents as well as the tourism industry, e.g. access roads, water supplies, sanitation systems. • Establish small-scale tourism infrastructure that benefits multiple businesses, such as market places and visitor information centres.
Tourism training and licensing	• Provide courses, licenses and exams in tourism subjects in ways that are accessible to local people, and provide qualifications that are appropriate for local enterprises: especially important are guiding skills, language skills, hospitality, site management and maintenance. • Provide training to increase the capacity of local people to manage a business enterprise, market it effectively, and provide good customer service; e.g. publish 'how to' manuals in appropriate languages.
Empowering local populations	• Ensure there is a role for community participation in planning tourism development. • Raise awareness about the potential and pitfalls of tourism, e.g. market surveys on tourism potential. • Disseminate information on tourism options for local communities, e.g. small- versus large-scale ventures, potential for collaboration with the private sector. • Arrange study tours to other tourism sites where people have the chance to talk to and learn from those who have attempted to engage in tourism enterprises. • Mentor people who are developing small businesses. • Ensure regulations/tenure arrangements give power to communities.
Working with the private sector	• Raise awareness among businesspeople, tourism associations, chambers of commerce and local decision-makers about the potential of tourism to alleviate poverty through both individual and communal benefits.

Continued

Table 6.3   Continued

Working with the private sector (contd)	• Encourage hotels, restaurants and resorts to make their procurement practices more pro-poor by using local goods (e.g. fresh produce, soap, furnishings) and services (e.g. security, laundry), and to promote complementary businesses (e.g. a hotel could advertise village-run bamboo rafting adventures). Consider a national tourism award for businesses which maximize their local multiplier effects. Enact policy which provides incentives for private companies to collaborate with communities (e.g. via partnerships or mentoring schemes). • Encourage hotels and lodges to adopt a human resources policy which provides security of employment, training and progression opportunities. • Mediate contracts between large tourism businesses and individuals or small business owners concerning supply of goods or services (e.g. employment). • Support development of effective small and medium-sized tourism enterprises and facilitate links with existing tourism flows and products (e.g. tea shops along a hiking route used by backpackers).
Information, staffing and extension	• Provide dedicated staff, such as community tourism officers or provincial government staff, in regions to advise and support communities initiating tourism enterprises, e.g. to provide information on business planning, and to improve the quality and competitiveness of local products. • Provide information to the formal sector on how to work with communities and enhance local benefits.
Protected area management	• Manage parks in ways that stimulate enterprise opportunities for neighbouring communities (e.g. craft markets, local guides). • Provide park visitors with information on local enterprises. • Give neighbouring communities a tourism concession inside the park, or allow controlled extraction of certain resources. • Collect a levy from each tourist for a development fund for surrounding communities. • Build capacity so that local communities can be involved in protected area management (e.g. sitting on parks boards) or management of communal lands.
Credit	• Provide access to credit for small and medium-sized enterprises.

Sources: Ashley and Roe (1998: 30–31); Deloitte and Touche et al. (1999); Goodwin (2006); Karammel and Lengefeld (2006); Scheyvens (2002a); Schipani and Oula (2006); UNWTO (2006a); Van der Duim and Caalders (2008)

a lasting impact on state agents and officials alike, impairing their ability to readjust to a new agenda involving fresh thinking in spheres such as poverty alleviation' (Öniş and Şenses 2005: 279). It is very difficult for proposed partnerships between the market and state to work in such circumstances—rather, the market continues to dominate, and this can certainly inhibit pro-poor initiatives.

There have, however, been some commendable efforts by a number of governments to seek ways of ensuring that tourism is not just an 'engine for growth', but that it directly benefits poorer areas of their countries and poorer peoples as well. Examples from countries such as Cuba, Bhutan and South Africa are not provided as models of development to be applied elsewhere; it is important that the approach suits the very different contexts of particular developing countries. However, such examples do provide evidence that an alternative path to PPT—which does not mean an approach limited to alternative *forms* of tourism—can reap substantial rewards, including greater control and self-determination, not just revenue-generation. However, they also indicate that there is a need for effective governance structures if tourism is to maximise benefits for the poor. It is relatively easy for donors or governments to embrace PPT rhetoric while failing to ensure this occurs in the context of an appropriate policy and regulatory framework. This strategy could entrench existing economic and social inequalities while threatening the environment in many countries.

While a 'hands-off' approach from government is not conducive to promoting PPT, it is also not appropriate for states to over-regulate—thus trade-offs are likely to be needed: 'The problem is to find the correct mixture of market orientation and state intervention that can lead to more sustainable forms of development . . . ' (Milne 1998: 47). Governments also need to find ways of supporting local industry through training and information, and through provision of a supportive policy environment. The greatest challenge for developing country governments is to work more seriously on efforts to transform mainstream tourism. As noted by Reid (2003: 42) 'considerable inventiveness' will be required for developing countries to chart a path which allows the interests of their own communities to rise above those of outside forces.

7 Tourism Reduces Poverty
Development Agency Approaches

INTRODUCTION

In the past many development agencies eschewed opportunities to develop the tourism sector in developing countries, based on the belief that this was a private sector, profit-maximising activity which entrepreneurs could be expected to develop. Donors were concerned they would end up supporting big business, rather than enhancing livelihoods of the poor. Tourism is an industry associated with hedonism and luxury, not the types of activities development agencies saw as fitting directly within their purview, that is, feeding the hungry, providing basic health and education services, and other such 'worthy' endeavours. A research exercise conducted at University of Plymouth in 2007 revealed that out of 24 bilateral and multilateral agencies reviewed, 10 had adopted specific tourism strategies or policies. The latter tend to see tourism as an important sector in terms of sustainable livelihood strategies for the poor, whereas other agencies seem concerned that a focus on tourism could detract from traditional development interventions in areas such as primary healthcare or education (Mowforth and Munt 2009: 310). This view that tourism is not a legitimate development sector is admonished by some commentators:

> A failure of development cooperation agencies to become involved in tourism represents a failure to capitalize on the opportunities it presents (in job creation, economic development, cultural interchange and cultural heritage management) and a failure to help steer it toward a sustainable path. (Van der Duim and Caalders 2008: 110)

As we know from previous chapters, however, the advent of a new poverty agenda in the 1990s has seen a significant shift in development agency priorities, such that poverty alleviation has become the rallying cry of the majority of the world's development agencies. Some donors have subsequently re-thought their position and have identified tourism as one of the few 'engines of growth' in less developed economies.

A range of donors including multilaterals such as the World Bank and UNWTO, bilateral donors like SNV (Netherlands) and GTZ (Germany), and non-governmental organisations (NGOs), have engaged directly with efforts to strengthen the tourism sector in developing countries. They have done this in recognition of the opportunities it provides for the poor in a wide range of areas including job creation, markets for goods and services, and provision of improved infrastructure.

This chapter outlines, in turn, the PPT efforts of multilateral agencies, bilateral donors, and NGOs. Due to space limitations, only a selection of initiatives and agencies can be profiled here. Note that these agencies' reasons for involvement in tourism for poverty alleviation are varied, from those taking a neoliberal, growth-oriented approach to others more influenced by alternative development and human rights ideologies. Later there is a discussion of lessons that development agencies can learn about the most effective ways of supporting poverty alleviation through tourism, and pitfalls to avoid.

MULTILATERAL ORGANIZATIONS

Multilateral aid is channelled through international organisations that receive their funding from multiple sources. The most significant multilateral organization that advocates for PPT is the UNWTO, but the ADB will also be discussed as it has funded a number of PPT initiatives in the Greater Mekong Subregion in particular. Similarly, the World Bank's resurgence of support for tourism in recent years will be highlighted. Other multilateral agencies which have supported tourism programmes and provided technical assistance to develop tourism in recent years include the African and Inter-American Development Banks, the European Union, and a wide range of United Nations agencies including UNDP (United Nations Development Program), UNESCO (United Nations Education, Scientific and Cultural Organization), and UNCTAD (United Nations Conference on Trade and Development). Some of the multilateral organisations tend to work within a more neoliberal growth-oriented framework than, for example, NGOs committed to pro-poor tourism. As noted in Chapters 2 and 3, there are concerns over whether such an approach is effective in overcoming inequalities and benefiting the poor.

UNWTO (United Nations World Tourism Organization)

The World Tourism Organization has a mandate from the United Nations to *promote* and *develop* tourism on behalf of its 161 government tourist board members and 390 affiliate members (tourism associations, airlines, educational bodies and hotel groups): it has no explicit interest in advancing the well-being of the poor. In recent years it has, however, sought to enhance the image of tourism internationally by showing how tourism can be practised in an environmentally sustainable manner and also bring benefits to the poor.

Specific roles played by the UNWTO include provision of practical know-how regarding tourism development, regulation, and guiding global tourism policy. Regarding the first point, the sharing of practical knowledge is often carried out via technical cooperation. Telfer and Sharpley (2008: 90) discuss how the tourism consultant business has boomed along with the UNWTO's establishment of a Technical Cooperation Service in 2004, which seeks to serve the needs of those planning for tourism growth in transitional and developing countries. Member governments request services that range from establishment of a system for recording and analysing tourism statistics through to helping to prepare tourism plans and strategies. In terms of a regulatory role, the second point mentioned, the UNWTO can influence international regulations regarding human mobility, trade and the environment. However, within the tourism industry it tends to encourage self-regulation rather than government regulation (Hall 2007b: 263). Some limitations to self-regulation were noted in Chapter 5. The third point mentioned was to provide policy advice. Hall suggests that the UNWTO's policy advice focuses on 'industry partnerships and trade liberalisation', further reinforcing where their interests lie (2007b: 263). Thus while the green (environmental) agenda and the pro-poor agenda have both led to new initiatives within the World Tourism Organization in recent years, their main motivation is still to promote economic growth through tourism. As one commentator observed, 'Anything the World Tourism Organization does outside tourism promotion is just window dressing' (Personal communication, tourism specialist: September 2005).

In addition, the World Tourism Organization has sought to lead the way in improving ethical conduct in the industry by releasing a Global Code of Ethics for Tourism in 1999. The Code attempts to balance the rights of countries hosting tourists with the rights of the tourist. It lists principles by which the actions of all stakeholders in tourism should be guided; however, in practice the Code focuses mainly on the rights of tourists and the industry, rather than the communities affected by tourism (Wheat 1999b). Thus while Article 5 stresses the right for host communities to benefit from tourism, in Article 6 the obligations of stakeholders in tourism development are seen in a relatively simplistic light which emphasises protection of clients rather than protection of the people in the places that are visited by their clients.[1] Such inconsistencies do not suggest that the UNWTO is truly committed to ensuring a fair deal for communities involved in tourism. Furthermore, the effectiveness of such a voluntary code is dependent on the willingness of governments and the private sector to implement appropriate changes—Richter argues they have not shown such commitment in the past; thus change would only happen comprehensively if there were regulations, and supranational agreements (2004, cited in Schilcher 2007a: 70). Indeed, it is suggested that a global tourism code of ethics

> will only tinker with the imperialistic nature of tourism. The roots of this . . . lie in a profit-driven global economic system that disregards social costs, and is . . . much larger than the tourist industry itself. (D'Sa 1999, cited in Hall and Brown 2008: 1028)

Mowforth and Munt (2009: 312) suggest that one of the most significant indications of the recognition of tourism as a legitimate sector which can lead to development and alleviate poverty was that in 2003 the World Tourism Organization was formally made a United Nations agency. The UNWTO's specific PPT programme was devised in the year prior to this and is named ST-EP: Sustainable Tourism—Eliminating Poverty. The neo-liberal origins of ST-EP are clear, as it emerged out of an earlier World Tourism Organization programme entitled 'Liberalization with a Human Face'. The UNWTO has also endorsed the MDGs:

> For poor countries and small island states, tourism is the leading export—often the only sustainable growth sector of their economies and a catalyst for many related sectors. It can play a key role in the overall achievement of the Millennium Development Goals by 2015. (UNWTO 2005a)

Through a non-profit body formed in 2005, the ST-EP Foundation, the UNWTO seeks to assist with a range of activities, notably:

- Capacity building seminars: held at regional and national levels, to build capacity of government officials.
- Research and publications: a number of major reports have been published focusing on topics such as 'Tourism, Microfinance and Poverty Alleviation' (2005), and 'Poverty Alleviation Through Tourism: A Compilation of Good Practices' (2006a).
- ST-EP projects: project identification missions had been held in 30 countries and over 150 potential projects related to sustainable tourism development were targeted for implementation. Eighty projects are underway. LDCs and the poorer regions of other developing countries are the primary beneficiaries of support via ST-EP projects. As well as working with NGOs on the ground to implement some of these projects, several donors have contributed funds or expertise including SNV, and the governments of Italy, France and Macao (China).
- Dissemination of information and awareness-raising: publications are all available on the UNWTO website, and the UNWTO has convened ST-EP forums at the tourism industry trade fair in Berlin.[2]

A survey of ST-EP projects listed on the UNWTO website reveals that most are either: a) associated with protected areas and ecotourism, or b) community-based tourism ventures focused on a particular locality.[3] These include a handicraft project in Ethiopia, a footbridge project in Kenya, and improving local guiding services in Bolivia. There are also a number of interesting regional initiatives funded, such as developing regional tourism routes or trails that take in a number of attractions, and marketing a region as a destination. For example, in May 2009 the ST-EP programme presented a marketing strategy to stakeholders in eight African countries regarding multi-destination circuits. There appear, however, to be few initiatives to connect local food producers with mainstream tourism enterprises, which has been identified in the PPT literature as an area of great potential.

In 2009, the Secretary General of the UNWTO, Taleb Rifai, was interviewed about his views on what the UNWTO had achieved and what direction it should take in future. Commenting specifically on ST-EP, he stated that their achievements had been mainly in increasing awareness globally about the potential of tourism to contribute to poverty alleviation, and he admitted that the organisation may not have made much of a tangible contribution to alleviating poverty (eTurboNews 2009d). While a wide range of good projects have actually been implemented through ST-EP, they do not address some changes at national and global levels which could also be of great significance. For example, it is relatively straightforward for donors to support communities in developing their own tourism enterprises. However, it is more difficult and controversial to endorse labour rights for all tourism sector workers worldwide, or to work with developing country governments to establish a policy environment conducive to controlling the activities of foreign investors and protecting local businesses.

UNWTO has also worked with private companies. For example, they support the Tour Operators Network for Poverty Alleviation at Destinations (TONPAD), which involves 35 countries which are trying to build sustainable enterprises and ensure direct benefits for people in destination areas (UNWTO 2006c: 6). In addition, UNWTO has entered into a public-private partnership with Microsoft, with whom they are working to improve the competitiveness and quality of tourism in developing countries by using information technology. As Bill Gates expressed,

> Microsoft wants to play a hands-on role to help countries and entire regions develop their knowledge-based economy, create jobs, spur growth and enable innovation. We can do this by providing easy and affordable access to technology and helping our partners build robust local software economies. (Travel Wire News 2006)

One initiative launched under this scheme in 2007 is a social networking site which allows socially conscious travellers to share information on ethical tourism, such as enterprises that help poor communities (UN

News Service 2007). While many countries in Africa would undoubtedly welcome assistance with upgrading their technology and software related to tourism, and this could enhance their market presence and efficiency, questions could also be asked about whether this is just a clever way for Microsoft to penetrate another marketplace and, eventually, profit from its development.

At a speech delivered by Geoffrey Lipman, assistant secretary-general of the UNWTO, to tourism industry executives in Sydney on 8 April 2009, he discussed how tourism could be a saviour to developing countries if their governments invested further in growth of tourism as a strategy to fight the global recession. He then admitted, however, that any increase in tourism in developing countries would bring broader benefits to the travel industry as these tourists visiting developing countries would fly on rich-world airlines, stay in rich-world chain hotels, and eat rich-world produced food (Personal communication, travel industry official: 9 April 2009). The tone of Lipman's statements seems representative of the UNWTO's overall approach to PPT, that is, that promoting tourism in the developing world is a win-win situation: it can help the economies of poorer countries while increasing the profits of travel companies in the west as well.

World Bank

Since the mid-1960s the World Bank has funded several hundred projects which utilize tourism as a developmental tool (Hawkins and Mann 2007). While the World Bank does not have a specific 'tourism for poverty allevia-tion' programme, it is currently providing significant funding for tourism projects and programmes around the globe with the intention that this will lead to development and reduce poverty over time. This is despite the fact that the Bank's directors are reluctant to name tourism as a specific industry focus as it has ' . . . been judged unstable and volatile' (Hawkins and Mann 2007: 359). It is important to note that in addition to the World Bank's efforts to provide technical assistance and loans to governments regard-ing tourism development, the IFC (International Finance Corporation) is another part of the World Bank Group that provides funding directly to the private sector, so a significant amount of funding to the tourism sector is provided via the IFC.

In the accounts of Mann (2005) and Hawkins and Mann (2007) con-cerning the World Bank's changing approach to tourism over the past forty years, it is fascinating to detect several phases which reflect different theo-retical understandings of the relationship between tourism and develop-ment (Table 7.1). In the first phase from 1966 and through the 1970s which they label as 'macro development', there was considerable investment in tourism infrastructure in line with a liberal economic perspective prioritis-ing modernisation and economic growth. In the 1980s, however, the World Bank closed its tourism department and pulled most of its funding from the tourism sector due to: a) the neoliberal climate of the time which emphasised allowing markets to drive growth, and b) criticisms of the social and economic impacts of tourism which then required agencies like the World Bank to spend more money when preparing their projects. The World Bank was prompted to invest considerable sums of money in tourism once again in the third phase in the 1990s, due to widespread calls to support environmental projects and sustainable development following publication of the Brundtland Report in 1987 and the Rio Earth Summit in 1992. To some extent, therefore, the World Bank was in this third phase responding to concerns raised under an alternative development approach. It was, however, the endorsement of tourism as a means of alleviating poverty at the UN General Assembly in 1999, a stance that accorded with the World Bank's new emphasis on poverty reduction, which led to larger sums of money than ever before being directed to the tourism sector in the past decade. Hawkins and Mann (2007) call this fourth phase 'micro development' but in Table 7.1 I have called it 'Creating an enabling environment for investment'.

In its renewed focus on tourism the World Bank endorses preservation of important natural and cultural resources and encourages participation of local communities in tourism; however, it also looks very closely at the overall investment climate and stresses that there needs to be a commitment from governments to 'make markets work for tourism' (Christie 2002: 36). Put another way, it is suggested that ' . . . the bank is a critical interlocutor because it lends to and advises governments directly, thereby *empowering their capacity to manipulate development*' (Hawkins and Mann 2007: 350—emphasis added). This 'capacity to manipulate' is linked to neoliberal logic. For example, it is suggested that any 'enlightened' government will recognise that in order to achieve development through tourism it is vital to adopt certain reforms, such as guaranteeing investors clear title to land (Christie 2002: 36). Yet to do this may mean undermining customary land ownership and traditional decision-making structures, something which those adopting a critical or alternative development perspective would see as contrary to attempts to make development 'pro-poor'.

ADB (Asian Development Bank)

Tourism is not a major sectoral focus for the Asian Development Bank; however, it fits well with the agency's interest in promoting private sector development. Many of the recent tourism-related projects funded by the ADB are associated with developing infrastructure such as roads, airports, water and waste management services, natural and cultural heritage conservation, and tourist information centres.

There has been a more concentrated effort to support tourism as a tool for economic development in the Greater Mekong Subregion, however, as evidenced by several major projects advanced here between 2004 and 2010.[4]

Table 7.1   Changing Support for Tourism at the World Bank, 1966–2006

Period	Focus	Description	Funding for tourism (in constant $)
1966–1979	Macro development	The WB began funding tourism projects as a means of generating economic development in 1966, soon after commercial air travel started to generate large numbers of tourists to long-haul destinations. Loans were provided to private sector and governments for investment in infrastructure, capacity building & wildlife conservation. This helped to launch new destinations e.g. Bali, Kenya, and Mexico	$1115 million
1980–1990	Disengagement	Tourism Department at WB closed. Previous rapid growth in tourism led officials to decide that the industry should be left to markets and the private sector. They were also concerned that tourism projects were complex and thus required lots of input, and that investments in tourism did not benefit the poor. Due to continuing demand, UNDP and World Tourism Organization funded tourism plans and gave technical assistance, although they could not facilitate access to finance.	$180 million
1991–1999	Sustainable development	Ideology of environmental and social sustainability infiltrated WB's approach to lending. WB also helped to fund the Global Environment Facility. Thus while the WB's line was that it still 'did not do tourism', conservation projects with tourism attached did get funding.	$600 million
2000–2006	Creating an enabling environment for investment	Identifies investment opportunities in tourism and analyzes constraints to investment. Encourages reforms to overcome these barriers. Provides detailed analysis of tourism value chains to assess efficiency of firms in the supply chain, with a focus on improvement of livelihoods.	$3.5 billion

Source: Based on Hawkins and Mann (2007); Mann (2005)

While initially this support was framed in terms of promoting 'pro-poor tourism', now the ADB has shifted to funding 'sustainable tourism development'. The ADB's technical assistance for the Greater Mekong Subregion Tourism Sector Strategy is part of a larger ten-year plan (2006–2015) for the Greater Mekong Subregion. In a rather ambitious, but also naïve way, the Strategy states that poor communities will have ownership of tourism programmes developed with other, more powerful, stakeholders:

> Poor local communities will be the primary beneficiaries in planning and owning their future in tourism development with the public sector, development partners, and nongovernment organizations providing policy, technical assistance, capacity building, and financial support. (ADB 2005: 45)

Despite due attention being made to PPT principles and PPT being frequently mentioned in the Strategy, it is not prioritised in indicative financing of the first five years of the project. Out of a total cost of $440.78 million, only $13.5 million is allocated specifically to the PPT section of the strategy, which is just 3 percent of the total cost. Meanwhile, $372.73 million is pegged for tourism-related infrastructure, a massive 85 percent of total expenditure. Pro-poor rhetoric by the ADB does not compensate for the disproportionate way in which these funds are being expended. As noted by Redman (2009: 24), 'It is unlikely that the poor will be the primary beneficiaries in the "owning and planning" . . . of this type of development'. Growth is being prioritised, but there is scant reference to equity.

Furthermore, civil society action groups believe that in its Safeguard Policy Statement draft of 2007, the ADB significantly downgraded its mechanisms for social and environmental protection, which is of major concern considering the amount of money they are investing in infrastructural projects (Redman 2009). The ADB attempted a consultation meeting about the proposed new policy statement in March 2008, but this was boycotted by most NGOs in the region as they interpreted it as a "step backwards for donor accountability, transparency, the rights of indigenous persons, housing rights and the environment" (BIC 2008: 1, cited in Redman 2009: 33).

Infrastructure development in central Vietnam funded by the ADB has been welcome in most contexts, improving transport and communications and associated possibilities for business development, including tourism. However, the negative implications of infrastructural improvements are often not considered. For example, a road was built around a lagoon adjacent to the tourist town of Lang Co, interfering with irrigation systems around the lagoon, cutting off some farmers' access to water so they can no longer have two crops of paddy rice a year. Redman (2009: 94) sees this example as representative of the public's 'lack of participation in the planning process with regard to tourism development . . . [and] a complete lack of awareness of various plans'. In some cases even the Commune People's

Committee did not know of development plans which Redman had access to. Redman (2009) suggests that such lack of community awareness and poor community involvement in planning significantly limits PPT's potential, because outsiders are deciding which activities to prioritise and local people are also unaware of the possibilities open to them.

This section has shown how a number of multilateral agencies have embraced tourism as a means of promoting economic growth and alleviating poverty, and due to this millions of dollars have been invested into a range of initiatives from community-based projects and capacity building (UNWTO) to technical assistance, an emphasis on working with the private sector, and large-scale infrastructural development (World Bank and ADB). To follow, I consider the nature of bilateral donors' support for PPT, which does differ from some of the multilateral forms of assistance.

BILATERAL DONORS

The introduction to this chapter noted that for many years donors avoided the tourism sector, seeing it as a private sector activity that did not require their intervention and which could not effectively deliver benefits to the poor. Bilateral donors, those giving country-to-country aid, seemed to subscribe to many of the critiques of tourism presented in Chapter 3, that is, that tourism is dominated by large corporations which exploit the labour and resources of developing countries, thus causing environmental and cultural degradation, entrenching inequality and deepening poverty (Britton 1982; Pleumarom 1994). Some were tempted to start funding alternative tourism ventures in the 1980s and 1990s, however, as support for community-based ecotourism or cultural tourism ventures was seen as taking a people-centred approach which could directly enhance the livelihoods of the poor.

It has only been in the last decade that a number of bilateral donors have developed programmes based on an understanding that mainstream tourism too has the potential to alleviate poverty. As noted in Chapter 1, tourism has been identified as a possible strategy to overcome poverty partly because tourism is a significant or growing economic sector in most developing countries with high levels of poverty. Tourism contributes up to 40 percent of GDP in developing countries compared with 10 percent of GDP in Western countries (Sofield et al. 2004: 2). There are still many bilateral agencies that do not specifically fund tourism initiatives, so the upcoming discussion will focus only on the activities of a few of the donors which have made a clear and sustained commitment to tourism for poverty alleviation in their work: NZAID, SNV and GTZ. It is noteworthy that PPT-related initiatives have also been funded by other bilateral donor agencies including those from Australia, Canada, Denmark, France, Ireland, Japan, Norway, Switzerland, the UK and the USA.

NZAID

The New Zealand government agency delivering bilateral aid is known as NZAID. It is by far the smallest of the bilateral donors considered here, but has nevertheless supported some effective tourism-related programmes, particularly in the Pacific Islands and Southeast Asian regions. The agency's early forays into the tourism field in the late 1980s and 1990s were driven by conservation logic, drawing on New Zealand's expertise in areas of forestry and conservation. This led to support for nature tourism and ecotourism. In addition, following a modernist approach to development there was a good deal of support for upgrading of transportation and communications infrastructure. When requested, NZAID also provided support with marketing and publicity (Scheyvens 2006). This is clearly shown in the examples of programmes funded by NZAID in Table 7.2.

There was a shift in approach at NZAID post-2000, however, linked to a new vision for the agency: 'a safe and just world free of poverty'. Then explicit recognition of tourism's potential as a tool for poverty alleviation was provided in 2007 when a pro-poor tourism workshop was hosted by the agency. Initiatives in the last decade have focused more on assisting with national-level planning for tourism development, building capacity of those working in the industry, and seeing tourism as a good option for supporting sustainable livelihoods. A sustainable livelihoods approach has also combined with NZAID's past focus on nature-based tourism in cases such as the Gunung Rinjani National Park Project, which sought to combine conservation and development. This was discussed in Chapter 3 (see Box 3.1), in a case study which showed how difficult it can be for donors to effectively support the most vulnerable groups in a community. This example also showed how donor funding to consultants who manage a tourism and development programme can constitute a large part of the overall budget, leaving comparatively small amounts of funding for community development and poverty alleviation initiatives on the ground.

NZAID has provided comprehensive support to tourism in Samoa, from supporting development of a new tourism development plan at a national level through to grassroots support for small-scale tourism enterprises. For example, owners and managers of beach *fales* (basic huts built on communal land—see Photo 7.1) were trained in financial management, health and safety, and service skills. NZAID also funded the *Samoa Beach Fale Owners' Manual*, written in both Samoan and English, which contains sections on looking after your guests, managing your beach *fale* and running your business. A Tourism Support Fund was established using NZAID monies to provide advice and financial grants for capital development to tourism operators. Under this scheme businesses can apply for up to two days of free advice on planning, management and marketing their enterprise. The Tourism Support Fund also reimburses up to 50 percent of the costs of capital works, up to a maximum of ST$10,000. This has enabled some small-scale operators to fund new signage, communal bathrooms or

Table 7.2 Trends in New Zealand's Official Development Assistance to Tourism

Period	Main focus of funding	Selected examples[5]
1980s	Infrastructure & training: transportation & communications	Runway resealing: Niue (1981) Civil aviation training: W. Samoa (1981) New control tower: Tonga (1985)
	Marketing & promotion	Visitor promotion: Niue (1983) Promotional campaign: Cook Islands (1986)
1990s	Transportation	Civil aviation assistance: Tonga (1994)
	Community-based ecotourism/tourism in association with protected areas	Ecotourism project: Fiji (1990+) Study of environmental tourism potential: W. Samoa (1991) Ecotourism project—World Heritage site: Solomon Islands (1992+) Nam Ha ecotourism: Lao PDR (1997+)
	Advice to industry	Small-scale business advice: Vanuatu (1999) Business advisory services, Kosrae: Federated States of Micronesia (1998)
	Marketing & promotion	Tourism promotion: Niue (1994)
2000+	Ecotourism and nature-based tourism	Nature Tourism Programme: Tonga (1999+) National park management, tourism and community development: Mongolia (2001+)
	Tourism Master Planning	Tourism Development Plan 2002–2006: Samoa (2001+)
	Ecotourism Planning	Development of National Ecotourism Strategy: Philippines (2001+)
	Capacity building	Training workshops for small tourism businesses: PNG (2005)
	Sustainable livelihoods	Grant funding and technical advice to help small-scale tourism operators rebuild post-tsunami (2009+)

Source: Hall and Page (1996); MFAT and NZAID reports from 1990–2010

an open-sided restaurant, for example. Forty percent of funding went to designated 'hardship areas' (Scheyvens 2005 and 2006).

NZAID's response to the September 2009 tsunami that hit Samoa is also telling. This tsunami was devastating for communities in the southeastern

Photo 7.1   Family-owned beach fales offer a sustainable livelihood option to some village dwellers in Samoa.
Source: Author

coast of the island of Upolu, where a lot of family-owned beach *fale* establishments are based. Around the village of Lalomanu alone, over 50 people lost their lives, and all of the beach *fales* along the coast were wiped out. Overall 44 percent of national accommodation stock was damaged or destroyed, and only 37 percent of the employees in these businesses still had a job one month after the tsunami struck (Robertson 2010: 11). Rather than just investing in rebuilding people's homes, NZAID has responded to the Samoan government's call to help to rebuild its tourism industry, the major sector in the economy. NZAID has thus provided NZ$4 million, part of which will be used for interest rate subsidies on loans from commercial banks to owners of high-end hotels to help them rebuild more quickly and cheaply, with the rest as grant funding and technical assistance to beach *fale* operators for rebuilding purposes (Robertson 2010).

SNV (Netherlands Development Organisation)

A Netherlands bilateral development agency, SNV, has been involved in tourism projects since the mid-1990s and has a strong commitment to endorsing sustainable tourism and involvement of communities in tourism development (see Leijzer 2003). Box 7.1 provides a case study of one of SNV's early tourism programmes implemented in a number of different places in Tanzania. This shows that most local people believed tourism did

---

Box 7.1 Contribution of Tourism to Poverty Alleviation in Barabarani Village, Tanzania

In 1996, SNV initiated a cultural tourism programme in 20 locations in Tanzania. Tours to these places now attract around 20,000 tourists annually and bring in $500,000 directly for those who organise the tours.

One of these places was Barabarani village in Mto wa Mbu ward, which is strategically located on the northern tourism circuit in Tanzania, which includes a number of renowned national parks. A number of groups work on cultural tourism in the area, and tourist numbers have grown significantly over the past decade. Barabarani can be thus described as a small but active cultural tourism hub. Muganda Michael (2009) conducted interviews with a wide range of key informants as well as using a questionnaire with 139 local households to get residents' impressions on whether tourism had contributed to community development and poverty alleviation in Barabarani over the past five years. Just under half of his respondents felt that the general quality of life of local people and their household incomes had improved or significantly improved due to tourism development, while a third felt that these things had worsened. Proximity to the road was a strong indicator of how people felt about tourism – that is, the small number of people who did not feel their locality had benefited greatly from tourism were those who lived in sub-villages far away from the tarmac road.

Most responses were overwhelmingly positive, with 80.6 percent of people feeling that tourism contributed to income-generating projects, 72.7 percent saying that tourism stimulated entrepreneurship, and a massive 97.2 percent enthusing that tourism improved their community's accessibility, including transport (e.g. roading) and telecommunications (e.g. internet access) (Michael 2009: 173). Many researchers suggest that direct employment opportunities are the main local benefit of tourism, but it is clear in some cases that more communal benefits can improve local facilities for a wide-ranging group of people.

---

contribute to improved incomes, but those who were not located near to the tourism development were far less likely to experience direct benefits.

Despite the apparent success of their cultural tourism programme in Tanzania, since 2000 SNV's approach to tourism has changed away from projects at the community level, to more sector-wide support. This involves, for example, providing advisory services to tourism organisations, developing institutional capacity of related organisations, and advice on tourism planning (Van der Duim and Caalders 2008).

There is a strong focus on developing commercially viable businesses and influencing the private sector, as can be seen in the first three of the following four services listed on SNV's website:

- Improving product quality and commercialization in tourism destinations

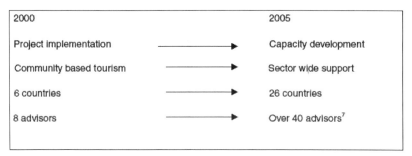

Figure 7.1   Changes in SNV's support for tourism.

- Developing market linkages and value chain development for tourism products and services
- Mainstreaming 'inclusive business'/pro-poor principles in private sector businesses, and
- Improving policy making and sector coordination.[6]

There has also been significant growth in the volume of their support for tourism (Figure 7.1). SNV now focuses on 'pro-poor sustainable tourism', based on the argument that 'With relatively little capital investment, tourism can yield high levels of employment and income for the poor, particularly in rural communities where biodiversity has remained intact' (SNV n.d.: 2).

Reflecting this change in approach, SNV now provides technical assistance to national government organisations, destination management organisations, training institutes and tourism business associations (Leijzer 2006). SNV's work in Lao PDR, for example, is detailed in Box 7.2, showing initiatives involving a wide range of stakeholders from provincial government to tour operators, and a university.

Box 7.2   SNV's Advisory Work in Lao PDR, Current and Planned[8]

- Managing a taskforce to implement the ecotourism strategy
- Consulting with the private sector and support of the Lao Tour Operator's Association
- Management of the Sustainable Tourism Network
- Securing funding for the Housphanh Tourism Action Plan
- Supporting implementation of the ADB/NTA Mekong Tourism Development Programme
- Advising Savannakhet PTO on developing a Provincial Tourism Strategy
- Curriculum developing and capacity building with the National University of Laos
- Developing funding mechanisms for tourism activity to strengthen biodiversity conservation in and around protected areas
- Reviewing ecotourism and protected area legal and regulatory mechanisms

---

Table 7.3   SNV's Advisory Services to Support Pro-Poor Sustainable Tourism[9]

Advisory Services	Description
Planning and development	Master plans, policies, strategies, laws Programmes and proposal formulationNetworks Tourism businesses and business associations Community-based tourism products Marketing and promotion strategies
Tourism management	Information systems Visitor management and interpretation systems Guide systems and services Establishing public and private sector partnerships
Education, research, monitoring and evaluation	Tourism education and awareness-raising Research methodologies Monitoring, evaluation and quality control Mainstreaming gender in tourism processes and product development

SNV's advisory services include planning and development, tourism management and education, research, monitoring and evaluation, as noted in Table 7.3. For example, in different districts of Vietnam, SNV is working to build the capacity of district government staff, establishing a tourism fee system to distribute tourism benefits to surrounding communities, setting up a Tourism Information Centre, training guides, and developing a trekking policy. SNV also worked with the government of Vietnam and consulted a wide range of stakeholders to develop a new law on tourism in 2005 which links tourism and poverty reduction, as was noted in Chapter 6.

GTZ

In 2006 German bilateral donor GTZ (Deutsche Gesellschaft für Technische Zusammenarbeit) had fifty projects with tourism components or with tourism as a main focus, and fifty qualified personnel working on these projects (Tampe and Lengefeld 2007). There has been a major shift in their approach to tourism over time, from an initial focus on tourism as a tool for modernisation through infrastructural development, human resource development and tourism promotion in the 1960s and 1970s, to the 1980s when they virtually withdrew from funding tourism due to harsh criticism of the industry from both German and international voices. The 1990s saw a revival of funding due to the global interest in sustainable development stimulated primarily by the United Nations Conference on Environment and Development in Rio de Janiero. The latest phase, by contrast, has been characterised by both a focus on supporting niche tourism and a strong desire to engage directly with mainstream tourism operators and assist them to transform their practices in a more pro-poor manner.

Table 7.4   Key Foci of German Development Organisations Funding Tourism Initiatives

Focus	Examples
Environmental protection and rural community development	Tourism development in relation to sustainable use of resources in and around national parks and protected areas
Tourism management and marketing	Assistance given to individual companies, but also to institutions from the local through to the supranational level. Tourism master planning also conducted at the national level.
Training, education and knowledge transfer	Workshops and seminars to build capacity of local actors engaging in tourism including community members, NGO staff and municipal officials. Topics include quality management, tourism planning and environmental education.
Education and public relations	Campaigns in Germany to raise the awareness of potential travellers about responsible tourism. This also includes GTZ's programme on 'Protection of Minors Against Sexual Exploitation' in partner countries.
Cooperation with the private sector; employment promotion	Support for trade associations, public infrastructure development and structural reforms. Also includes GTZ's PPP (public private partnership) projects – e.g. a partnership with International Business Leaders Forum and the hotel chains of Marriott, Starwood and Intercontinental gives socially disadvantaged youths the opportunity to receive vocational training.

Source: Derived from Tampe and Lengefeld (2007)

Table 7.4 lists some of the key foci of assistance by German development agencies, of which GTZ is the major agency involved in support for tourism. Similar to NZAID, their work has had a strong focus on tourism in terms of its potential contribution to environmental sustainability. They have also supported tourism planning, management and marketing at a wide range of scales. For example, their FODESTUR project with seven countries in Central America sought to develop a regional strategy for sustainable development of tourism and an umbrella brand for tourism products in these countries. The German development agencies have also educated German tourists about responsible travel, and supported economic development initiatives including cooperation with the private sector. As an example of the latter, GTZ initiated public-private partnerships with Studiosus and Aventoura, tourism operators who bring German tourists interested in development issues to visit GTZ projects (Tampe and Lengefeld 2007).

In recent years GTZ's overall approach has broadened further such that, a) social sustainability is central to their concerns, and b) tackling change in mainstream tourism, or as they put it, "mainstreaming sustainability", is a major focus. As part of this approach to mainstream sustainability, GTZ has promoted Corporate Social Responsibility and thus has worked closely with the tourism industry, labour unions and NGOs to discuss social standards and working conditions in the tourism sector. These issues include fair wages, and abolishing the use of forced labour and sexual exploitation in the industry. Rather than just focusing on the accommodation sector, they have also identified the importance of examining working conditions of local suppliers of goods and services to the tourism industry. GTZ has worked directly with all-inclusive resorts in the Nicaragua, Jamaica and Dominican Republic, assisting them to find ways of contributing effectively to poverty alleviation (Tampe and Lengefeld 2007).

The three bilateral agencies just discussed have definitely changed their focus over time, from seeing tourism as a mainstream development strategy associated with economic growth, to a more cautious approach in the 1990s associated with supporting only environmentally friendly, niche tourism development. In the latest decade, there has been a noticeable shift to support national-level tourism planning and the transformation of mainstream tourism as part of a more pro-poor tourism approach.

NGOs

NGOs have become increasingly important development actors in recent decades (Kennedy 2008). NGOs do not have a profit motiv. They can be effective in delivering development assistance in the context of weak states or states burdened by corruption or bureaucracy. Once considered fringe development actors, their legitimacy and scope has grown over time through their provision of humanitarian assistance, education and health services, development of infrastructure and social development initiatives.

Kennedy (2008) suggests that there are three main types of NGOs involved in tourism which have made a significant contribution to tourism as a poverty alleviation strategy (these accord with the first three categories in Table 7.5). The earliest NGOs dealing with tourism and development tended to be very critical of this industry and thus played watchdog and advocacy roles. This included local action groups opposed to the impacts of tourism development in their area, as seen in the discussion of the Consumer's Association of Penang in Chapter 3, and issues-based organisations, such as ECPAT (End Child Prostitution in Asian Tourism). Another example is Indian NGO Equations, which is concerned with empowering communities to protect themselves against the negative impacts of tourism.

Table 7.5   Types of NGOs which Deal with Tourism

NGO type	Purpose
Educational and advocacy	Raise awareness in western countries about how to be an ethical traveller. Play watchdog roles and advocate nationally and internationally on behalf of communities and vulnerable groups that are being exploited by tourism. Seek to change the way in which mainstream tourism works. Examples: Equations (India); ECPAT; International Institute of Peace through Tourism; International Ecotourism Society; Tourism Concern.
Volunteer tourism organisations	Send tourists to work on development projects around the world, which may meet one or more of the following purposes: assisting others who live in poverty, raising awareness of voluntourists about global inequalities, building relationships between people in different parts of the world, and stimulating action towards social justice in western countries. Examples: Cross Cultural Solutions; Ladakh Farm Project.
Tour company foundations	Companies can have not-for-profit foundations which are funded through the profits of the parent company and voluntary donations. They tend to partner with NGOs in their home country and the developing world and then give grants to support community development projects in the places they visit. Examples: Intrepid Travel; GAP Adventures.
Local community development	Assist communities to develop alternative livelihood strategies which can help them to protect the integrity of their natural resources and culture while also bringing in a source of income. These agencies focus mainly on local-level support.
Sustainable livelihoods: national and regional approaches	Work at higher levels to influence the policies and institutions which frame possibilities for sustainable development at the grassroots level. For example, Oxfam Caribbean seeks to influence national-level policies and a regional trade agreement which directly impact on the livelihood options of many poorer people.

Source: Kennedy (2008) and author

Equations conducts an annual audit of the tourism industry's operations in India, effectively monitoring government policy and large-scale tourism development, as well as passing monitoring skills on to local communities (Equations 2009). There is now a greater focus from some NGOs on raising awareness of tourists about how to travel ethically, and on working *with* the industry for change. British NGO Tourism Concern provides a good example of this new approach in the upcoming discussion. Another organisation seeking to influence change in the travel industry is the Travel Foundation, a sustainable tourism charity which works with leading travel companies to persuade them that CSR is good for business. It has 130 members in the UK, from small independent tour operators to airlines and multinational corporations, and has worked in 12 countries (The Travel Foundation 2010).

In recent years, there has been quite significant growth in efforts of other types of NGOs which see tourism's development potential in a more positive light than the early advocacy NGOs. These include the volunteer tourism organisations such as Cross Cultural Solutions and Learning from Ladakh project, which were discussed in some detail in Chapter 4 of this book. Kennedy identifies such organisations as a second type of NGO involved with tourism.

Kennedy (2008) also discusses tour company foundations, that is, private travel businesses which have established a sideline foundation in order to put money back into community development in the places they visit. Companies such as Intrepid do this, and they report major growth in interest from tourists in recent years to support such initiatives. A major benefit of the these foundations is that the tour companies regularly visit the same communities as part of their travel itineraries, so they can develop relationships which enable them to get a good sense of community needs as well as monitoring progress with initiatives supported by their grants or donations. Another version of this is when a charitable organisation is formed to link travellers to development initiatives. For example, Travaid is a charitable organization established in the UK in 2009 which identifies and screens worthwhile environmental and social projects that travellers can donate to. By developing partnerships with the travel industry (e.g. airlines, hotels and tour operators), it then sets up an online system whereby tourists booking through these agencies can donate to trusted projects. Travaid thus provides certainty to the travel industry and its clients regarding the value of various projects, including providing them with progress reports on the projects it endorses.[10]

To Kennedy's three categories of NGOs involved with tourism I would add two more. The fourth comprises NGOs that have in the last ten to twenty years started to work directly with local communities to support them in developing alternative livelihood strategies. This may range from training for people wishing to establish a community-tourism venture, to business advice for women's groups which wish to sell crafts in tourist markets. Communities have generally welcomed the support of NGOs in these endeavours, often for the reasons outlined in Chapter 3, which highlights the challenges of running a successful community-based tourism initiative. Communities need capacity building, access to credit and technical support, all of which an NGO

can provide. Support from an NGO can also help communities get a
al from tourism. For example, Africa Wildlife Foundation helped to
te 14 agreements that had been established by Chief Mukuni with
urism industry businesses (e.g. rafting companies and safari lodges)
in the Victoria Falls area. After 7 of the 14 moved to formal leases, the revenue generated has, rather than going directly to the chief, been used to fund 24 pre-school teachers, and provided resources for schools and a local health centre (Metcalfe and Kepe 2008: 251).

The fifth category of NGOs may have started out working directly with communities, but now increasingly work at higher levels. While there are potentially hundreds of NGOs providing support for community development through tourism, there are very few which see it as more strategic to work at the national or regional level to influence the frameworks and institutions which shape possibilities for development of sustainable livelihoods at the grassroots level. Oxfam Caribbean is one such NGO, and the upcoming case study documents how it is endeavouring to influence government policy and trade agreements.

Kennedy's research on NGOs involved in tourism concluded that NGOs play a unique and valuable role as development actors, and that they can thus contribute significantly to tourism development initiatives:

> Partnerships between tourism NGOs in the developed world and either community leadership or NGOs in developing countries create one of the most effective strategies for tackling poverty reduction as they allow locals to assume control and leadership in creating solutions locally and avoid dependency. (Kennedy 2008)

This view is also supported by Wearing et al. (2005), who conclude that because NGOs are not motivated by a focus on generating profits for industry, they have prioritized development approaches that include community perspectives, emphasize host-visitor interaction, and are culturally and environmentally sensitive. Furthermore, NGOs tend to work in partnership with local communities and facilitate their empowerment. Of the two NGOs profiled next, Oxfam Caribbean works with communities while Tourism Concern does not do this so much; however, both organisations are involved in initiatives to transform mainstream tourism and they work to influence policy at the national level and beyond.

Oxfam Caribbean

Oxfam Caribbean provides an example of how an NGO can work effectively with both government and the private sector to build linkages between tourism and agriculture which enhance livelihood outcomes for local people (Meyer 2007). In 2003 Oxfam established a Market Access Initiative (MAI), which aimed to: 'increase the power of small-scale rural

farmers through advocacy and lobbying for the implementatio
positive policy framework which creates an enabling environment
2008: 2). Oxfam then provided support in terms of production, 1
ing and purchasing. For example, a marketing company was set
Oxfam Caribbean to foster cooperation and communication between the
tourism and agriculture sectors. To encourage hotels to purchase from
local farmers, incentives are being developed including accreditation of
hotels that buy locally, marketing material about the scheme to be used
for hotel promotion, and tax benefits for those that contribute to pover-
ty-reducing objectives (Meyer 2007: 576–579). In addition, Oxfam has
supported four farmer cooperatives so farmers can pool their resources,
market their produce effectively and negotiate with hotels (Ashley et al.
2006: 3).

At a higher level, Oxfam provides advice on the policy framework at the
national level and has been involved in efforts to influence Caribbean trade
policy at the regional level.

For example, they worked with the Caribbean Policy Development Centre, which lobbies against unfavourable trade regulations at the regional
and international levels (Scott 2008).

Tourism Concern

Tourism Concern is a UK-based campaigning NGO advocating for human
rights (see Tourism Concern 2009), though it began with more of an
emphasis on education. In its first few years, in addition to supporting campaigns at the grassroots level, the agency focused on producing reports and
educational materials to provide information and open up opportunities
for dialogue. They later shifted their focus more centrally to campaigns
at a range of levels, ' . . . lobbying power brokers in industry and government both nationally and internationally . . . mounting public campaigns
to encourage holidaymakers to take action . . . producing reports and literature' (Barnett 2008: 996).

Unlike other campaigning NGOs whose main emphasis is on critiquing the tourism industry, Tourism Concern's Mission is more positive, that
is, 'to ensure that tourism always benefits local people'. The agency does
not then see tourism as an inherently negative force; rather, it is seen as
having potential to both benefit communities and build good relationships
between otherwise distant people. As the current director wrote, 'We are
passionate advocates for a relationship between hosts and guests shaped by
dignity and respect' (Barnett 2008: 996).

While Tourism Concern remains independent of industry, it does not
seek to work apart from the tourism industry: rather, it engages with industry bodies in a variety of ways (see Table 7.6). Thus Tourism Concern could
in no way be dismissed as an 'anti-development' organisation; rather, they
want to see ethical development of tourism, particularly in developing

countries. Some of their endeavours to find positive strategies for improving the sector include:

- Providing training on CSR and introducing the concept of CSR to UK and European tour operators
- Lobbying policy makers both nationally and internationally about tourism issues
- Facilitating discussions internationally on fair trade in tourism which led to development of principles for fair trade in tourism
- Developing labour audit and social impact assessment tools for tour operators (Barnett 2008: 996–997).

Table 7.6   Key Ways in which Tourism Concern Works

Influencing tourists, governments and the tourism industry	<ul><li>Sending speakers to travel industry meetings to present on ethical tourism</li><li>Engaging in discussions on tourism and trade led by UN agencies</li><li>Developing tools that the private sector can use in their work, such as a social impact assessment tool for tour operators</li><li>Challenging both industry and governments to be more accountable for their actions</li><li>Using campaigns to expose significant problems caused by tourism.</li></ul>
Campaigns and advocacy in the case of serious problems caused by tourism	<ul><li>E.g. 'Tsunami of Tourism' campaign involves working for the rights of communities affected by the Indian Ocean tsunami, such as those being pressured to move inland in what some see as a veiled attempt to make way for coastal tourism development.</li><li>'Our Holidays, Their Homes' campaign – focused on people such as the Samburu in northern Kenya who were being displaced from their homes due to tourism.</li><li>'Sun, Sand, Sea and Sweatshops' campaign – raised concerns about the widespread problem of poor working conditions and lack of labour rights of tourism employees, particularly in the developing world.</li></ul>
Creating alternatives	<ul><li>Seeking fair trade in tourism through supporting tourism workers and providers, e.g.:<ul><li>Publish an Ethical Travel Guide, which lists a wide range of travel options in different parts of the world</li><li>Worked with the Mexican tourism ministry to develop a training manual for community-based tourism groups in that country.</li></ul></li></ul>

LESSONS FOR DEVELOPMENT AGENCIES

The preceding sections discussed initiatives that a range of development agencies, from large scale multilateral donors to small NGOs, from watchdog and advocacy groups to funders of major economic development initiatives, are implementing in order to ensure that tourism has greater benefits for the poor. While some very interesting approaches have been utilised by development agencies, it is also clear that they often come up against barriers to their work. Thus despite a decade of promotion of tourism as an effective development strategy and the implementation of a range of PPT programmes, it is estimated that only 10 percent of a country's tourism receipts usually reach the poor (Mitchell and Ashley 2007: 21–22).

This section will now consider what lessons development agencies can learn in order to bring better outcomes to the poor in future, and it also suggests benefits of aligning themselves with governments and working more closely with the private sector in order to achieve their poverty-alleviation aims.

Target and Empower Poorer Sectors of Society

As noted in Chapter 3, while development agencies may go to significant lengths to support communities establishing tourism enterprises, it is very difficult for them to ensure that the direct economic benefits of tourism will spread beyond those who are already better off. Too often elites and/ or established entrepreneurs from outside the local area secure the benefits of tourism development. This can build up significant resentment. When donors provide direct funding for tourism enterprises, their assistance (for example, with the cost of building a lodge) can easily be seen as a 'handout', and one that is accessible only to those with existing power in a community.

In order to effectively engage poorer sectors of a society in tourism initiatives, a comprehensive approach must be adopted involving:

- Collecting detailed information on the composition of 'communities' including who are the poorest of the poor and what are their capabilities and resources
- Building awareness of community members about the potential and pitfalls of engaging with tourism
- Empowering poorer members of communities to effectively engage in and benefit from tourism enterprises, for example, through providing training/capacity development in required skills, study tours, access to credit, and mentoring (e.g. by local NGO personnel or locally-based effective businesses)

In support of these points, Cole (2006), who has conducted extensive research in specific locations in Flores, Indonesia, argues that community involvement in tourism should be based on their empowerment. First, communities need to understand what tourism is as a process and who tourists are, as without this information they cannot make an informed choice as to whether, or how, to proceed with tourism development. Secondly, there must be strong ongoing communication between the local community and other tourism stakeholders, which is something which Cole suggests can be facilitated through creation of a tourism forum. In Flores, the first tourism forum involved Cole sharing her research results in a one-day seminar which involved villagers, the Department of Tourism, Department of Education and Culture and local guides. They developed a code of conduct for tourists taking village tours as part of that first forum, and also discussed responsibilities of themselves and other stakeholders, which were later shared. For example, the government officials expected villagers to keep their village clean if they were going to accept tourists and villagers said they expected the government to provide them with appropriate training opportunities. The villagers were also sufficiently confident to express, however, that government should not attempt to direct tourism in the villages, particularly with respect to matters of tradition: 'In a very public forum the government was told to limit its heavy-handed approach in the villages' (Cole 2006: 640).

Allowing sufficient resources and time for such work with poorer sectors of communities at every stage of the project cycle is important if pro-poor tourism is to be realised. However, this often does not happen in practice because of the huge gulf between those implementing projects and the very poor, and due to differences between owners of successful mainstream tourism operations and the poor:

> One of the huge challenges of pro poor tourism which attempts to work at both the grassroots level and the high end [is that] . . . it becomes a clash of cultures, a confrontation between affluence and poverty . . . Such an undertaking simply cannot be done without sensitive, socio-culturally grounded preparation, implementation and monitoring throughout the project cycle. (Jean McKinnon, Kinsa Associates, personal communication: July 2006)

There must then be strong, ongoing support for communities attempting to engage in tourism enterprises for the first time. A piecemeal approach which collects information through community consultation forums and does not follow through with recommendations is problematic, but this has happened too often in the past. It may be necessary to engage a local facilitator or NGO to support such groups in an ongoing fashion in order to ensure they have sufficient training, that they know how to access loans, and even to monitor their participation in public meetings or decision-making forums concerning tourism to ensure they are able to speak out on issues of concern.

In many cases the poor simply cannot access tourism opportunities because they do not have the required skills and/or credit to invest in an enterprise—or even merchandise to start their business. Even a fruit seller on the beaches of Goa or Bali needs a tidy plate and a knife, and some cash in order to buy good quality produce that they can slice attractively to be sold to sunbathers. Development agencies can help with skills development by funding training courses for guides, business owners, craftspeople and the like. They may also produce training manuals in local languages as shown in the example of NZAID's support for the *Beach Fale Owner's Manual* in Samoa, as mentioned earlier. It is possible to build benefit-sharing mechanisms into some development initiatives to ensure wide, communal benefits are felt even by those who are not directly involved in tourism. This could include, for example, a community tourism venture whereby the income is relatively well distributed because tourists pay villagers directly for food and lodging and the cooking and food sales are distributed by roster (Lyttleton and Allcock 2002).

Provide Communal Benefits

Partly in recognition of the difficulty of delivering individual benefits from tourism to large numbers of poor people, recent PPT publications have recommended that communal benefits be built into the planning of new tourism development enterprises (UNWTO 2006b). This point was made in relation to government investment in tourism infrastructure in Chapter 6, but applies equally to efforts of development agencies to support PPT. While a small number of the poor have direct access to income, larger numbers have benefited from improved infrastructure (e.g. water supply systems), more regular transportation services, or training opportunities which have increased their skills base and confidence even when they have not always led directly to employment opportunities. With respect to the dual benefits of infrastructural improvements, Endo asserts that,

> If a developing country is serious about using tourism as the engine of economic growth, proper resources should be allocated to create good hard and soft infrastructures. Improved basic infrastructures also contribute to the welfare of the general public in host economies. (Endo 2006: 613)

Harrison (2008: 858) concurs, noting that investing in infrastructure such as roads and jetties will help to spread the benefits of tourism more widely. Similarly, a World Bank study of Tanzania's Tarangire National Park which looked specifically at the issue of benefit dispersal found that 'project rewards' such as wells, roads, schools and dispensaries were the most effective way of spreading benefits. Cash benefits, meanwhile, flowed only to a small proportion of possible beneficiaries and cash was sometimes misappropriated (Parker and Khare 2005: 41). The case study of cultural tourism in Barabarani village discussed in Box 7.1 also provided an example of communal benefits via improved access of the community to both transport and telecommunications.

In another example, the main hope of the community running a nature tourism enterprise in Koroyanitu, Fiji, was that the project would improve transport and children's access to education: ' . . . while accepting the need for conservation, the priority of the villagers . . . is to overcome their remoteness from schools, markets, and services' (MFAT 1995: 16). People's patience regarding the slow pace at which individuals were gaining benefits from the nature tourism project at Koroyanitu was thus helped by the fact that the truck used to bring tourists to the area was also able to be used to transport children to school and to take people to the marketplace in Lautoka.

Provide Support at Multiple Levels

Often it is assumed that benefits of tourism development will somehow 'trickle-down' to the poor, as noted in Chapter 3, through jobs created or goods and services needed by the industry. In practice, however, the poor are unlikely to receive significant benefits from tourism unless there is an overarching policy framework which asserts the government's strategic commitment to PPT, as discussed in Chapter 6, and unless support for PPT is provided at multiple levels.

The most effective tourism development initiatives by development agencies that contribute to poverty alleviation have involved support at multiple levels. Building on the Samoan example already discussed, NZAID supported policy in the form of a new Tourism Development Plan focusing on sustainable tourism; it supported the Samoan Tourism Authority through funding for community awareness–raising, development of manuals and training sessions for small-scale beachside accommodation operators; and it provided a business advisory service and a Tourism Support Fund which helped some operators of small-scale beachside accommodation to upgrade their facilities.

Ensure Commercial Viability

In the past too many development agencies have made unrealistic promises to potential stakeholders in tourism development about the benefits tourism can bring. This is particularly of concern when they have not ensured there is a viable tourism product or service which could be offered by a community, or when they have not fully considered whether tourists are likely to venture to a remote area, or country. An example of the latter is Niue, a beautiful but remote island in the South Pacific, which is only accessible once a week by a relatively expensive flight. Nevertheless development officials and consultants have invested considerable energy and funding into developing tourism on this island.

Another problem with development agencies seeing tourism as a panacea to the development woes of a particular community or place is that they can invest tens or hundreds of thousands of dollars into funding an initiative which will only bring back a fraction of this money to communities in terms of revenue earned once tourism is up and running. This, Butcher (2006) argues, is a case of 'charity replacing the market', whereby a development agency's funds artificially prop up a tourism business which is doomed to failure under real market conditions. Harrison and Schipani (2007), discussing what they call DACBT (donor-assisted community-based tourism), provide a noteworthy account of its limitations using an oft-cited example of 'successful' ecotourism in Nam Ha, Lao PDR. At Nam Ha tourists experience one- to three-day treks or boat trips. The ecoguide service operated 1,331 tours between 2001 and 2005, earning gross revenue of $137,794. This project has been praised for its benefit-sharing mechanisms, including diversion of a proportion of guest-house fees to poorer families who suffer rice shortages (Lyttleton and Allcock 2002: 45). $9,485 was also put into village development funds. Meanwhile, people from local villages earned money from providing accommodation and meals to trekkers. However, the project *received* almost half a million dollars in aid money between 1999, when the treks started, and 2002. Even taking into consideration other benefits to these once very poor villages in Nam Ha, including new infrastructure that was developed with donor money and the equipment and training for guides, this is a huge donor investment in comparison to the economic benefits gained from the venture to date.

Harrison and Schipani (2007) compare Nam Ha with another small-scale tourism development in Don Det which is private sector-led. In the latter, owners of simple guesthouses typically gained capital to start their ventures through sale of family livestock or other assets. While charging only around $1 per night for accommodation, they make good profits due to also owning restaurants. Others earned money from taking tourists on boat trips and renting bicycles and inflated inner tubes for tourists to float on the river. Small taxes were paid monthly to the government by guesthouse and restaurant owners, and the boat owners' association paid money into a village fund which was used for activities such as painting the local primary school.

The authors conclude that while the Nam Ha project specifically targeted the poor and sought their participation and empowerment, it is heavily dependent on donor funding and thus its economic sustainability comes into question. Small-scale tourism ventures led by the private sector such as Don Det have an advantage in that they develop in response to market demand, usually from the mass tourism sector, whereas DACBT may be initiated because of a perceived need for improved economic opportunities for a group of people and considerable effort may need to go into attracting 'alternative' tourists to experience such ventures (Harrison and Schipani 2007).

Allow Sufficient Time to Engage with Stakeholders on Community Development

Many NGOs seek to work to promote community development through tourism. In light of the issues that arise when working with communities, as explained in Chapter 3, it is important to allow sufficient time to develop relationships and get programmes off the ground. As noted by an NZAID staff member commenting on the challenges encountered by managers of tourism projects:

> one of the problems with any donor is that your temptation is to go fast in order to achieve your goals and your project timetables and your expenditure timetables and all those sorts of things and the key is that . . . you have to move as fast as the community is prepared to move and I guess that comes back to community processes. (Interview, Wellington, May 2003—cited in Schellhorn 2007: 245)

Donor structures and procedures can otherwise impede possibilities for active participation by communities in the planning and management of tourism endeavours: ' . . . the institutionalised performance pressure has the operational effect of shifting emphasis away from more cost- and time-intensive activities (such as community development) to deliverables that indicate measurable economic progress' (Schellhorn 2007: 254).

Engage with the Private Sector

Chapter 5 provided a number of examples of ways in which private-sector tourism bodies, from multinational resort operations to small joint venture campsites, were working to ensure they delivered direct benefits to the poor. It would be remiss, indeed, illogical, for development agencies to ignore the private sector when espousing PPT.

While the private sector has often been criticised by academics and development practitioners in the past, there is now a greater focus on working *with* the industry for change. For example, this chapter has noted how agencies like Tourism Concern, SNV, GTZ and the Travel Foundation are promoting change in the tourism industry through their work. There is also evidence that the mainstream tourism players are ready for change, both through greater attention being paid to Corporate Social Responsibility (see Chapter 5), and through trends which show consumers are demanding more ethical holiday experiences (see Chapter 4). While it is important to engage with the private sector, this requires care. The reason that many donors have been reluctant to support tourism development in the past is that they are concerned they will end up subsidising big business.

There are particular ways in which donors can provide support for reform of private sector practices to make them more 'pro-poor'. Some of these points are highlighted in Table 7.7. For example, they can strengthen the capacities of local hotel or tourism association bodies and help these bodies to recognise the value of pro-poor tourism initiatives. Siem Reap province in Cambodia, home to the country's key tourism drawcard, Angkor Wat, meets only 50 percent of its demand for vegetables, and imports up to 90 percent of its fruit needs. During the wet season most farmers focus on rice production and consequently the supply of vegetables and fruit diminishes and prices for these products can quadruple, with Vietnamese and Thai imports filling the gaps. The Siem Reap Hotel Association has thus been

Table 7.7   How Development Agencies Can Support Pro-Poor Tourism Strategies with the Private Sector

Support appropriate policy development and programmes to encourage . . .	• Fair employment conditions and practices for workers in the service sector, considering addition of health insurance and pension schemes • Hotels and lodges to adopt a human resources policy which provides security of employment, training and progression opportunities. • Hotels and restaurants to develop partnerships with local suppliers, e.g. of produce, furnishings, art and crafts, soap, linen, tours, as well as laundry and security services • Assistance to microenterprises, e.g. advice and support for guides, craftspeople and entertainers
Support farmer associations and government staff from associated sectors like agriculture and fisheries to . . .	• Improve the quality and supply of produce • Build linkages with the tourism industry
Support business or tourism associations to . . .	• Establish mentoring schemes • Facilitate linkages between mainstream and alternative tourism businesses • Adopt a code of ethics or code of conduct guiding practices of members • Implement 'adopt a farmer'-type schemes
Training for tour operators, guides and information centre staff . . .	• To ensure local guides and locally owned services are supported • To develop brochures and other information sources to inform clients about how to behave/dress in a culturally and environmentally sensitive manner • To develop brochures and other information sources to provide accurate information on local history, culture and nature

Source: Adapted from Karammel and Lengefeld (2006)

exploring ways to increase sourcing of local produce. A relevant role for donors could be convening meetings to bring together relevant stakeholders, including individual farmers, farmer associations, microfinance NGOs and the government's agriculture ministry, and then establishing whether further outside support is needed (UNDP, cited in Epler Wood and Leray 2005: 28).

Through a coordinated approach involving government agricultural staff, development agencies focusing on rural development and so forth, donors could help farmers to improve the quality and supply of fresh fruit and vegetables to hotels and resorts. For example, farmers in Cambodia could learn from the success of an NGO, Hurredo, in the capital city, which has successfully filled a market niche by supplying upscale tourist hotels with high-quality, low-pesticide romaine lettuce, with demand in excess of what they can supply. Farmers could also be given assistance with food processing, with developing business plans which would receive bank support, and with marketing (Strategic Management Solutions 2004).

Another strategy for donors may be to work with district councils and/ or NGOs in an integrated way to develop effective marketplaces so that craftspeople or local farmers producing quality produce have a regular, safe and attractive place from which to sell their goods, whether to local households, businesses, expatriates, hotels or the tourism industry directly (Strategic Management Solutions 2004).

Avoid Common Biases

Table 7.8 outlines a number of typical biases found in the efforts of development agencies targeting tourism as a means of poverty alleviation. Some of these points apply equally well to governments, as discussed in Chapter 6.

Firstly, development agencies have typically used tourism as a tool to improve the well-being of rural dwellers. They should not overlook the fact that people living in tourist towns and cities (e.g. in Siem Reap, Khatmandu or Capetown) which attract many tourists could also gain substantially from pro-poor tourism endeavours. As noted by ESCAP, 'When one considers that within the Asian region more than 50 percent of people now live in urban areas and the proportion of poor in these areas is steadily growing, there is an urgent need to understand the use of tourism as a tool for development' (2003: 30). Good examples were provided in Chapter 6 to show that there is real potential for tourism in urban areas to bring benefits to the poor, with the nightly food court on a city street in a formerly crime-ridden area in, Medan, and with collaboration between the city government and private sector to develop tourism and provide opportunities for unemployed youths in Baguio.

Secondly, development agencies, like the governments of the countries in which they work, tend to assume that the main market for tourism is

Table 7.8　Biases That Development Agencies Should Avoid When Promoting PPT

Bias	Reality
Focus on rural tourism development	Many tourist attractions are located within, or near to, urban areas, and half of the world's population lives in urban areas. The lives of the urban poor could be significantly enhanced by urban PPT.
Focus on attracting international tourists	Domestic and regional tourists make up a far higher percentage of total tourists than the international market, and while they may not spend as much money per person, they have other advantages: e.g. they are less fickle (not so likely to cancel travel plans on a whim or due to potential conflict, etc.), and less seasonal in their travel preferences. Furthermore, when overseas-based nationals travel home (i.e. diaspora tourists), they often invest significant funds into social institutions, healthcare and education facilities. Domestic, regional and diaspora tourism should be valued (see Scheyvens 2007b).
Targeting higher spending tourists	It can be more beneficial to attract lower-spending tourists, including domestic tourists and independent backpackers, who spend less on a daily basis but: a) stay longer, b) spend their money on locally produced goods and services (thereby increasing the multiplier effects of tourism) and c) travel to less developed regions of a country. Furthermore, there are relatively few locations where the 'high value: low volume' motto actually works. A niche product is needed for this, such as mountain gorillas, or a unique destination, such as Bhutan.
Focus on community-based tourism projects	Many community-based tourism projects are not economically viable or are unsustainable, yet donors have sunk major funds into developing such initiatives. Greater gains could be made from efforts to ensure mainstream tourism delivers more benefits to the poor.
Avoidance of the private sector	Individuals, communities and governments cannot develop the tourism sector on their own—it is a business, so it is vital to network with the private sector and encourage them to support PPT initiatives.

foreign. However, domestic tourism accounts for 90 percent of all tourism movements (Fayos-Sola and Pedro Bueno 2001, cited in Endo 2006: 613). In Asia, especially, domestic and regional tourists have grown enormously (see Photo 7.2). The domestic and regional markets are incredibly important economically, plus they are less susceptible than the international market to fluctuations due to political upheavals, health scares and the like (Ghimire 2001; Scheyvens 2007b). For example, although international tourist numbers to Nusa Tenggara province in Indonesia dropped from 245,049 in 1997 to 179,666 in 2006 due to the effects of the Asian economic crises, SARS (sudden acute respiratory syndrome) and the Bali bombings, domestic tourism showed robust recovery and actually grew from 158,894 to 246,911 in the same period (Schellhorn 2007: 138). Domestic tourists can contribute significantly to local economic development because they typically purchase more locally produced goods and services than other categories of tourists, thus supporting small-scale enterprises and the informal sector (Goodwin et al. 1998). For example, Bowden's (2005) study in China found that it was the rapid growth in domestic tourism, not international tourism, that was fuelling support for small-scale, labour-intensive forms of tourism. Importantly, these forms of tourism, which involved guesthouses, ferry services, sale of handicrafts and small restaurants, were leading directly to poverty alleviation in some areas. Governments interested in promoting poverty alleviation through tourism need to recognise that people from poorer communities who do not have the skills, networks or resources to cater for higher-end tourists can often effectively provide goods and services to domestic tourists, and they can do this by utilising local resources rather than needing outside capital.

Some governments are starting to value domestic tourism. For example, following the Bali bombings and other health and security matters, which

Photo 7.2   Thai tourists pose for a photograph in a historic area of Hue, Vietnam. *Source:* Author

together led to a softening of the international tourism market in Indonesia, the government initiated a new domestic tourism campaign, *Ayo Jelajah Nusantara* or 'Let's travel around Indonesia'. To support this campaign it was decreed that all government offices and schools would be closed on Saturdays, and public holidays would always be contiguous with weekends (David et al. 2005). This may have contributed to the robust recovery and growth of the domestic tourism market in Nusa Tengarra province: in 1997, domestic tourists here numbered 158,894, but by 2006 their numbers had grown to 246,911; meanwhile international tourist arrivals dropped from 245,049 in 1997 to 179,666 in 2006 (Schellhorn 2007: 138). The Indian government also supported domestic tourism in the past by introducing a subsidised holiday scheme for its employees, which has boosted tourism to some areas enormously: '[The] Leave Travel Concession, has done wonders for domestic tourism in India. A whole infrastructure, consisting of moderately priced accommodation, catering services and tour packages have thrived around this scheme' (Shah and Gupta 2000: 41).

Diaspora tourism, which is significant in a wide range of countries, from the Pacific and Caribbean Islands to the Philippines, China, India, Bangladesh, and Ghana, may exhibit benefits in addition to those already mentioned. When a country's nationals return home for a holiday and/or family gathering, they bring foreign currency as well as rekindling their cultural links and ensuring enduring economic and social ties with their country (Coles and Timothy 2004). Contributions from people returning to their home country for a holiday can be significant, and can include 'financial remittances, technology and skills transfer, material and equipment donations' (Asiedu 2005: 1). For example, donations by American Chinese originally from Taishan County to the Taishan Overseas Chinese Affairs Office between 1978 and 1998 amounted to $14 million and funded numerous educational, medical, infrastructural and cultural projects in the area (Lew and Wong 2004: 209). In Ghana, migrants' home regions in particular have benefited from their assistance:

> Individuals, communities and institutions have received donations of cash, drugs, materials and equipment that have helped in the sustenance of their operations. The sectors that have derived most benefit—health, education and institutions for the socially and physically handicapped—also happen to be the most financially and materially hard-pressed in the country. Migrant funds have therefore aided poverty alleviation in the recipient regions. (Asiedu 2005: 9)

Thirdly, a number of developing countries have developed tourism plans in the past which target higher-spending tourists. Their logic is that it is more sustainable to attract smaller numbers of these higher-spending tourists than to go for mass tourism or to encourage budget tourists, such as backpackers. This logic is flawed, as backpackers often stay longer in a country and thus spend more over the duration of their visit, they seek 'out-of-the-way' destinations and thus bring money to places that other tourists avoid, and because they stay in locally owned accommodation and eat at roadside stalls and family-owned restaurants, their dollars have very good multiplier effects (Scheyvens 2002b). Backpackers are also resilient tourists. Schellhorn (2007: 176) writes that in the immediate period following the Bali bombings, tourism numbers to the Gunung Rinjani National Park in the adjacent island of Lombok were very low, yet a few hardy backpackers still came along: 'The locals refer to these brave types as *"turis nakal"*, literally meaning "naughty tourist" ("even if there is a problem, they come").

Fourthly, as already discussed, many development agencies have limited their involvement in tourism to support of small-scale alternatives which are communally owned or managed, but which only involve a small percentage of the tourism market. While much hope has been held out for these forms of tourism, as Chapter 3 noted, it can be very difficult to deliver economically viable, community-based tourism initiatives in practice. Constraints include the lack of a commercial product, poor location in relation to tourist markets, and lack of engagement with the private sector. The outcome is that, for example, too many community lodges or bungalows, built with the hope that local people would benefit from a rush of ecotourists once a protected area was established, sit idle around the world. In such cases, little thought has been given to working with existing tourism flows and products:

> Instead of focusing on domestic tourism, they focus on international tourism, and instead of linking up with existing flows of tourism, they try to create new products for new markets. In many cases, the often already existing or emerging market for individual tourists (backpackers, students and domestic tourists) would be more interesting for the type of enterprises and community projects involved. (Van der Duim and Caalders 2008: 121)

The UNWTO's publication entitled *Poverty Alleviation Through Tourism—A Compilation of Good Practices*, which aimed to provide ' . . . concrete examples of projects and good practices in tourism that have effectively contributed to reduce poverty levels' (UNWTO 2006a: 1), failed to provide much inspiration in this regard. Only one of the 26 case studies from over 20 countries could be regarded as mainstream tourism—that is the FODESTUR project mentioned previously, which is supported by GTZ, a multi-level, inter-government plan which aims to promote Central America as a tourism destination. The rest are alternative forms of tourism, either community-based tourism, cultural tourism, agrotourism, ecotourism or a mix of these. The benefits from these forms of tourism, while significant locally, did not reach a wide number of people.

The PPT Partnership register, published from 2005 to 2007, sought to list initiatives that clearly demonstrate PPT outcomes. However, it was sometimes a struggle to find appropriate contributions. As the editor, long-time PPT advocate Harold Goodwin, noted, ' . . . there is too often an unwritten assumption that if tourism is community based then it must be pro-poor. Or equally falsely, that if tourism is to be pro-poor it must be community-based. Progress has been painfully slow' (Goodwin 2007: 1).

By focusing only on alternative forms of tourism, the potential of the mainstream tourism market, which accounts for over 90 percent of tourism flows, to contribute to pro-poor development has been overlooked. It is not recommended that development agencies should focus solely on supporting alternative forms of tourism, as regardless of the virtues of alternative tourism, the reality is that 'much of third world tourism today is not small-scale, ecologically oriented, or even broadly participatory' (Clancy 1999: 5). Furthermore, alternative tourism will not always be regarded by communities as more beneficial to them (Weaver and Oppermann 2000). Mass tourism, for example, may be preferred if it brings in more money to local communities. Local communities may also favour larger-scale tourism enterprises if they feel these are more likely to be competitive. Thus, for example, while ' . . . small is beautiful in the context of ecotourism . . . small is also vulnerable' (Thomlinson and Getz 1996: 197). Mass tourism could actually be perceived as less culturally invasive by a local community if it involves busloads of tourists coming to them once a day for a cultural performance and to buy and then returning to their hotels, rather than cultural tourism whereby outsiders stay in their homes for a few days.

Thus there is a need to examine mass tourism and to further the idea that 'mass tourism itself can be practised in ways that minimize and mitigate its obvious disbenefits' (Husbands and Harrison 1996: 1). Donors could contribute more broadly to poverty alleviation goals if they looked beyond alternative, small-scale, community-based initiatives and considered ways of promoting what an idea by Weaver (2001) raised in Chapter 5: 'sustainable mass tourism'. Thus, rather than helping a community establish bungalows, for example, it may be more sustainable and more lucrative for the community if a development agency simultaneously encouraged the government to review its labour rights legislation while also helping the community to access training in service-sector skills and to gain work experience in nearby resorts.

Fifthly, there have been insufficient efforts by development agencies to date to work with the private sector. This is despite the fact that a real strength of the PPT partnership's efforts has been to encourage engagement with the mainstream tourism industry, challenging tour operators, tour agents, tourism industry bodies and the like to think of ways in which their operations can bring more benefits to the poor. While some good efforts from SNV, Tourism Concern, GTZ and others have been listed previously, there could be opportunities to deliver more benefits to the poor if development agencies generally were to seek to engage constructively with the private sector. The UNWTO's compilation of good practice in tourism for poverty alleviation led to the conclusion that ' . . . close collaboration between communities . . . the private sector, technical cooperation bodies and local authorities has been crucial for the success of all projects' (UNWTO 2006a: 10).

CONCLUSION

It is only in the last decade that a wide range of development agencies have sought to support poverty alleviation via the development of tourism. The coining of the term pro-poor tourism in 1999 has coincided with broader legitimacy for tourism as a development strategy, leading to this being built into the policies, strategies and plans of a number of bilateral and multilateral development agencies and NGOs. This interest is welcome, as it may help development agencies to support governments of developing countries to utilise tourism as one strategy for development of their communities and their country, rather than pursuing what Reid (2003) warns against, that is, tourism development in its own right.

While tourism for poverty alleviation is now strong in terms of rhetoric coming from development agencies that support it, in practice its results have been more mixed, with attempts to benefit the poorest of the poor being particularly elusive. The approach taken by different agencies has a direct impact on how, and whether, they benefit the poor. Neoliberal orthodoxy is a key driver behind initiatives of some agencies discussed in this chapter, such as the World Bank, ADB and UNWTO, even though these organisations also draw quite heavily on alternative development rhetoric (e.g. 'participation', 'empowerment', 'capacity building') in their written documents. As Storey et al. note, such ' . . . alternative development concepts and terminology . . . have been selectively incorporated into the mainstream' (2005: 35). However, it is also important to acknowledge that many people have benefited from programmes initiated by these multilateral organizations as they are able to draw on a wide variety of resources and provide good support for essential tourism infrastructure (e.g. transport and communications) and they are able to provide quality technical advice.

Other development agencies endorsing PPT have approached this through niche markets such as community-based tourism and ecotourism. This was the case with many bilateral donors in the 1980s and 1990s, and is still a popular way for NGOs to support tourism development. This too has problematic dimensions, as huge investments of the time and resources of development agencies have often gone into community tourism projects which yield a trickle of tourist dollars in return. Nevertheless some communities are very grateful for the support they have received, which has enabled them to expand their livelihood options. Others are working from

a human rights and social justice framework, which seeks to emp
poor, uphold the rights of vulnerable peoples in particular, and
cacy work with relevant stakeholders such as tourists, governn,
tourism corporates.

This chapter has revealed some very innovative attempts by development
agencies to engage with the private sector and to transform mainstream
tourism. Thus, for example, we saw that Tourism Concern was campaigning for the rights of tourism workers internationally, and that the Travel
Foundation had over 130 members, from small companies to those working
in multiple countries, with whom it was working with to ensure more commitment to Corporate Social Responsibility. Meanwhile the NGO Equations audits the operations of the tourism industry in India annually and
monitors relevant government policy. The World Bank has funded studies
of value chains in tourism, which are helping to identify gaps that could be
filled by poor people providing specific products and services to the tourism
industry. Meanwhile the German development agency GTZ is educating
German tourists about ethical and responsible travel and it works with
owners of all-inclusive resorts in the Caribbean to bring more benefits to
the poor. Such examples point to ways of ensuring tourism makes a real
difference to the lives of the poor in the future.

8   Conclusion

INTRODUCTION

Chapter 8 summarises and reflects upon the main points made in the book, with the overall aim of evaluating the potential of pro-poor tourism to contribute effectively to poverty alleviation. Tourism, as is regularly noted, is a unique industry for developing countries as it brings consumers to the places occupied by the producers of the products and services they are buying. As a service industry it is also labour-intensive, offering many income-earning opportunities. This offers great potential for economic growth and job creation as well as providing an incentive for protection of the unique environments and support of the cultures which often attract tourists to developing countries. Yet despite all of this, and despite the fact that poorer countries have experienced higher rates of growth in tourist arrivals than many wealthier countries, the evidence that tourism contributes directly to poverty alleviation is sporadic and often tokenistic, and there is much contradictory information to consider.

In previous chapters it was noted that many countries are aiming to grow their tourism sector rapidly, doubling or tripling tourist arrivals in a 10- to 15-year period. While inherently this is of concern from a sustainability perspective, it is particularly disturbing when it is suggested that such growth, should it be achieved, will automatically bring benefits to the poor. Thus, for example, the International Council of Tourism Partners asserted, with relation to its projection for increases in tourism export income in Africa, that 'Tripling it [tourism revenue] means more direct tourism revenue, but it also amplifies all of the ancillary value chain benefits and increases the contribution to the Millennium Development Goals—particularly the eradication of extreme poverty' (Travel Wire News, 2005). Throughout this book it has been asserted that growth in tourism will not automatically reduce the incidence of poverty. Countries in both the West and the developing world that have experienced rapid rates of growth in recent decades have also often experienced increases in inequality overall.

In addition, the global economic recession of 2008–2009 provided another warning of the dangers of investing too much hope in a single industry to deliver widespread economic outcomes. This recession, as already noted, led to a 4.3 percent decline in tourism arrivals in 2009, with an associated decline of 5.8 percent in international tourism receipts and a loss of around 5 million tourism-related jobs (UNWTO 2010). This global economic slowdown should not be understood as a unique or 'one-off' event: the tourism industry constantly needs to adapt to crises in order to survive. Other crises will come in the future, whether caused by natural disasters, health scares, political instability, conflict or further economic difficulties.

Notions of PPT which have emerged in the last decade suggest to some that there is a simple win-win scenario between tourism growth, development, and reduction of poverty: this is unrealistic. Given the scale of poverty and its entrenched and multidimensional nature, as explained in Chapter 2, we must seriously consider whether a fickle and somewhat frivolous industry like tourism can hope to significantly improve the well-being of over a billion of the world's population that are poor.[1] While there is a great deal of rhetoric on the virtues and promise of pro-poor tourism, strenuous efforts will be needed to deliver on its potential especially developing the capacity of communities and partner governments to manage tourism programmes appropriately, and encouraging the private sector to be driven by something beyond the profit motive.

In this final chapter of *Tourism and Poverty* I begin by reflecting on a number of questions which were highlighted in Chapter 1 of this book. In responding to these questions, I will draw conclusions about the relationship between tourism and poverty alleviation. In the second part of the chapter a section on 'ways forward' looks at how tourism can contribute more effectively to poverty alleviation. Readers who have skipped straight to the book's conclusion for 'answers' might like to also refer to latter sections of the previous three chapters, which have considered, in turn, how the private sector, governments, and development agencies might more comprehensively address poverty in our world through tourism development.

REFLECTIONS ON PRO-POOR TOURISM

Six key questions were posed in Chapter 1 after introducing readers to both the promise of tourism as a tool for poverty alleviation, and reasons for caution. They are considered now in turn.

The Motives of Agencies that Support Pro-poor Tourism

The first question asked in Chapter 1 was 'what are the motives of various agencies that have jumped onto the pro-poor tourism bandwagon?' In order to assess the potential for tourism to contribute to poverty alleviation, we need to carefully scrutinize the motives of relevant agencies to see whose interests are central to their agenda. The views of different stake-holder groups on the notion of poverty alleviation through tourism vary widely, even when most speak out in favour of the concept. While a number of agencies have been keen to adopt PPT rhetoric, it is likely that for some the interests of the poor are peripheral to their main operations. In practice, some prioritize the interests of the tourism industry as a whole, that is, in growing the sector, expanding markets and enhancing profits, while others focus more directly on utilizing this large, global industry to improve the well-being of impoverished peoples.

Chapter 5 discussed the private sector, showing that while some businesses are showing a genuine commitment to the ethics and the ideals of Corporate Social Responsibility, many others which profess to support PPT are actually implementing only superficial changes. There is thus a real danger that, like a number of trends before it (e.g. 'ecotourism' in the 1990s), PPT will remain something of a fad, a new way of dressing up the tourism industry to reclaim its credibility not just as an engine of growth but also as a 'soft' industry that is both socially beneficial and environmentally benign. Tourism industry players put on 'green lenses' in the 1990s, and along with a revival of interest in the environment due to the rising profile of climate change issues, a commitment to poverty reduction seems to be a key focus for the industry in the first decade of the new millennium. It can be argued then that the majority of tourism businesses and organisations are attracted mainly to the rhetoric of PPT—whatever will work to enhance the image of the global tourism industry and continue to encourage increases in travel and tourism. This is not to dismiss some genuine efforts from tourism industry players to enhance the well-being of the poor, however, as will be explained.

Governments of developing countries, meanwhile, have too often uncritically taken on board the neoliberal agendas of their international funding agencies. Thus, as discussed in Chapter 6, they come up with wildly enthusiastic estimates of future growth in the industry without considering adequately how tourism can be planned for in a sustainable manner to deliver poverty alleviation goals. Similarly some multilateral development agencies such as the ADB were shown to be preoccupied with growth. Chapter 7 explained how the ADB's Greater Mekong Subregion Tourism Sector Strategy, while purporting to support PPT, dedicated only 3 percent of the budgeted $440 million specifically to pro-poor tourism. It is difficult to find examples of PPT advocates seriously grappling with the implications of a growth-oriented strategy, particularly in terms of environmental sustainability. As noted earlier in this book, tourists place heavy demands on limited resources, and the issue of carbon emissions from air travel cannot be ignored. Similarly, the social and cultural impacts of growth of tourism on local communities need to be carefully monitored and managed. Whether a strategy of growth will improve the lives of the poor is still debateable.

However, to generalise that all PPT initiatives are more about window-dressing than implementing real change, or that a preoccupation with growth precludes tourism that can benefit the poor, would be unfair. The motives of many agencies promoting PPT are sound, varying from altruism to advancing social justice and human rights aims. Some of the companies profiled in Chapter 5, for example, were working to secure more procurement of locally produced goods and services, which was translating into jobs and income for local communities, and others had established community development funds which supported social development initiatives. Meanwhile a number of the voluntourism and justice tourism organisations discussed in Chapter 4 were seeking to deepen the understanding of tourists about global injustice and to build solidarity between those visiting a place and the host community. Similarly, German development agencies discussed in Chapter 7 had been involved in initiatives to raise the awareness of German tourists about the ethics of responsible tourism, and GTZ had not shied away from addressing the sensitive issue of the protection of minors from sexual exploitation through tourism. Bilateral and multilateral donors and NGOs are also regularly involved in supporting community involvement in tourism as a sustainable livelihood option, which has helped to reduce the vulnerability of poorer communities and has also led to opportunities for skill development and business experience. Some significant initiatives beyond the local level were seen in the form of Oxfam Caribbean's efforts to influence regional trade policy, the Travel Foundations's efforts to encourage Corporate Social Responsibility among over 100 British tourism businesses, and the Bhutanese government's commitment to a balanced approach to development centring around promotion of 'Gross National Happiness'.

Another motive of some international agencies supporting PPT is to overcome inequalities as a strategy for building secure societies. For example, the World Tourism Organization refers to how tourism can be used in the 'war on poverty' (UNWTO 2005a). This language seems to be related to the choice of words used in the 'war on terror' waged by the United States' government in Iraq and Afghanistan. The two 'wars' are not unrelated. Democratic governance and security are seen as key components of a neoliberal poverty agenda (Wilkin 2002). In part the interest of organizations like the UNWTO in using tourism for poverty alleviation could then be motivated by the terrorist attacks in the United States on 11 September 2001, which some analysts interpreted as evidence that 'endemic poverty underlies instability in many parts of the world' (Sofield 2003: 350). Pro-poor initiatives may be seen as necessary to overcome the types of inequalities which have been identified since 9/11 as contributing to global insecurity.

Tensions between Profit-seeking and Poverty Alleviation Goals

The second question asked in Chapter 1 was, 'moving beyond the hype about Corporate Social Responsibility, can an industry driven by profits ever be expected to prioritise the interests of the poor?' We are continually told that tourism can benefit poor people *and* big business; or that tourism growth can bring profits to the industry *and* result in a bigger slice of the tourism pie for the poor. While this may appeal to those from the private sector, and those wishing to influence mainstream tourism providers to change their practice, it is in fact quite misleading. This book has shown that there are certainly many instances where tourism enterprises are bringing direct and indirect benefits to the poor, and there is also a good deal of untapped potential to increase these benefits for the poor. However, maximising profits while alleviating poverty is not necessarily a win-win connection.

Major players in the tourism industry, as in any industry, are centrally concerned with profit maximisation (Ashley and Haysom 2006; Zhao and Ritchie 2007). Why then should we assume that they might have some ethical commitment to ensuring their business contributes to poverty alleviation? In reality there is likely to be a need for trade-offs (Kontogeorgopoulos 2004). Yet Chok et al. (2007: 51) suggest that many advocates of PPT have not been realistic about the types of trade-offs required to ensure that tourism benefits the poor:

> Tourism development that generates net benefits for the poor and protects the environment . . . will place restrictions on human activity and challenge our current rapid expansion development model. In other words, there may be strong moral imperatives but weak profit margins.

Certainly when one examines what real changes PPT has brought about in the practice of the tourism industry, the examples appear tokenistic rather than transformational. An example was provided in Chapter 5 with the PPT Pilot Programme in South Africa, which in the case of Sun City led to only two minor enterprises, one producing recycled drinking glasses and the other manufacturing greeting cards. Companies involved in the Pilot Programme reflect a general trend among tourism enterprises whereby many will happily engage in philanthropy but most are not willing to make more significant, long-term changes to their business strategies and practices to make them more pro-poor (Ashley and Haysom 2006). Such more significant changes could include implementation of comprehensive policies that support labour rights (including training, health and retirement schemes), a commitment to joint ventures whereby the resident community's contribution is their land and/or cultural knowledge rather than financial capital, programmes to mentor small-scale entrepreneurs, and implementation of procurement policies that maximise opportunities for local producers and service providers. It is notable that there are examples of such initiatives already, as shown in Chapter 5. However, far more businesses need to adopt such changes otherwise the PPT approach can only hope to benefit a minority of people.

The Extent of Tourism's Impacts on Poverty Alleviation

The third question asked in Chapter 1 was, 'is a pro-poor approach to tourism likely to impact significantly on the extent and severity of poverty?' On this point, the jury is still out. PPT is commonly defined as tourism that generates net benefits for the poor. This definition has recently come under fire, however, as it still allows wealthier people to benefit *more* than the poor, thus ignoring distributive justice (Schilcher 2007a). In a heading within their article, Chok et al. thus refer to 'Pro-Poor Tourism: Where Tourism Benefits the Poor (Along with the Rich)' (2007: 37). Most assume that if tourism leads to a reduction in the number of people living in poverty (the World Bank's poverty headcount approach), then it is pro-poor. However, concurrently growth in tourism may deepen the poverty of some people and make the rich disproportionately richer, so while the number of people living in poverty decreases, inequality increases. This will particularly be so if a government follows neoliberal orthodoxy which promotes growth and openness to market forces growth and ' . . . displaces redistributive strategies' (Schilcher 2007a: 73).

What is clear is that it is difficult to reach the poorest of the poor. It is hard to improve the well-being of the poorest among the poor as they often do not have the resources, skills, networks, or confidence to directly participate in tourism enterprises. This leads Mowforth and Munt (2009: 349) to the conclusion that,

> Pro-poor tourism is not . . . a tool for eliminating nor necessarily alleviating absolute poverty, but rather is principally a measure for making some sections of poorer communities "better-off" and of reducing the vulnerability of poorer groups to shocks (such as hunger).

Nevertheless, tourism is directly aiding the poor in a number of contexts. For example, Donaldson notes that for residents in the Upper Road of China's Tiger Leaping Gorge, rural incomes have been bolstered by villagers catering to the food, accommodation and transport needs of weary backpackers, such that ' . . . tourism has tempered the rough edges of absolute poverty' (2007: 334).

From a contrary perspective, rather than suggesting that tourism might 'solve' poverty, the available data could in some cases be used to show that tourism has impacted negatively on the lives of the poor. Thus, for example, Manyara and Jones (2007) cite evidence that in Kenya, the incidence of poverty is greater in those areas with high tourist activity, while Mbaiwa (2005) notes that despite rapid growth of tourism in the Okavango Delta in Botswana since 1990, poverty has increased in rural areas. Plüss and Backes further claim that in 10 of the 13 countries which are home to 80 percent of the world's people who live in extreme poverty, tourism has not been able to reduce poverty (2002: 10). Thus it seems we must look very carefully at how the statistics are portrayed by PPT advocates and be careful to ensure that we do not exaggerate tourism's potential as a tool for poverty alleviation.

Another reason that some might doubt if tourism can impact significantly on the extent of poverty is that poorer countries still receive far fewer tourists overall than richer countries. The fact that the vast majority of international tourists still visit western countries, particularly Europe, leads Hall to conclude that 'the potential of tourism to contribute to the economic development of the developing countries . . . would appear to be questionable unless there are massive shifts in flows of international arrivals' (2007a: 112). Furthermore, tourism receipts are still less than 5 percent of GDP in the majority of developing countries (Blake et al. 2008: 109).[2]

It is also difficult to measure the exact contribution of tourism to an economy when developing country governments often provide foreign investors with tax exemptions, and allow them to import items duty-free. Even where governments do earn substantial revenue from tourism, there is no guarantee this will be invested in sectors which directly benefit the poor. For example, more may be spent on the military than on education or health (Gössling et al. 2008). This leads Gössling et al. to claim that:

> While it is clear that tourism growth has brought high levels of social development for some countries, it is also clear that using tourist arrival numbers as a measure of socioeconomic development over-simplifies tourism production systems, omitting much of the complexity of tourism-derived income generation and the socioeconomic benefit it brings. (2008: 895)

The Challenge of Facilitating Change in Mainstream Tourism

The fourth question posed in Chapter 1 was, 'can PPT effectively work on a large scale, influencing mainstream tourism initiatives?' Influencing a wide range of mainstream tourism stakeholders to make their practices more pro-poor remains a major challenge. For example, readers may have noted that a number of inspiring examples of pro-poor initiatives used in this book, involving industry, government and non-governmental organisations, came from South Africa. But even though a wide range of agencies in South Africa have a strong commitment to promoting fair trade in tourism and using tourism as a means of black empowerment and regenerating local economies (Binns and Nel 2002), most mainstream tourism industry ventures carry on as usual.

It is at the level of large, private sector stakeholders that perhaps the greatest changes in support of PPT still need to occur. As noted earlier, the majority of such businesses have mostly only supported token changes towards PPT. Hoteliers and resort owners may willingly use grey water on their gardens and provide donations to societies that protect turtle nesting sites, but they are less keen to develop partnerships with the poor,[3] to involve community representatives in decision-making, or to support implementation of effective labour rights legislation. Instead, in order to remain competitive, pay rates and labour conditions of tourism workers may be compromised (James 2004). They may support token community tourism projects that assist a small number of people, rather than making long-term changes so that their practices, including employment, training and procurement, are more pro-poor.

It will be difficult for well-intentioned governments to move beyond the rhetoric and into the practice of prioritising the interests of the poor if powerful elites and private sector lobby groups (such as hotel associations) with strong political connections resent PPT initiatives, such as positive discrimination towards poorer tourism providers. Thus a supportive policy environment is important, but not sufficient, to promote PPT.

If the WTTC wants to demonstrate a strong commitment to reducing poverty, rather than making platitudes about the need to build capacity among communities and to find ways in which they can gain more of the benefits of tourism, it should influence its members to consider joint venture arrangements with local communities, to endorse acceptable labour standards in the industry, and to minimise leakages from conventional forms of mass tourism.

The Importance of Challenging Inequitable Structures

The fifth question which arose in Chapter 1 was, 'can PPT effectively challenge inequitable institutions and structures that are in place, to a greater or lesser extent, in every country?' To date, PPT researchers and advocates have not grappled sufficiently with power (Church and Coles 2007: 271), an issue which certain tourism researchers have tried to emphasize for some time (Bianchi 2004; Hall 1994; Mowforth and Munt 2009; Telfer and Sharpley 2008). Major agencies that endorse a consensus on poverty are said to show an 'inability or unwillingness to address major issues pertaining to power and its distribution both at the domestic and international levels' (Öniş and Şenses 2005: 285). Similarly, the relative lack of power developing countries have in influencing the actions of foreign investors, due to the competition for their funds from elsewhere, and their lack of power in regional and international trade negotiations is not typically raised as an issue of concern. PPT does not seem to discuss how the actions of local elites, company directors and government leaders may influence whether tourism is working in the interests of the poor. Pro-poor policies are put forward then to take place in the context of existing structures or power hierarchies, considerably limiting their potential.

Chapter 3 highlighted research which revealed the challenge of tourism delivering tangible benefits to the poorest members of society. Even within poorer communities it is those with capital, connections, confidence, and foreign language skills—that is, those who definitely do not belong to the category 'poorest of the poor'—who have gained the greatest benefits from tourism development (Zhao and Ritchie 2007: 130). The poor tend not to carry much weight in their own right. For example, in Cancun, Mexico, large suppliers of fresh produce often give bribes to hotel chefs and buyers (Torres and Momsen 2004). It is very difficult for small farmers to compete in this environment. Meanwhile in Samoa, members of landowning groups rely on the goodwill of *matai* (clan leaders/chiefs) to release suitable land for them to use for their accommodation or restaurant enterprises, and to guarantee loans from the Samoan Development Bank.

It is not just elite capture at the local level which is a potential problem, however. Bianchi argues that we need to understand the power relations and discourses that shape tourism policies and plans, as well as highlighting the way in which the 'entrenched power of regional economic and political elites, is likely to undermine the prospects for a just model of sustainable tourism' (Bianchi 2004: 495). Efforts to spread the benefits of tourism more widely have often been constrained due to nepotism and corruption. For example, a government authority which asks for tenders regarding development of new tourism infrastructure (e.g. the tarsealing of a road which leads to a renowned temple or waterfall) may feel pressured to award that contract to a particular influential family business from a nearby town, even though the business is widely known for its maltreatment of workers and use of inferior materials in its roading work. As noted in the example from the Maldives in Chapter 3, governments and elites may collude to create conditions which ensure that tourism will mainly benefit those who are already wealthy. Similarly in Egypt, the government almost gave away coastal land to developers,[4] who have since made huge profits from the hotels they built (Richter and Steiner 2008).

In Duffy's (2002) examination of ecotourism in Belize, meanwhile, she exposed linkages between the tourism industry, elites, and money laundering, land speculation, the illegal drug trade, and trafficking of Mayan artefacts. This makes the aforementioned Samoan example seem like elite capture at its tamest. Duffy shows that 'ecotourism is part of a wider arena of legitimate business interests that intersects with illicit networks sustained by political corruption and global chains of traffickers' (Duffy 2002: 132). For example, when the government built a tourism village in Belize City selling crafts and souvenirs to make it more appealing to cruise ship visitors and ecotourists alike, they gave the contract to construct the village to a person who allegedly had been involved in drug smuggling and money laundering, allowing him to use cash to buy entire island resorts (Duffy 2002: 140).

The prevalence of such inequitable structures leads some researchers to conclude that, 'PPT will not "cure" corruption and cronyism, nor can it rid a place of patriarchy and racism. As a tool, tourism is overly burdened with ideals it cannot realise' (Chok et al. 2007: 51). It is certainly unlikely that PPT will work in every country and every context. Where inequalities are particularly entrenched, where corruption is rife, where human rights violations go unchecked by the ruling powers, and where existing structures preclude the empowerment of the poor, it will be difficult for PPT to contribute effectively to poverty alleviation. Factors which by contrast *are* conducive to PPT could include the following: a government that attracts foreign investors while also ensuring there are clear performance standards to maximise benefits for their country (e.g. requirements for local procurement or joint ventures); a legal and policy environment which is supportive of development initiatives by nationals of a country—for example in Samoa, the government supports communal land tenure and this has led to high levels of local ownership and control of the industry; support for freedom of expression, with strong NGOs and advocacy groups which play a watchdog role regarding tourism development; and good labour rights legislation along with appropriate incentives for upskilling employees or employing vulnerable peoples (e.g. youth at risk).

Tourism Highlights Inequalities

The final major question raised in Chapter 1 was, 'can PPT help to overcome the vast inequalities between tourists and local people, when international tourism is to some extent based upon, and highlights, the inequalities between the wealthy and the impoverished?'[5]

Tourism is structured around differences, between people, places, and environments, but also differences in wage rates, labour laws, health and safety regulations, and ease of access to sex and drugs. Thus poor countries may be attractive to resort developers partly because they offer cheap labour, which both lowers construction costs and ongoing labour costs when running a resort: 'to some extent tourism always feeds off the poverty of host regions' (Plüss and Backes 2002: 12). Even budget travellers such as backpackers can somehow raise the funds to set out on extensive sojourns through 'exotic', 'adventurous' locations around the world, where they may seek out people living in 'traditional villages', go on a tour of a shanty town or favela, and have opportunities to mix with 'the locals'. Zoomers highlights this contradiction when reflecting on differences between Andean villagers and tourists on the Inca route:

> promoting tourism means creating a world of extremes. It is an encounter of two opposing worlds: poor indigenous groups in their daily routines and well-to-do gringos in their time off, each with their own expectations and cultural orientations. (Zoomers 2008: 979–980)

These same 'locals' of course are unlikely to have the means to travel outside their own region, let alone internationally—except if they gather the resources to leave for a foreign destination as economic migrants:

> For the majority of the Andean poor, migrating is a better and quicker way to escape poverty than waiting for tourists. But they arrive unknown and unloved at their destinations, in stark contrast to what tourists experience when visiting exotic destinations. (Zoomers 2008: 981)

At the other end of the scale are luxury tourists who have heavy resource demands for both local resources that might be in short supply (e.g. energy, fresh water) and for imported goods. This just compounds situations of inequality. Disturbingly, the gaping inequalities in our world are fuelling conflict. Thus Hall seriously refutes some suggestions about the benefits of PPT:

> The notion espoused by the UNWTO that "tourism exchanges benefit primarily the countries of the South" is a ridiculous one and hides the reality that not only is the consumption of tourism the domain of the wealthy, but in many ways so is its production. (Hall 2007a: 116)

Advocates of PPT do not outwardly discuss nor attempt to address such inequalities. This leads Harrison (2008: 858) to complain that there is tacit acceptance by proponents of PPT with the status quo, such that they 'accept a neoliberal approach to development and tinker with the capitalistic international tourism system at the edges'.

WAYS FORWARD

While the foregoing responses to the six questions that were posed in Chapter 1 are not particularly positive, and they raise some significant constraints to tourism working in a pro-poor manner, they also show that there is reason for hope. In this section on 'ways forward' I will take a hopeful perspective and make suggestions for useful strategies for development agencies, governments and private sector interests wanting to support tourism as a tool for poverty alleviation.

Bring Ethics and Equity More Centrally into Tourism Development

If PPT is to work as a comprehensive approach, it will require what Chok et al. (2007) call a fundamental shift in ideology, from relying on supposed altruism, to a more solid foundation of ethics. Tokenistic efforts to employ a few people to weave mats for a resort on the one hand, or to encourage guests to contribute to a community development fund on the other, do not provide sufficient evidence that an industry which is focused on making profits by catering for the hedonistic pursuits of the world's middle and upper classes can actually be transformed. A number of researchers support the need for a more ethically grounded approach to pro-poor tourism (Higgins-Desbiolles 2006; Schellhorn 2007), which suggests that development policies focus less on growth and more on equity (Schilcher 2007a). This accords with Harrison's assertion that tourism studies needs to regain 'a moral dimension which was there in the 1970s and 1980s' (2008: 865).

It is useful to reflect back on the 1980 Manila Declaration, prepared during this period in which moral imperatives were more at the forefront of tourism debates, which stated: 'world tourism can only flourish if based on equality and if its ultimate aim is the improvement of the quality of life and the creation of better living conditions for all peoples' (WTO 1980: 1). If 107 state delegations were at the meeting where this enlightened declaration was made 30 years ago, it is anomalous that some current PPT advocates accept that tourism will typically bring more benefits to the non-poor than to the poor.

An example of how a moral dimension is missing from discussions of PPT can be seen in the case of a study of tourism 'value chains' in Danang, Vietnam. In this study 'massage' was counted as just another sub-sector which brought in money from tourists and which could potentially benefit the poor (Mitchell and Phuc 2007). No comment was made on the fact that this term is commonly used in Vietnam as a euphemism for the sex trade, and that sex tourism in Vietnam has been associated with forced prostitution of children (Duong 2002). In a related point, Harrison takes issue with the simple definition of PPT as 'tourism that delivers net benefits to the poor' as this does not account for the reality that some forms of tourism such as sex tourism may be incredibly exploitative—yet this could still be seen as PPT if it delivers income to the poor (2008: 859).

Promoting social equity through tourism, however, may not align with the interests of a number of current advocates of PPT, including both donors who are driven by neoliberal poverty alleviation agendas, and those agencies which act in the interest of the tourism and travel industry, such as the WTTC and PATA. Many tourism organisations and development agencies supporting PPT still take a relatively soft approach, suggesting that strategies involving self-regulation—such as voluntary codes of conduct—will be sufficient. This is most likely, however, to result in relatively small direct benefits for the poor, while continuing with a growth ethos that maximises benefits to the non-poor.

For something to be called pro-poor tourism then, Schilcher argues that the poor should capture disproportionate benefits:

> The tourism industry must be "moulded" so that "the poor" and "poorest" receive a proportionately higher share of tourism's benefits than people above the poverty line in order to reduce poverty-enhancing inequalities'. (2007a: 68)

This accords with Smith and Duffy's view (2003), in which they draw on the writing of Rawls (1973) to call for principles of distributive justice to inform tourism development, as so often tourism has led to a concentration of resources and power in the hands of a few. Reid (2003) also advocates for distributive justice. For PPT to have more of a re-distributive effect, the state would need to play a much stronger role, as explained in Chapter 6. For example, a government could specify that a certain proportion of tax revenue generated by tourism will be used to provide programmes that target the poor as beneficiaries. This could include the development of transport infrastructure linking isolated communities more effectively to markets, or provision of better health and education facilities to vulnerable and impoverished people (Mitchell and Ashley 2007a). Furthermore, redistributive justice could require greater ownership of tourism products by poorer people, and access of the poor to assets such as skills, credit and land (Schilcher 2007a: 71).

Specifically Target the Poorer Sectors of Society

With a more targeted approach the poorer sectors of society could benefit from tourism to a larger degree. In order to effectively engage poorer sectors of a society in tourism initiatives a comprehensive approach must be adopted involving: a) collecting detailed information on the composition of 'communities' including who are the poorest of the poor and what are their capabilities and resources; and b) providing adequate resources to empower poorer members of communities to effectively engage in, make decisions about, and benefit from tourism enterprises (e.g. through information on tourism pros and cons, providing training/capacity development in required skills, study tours, access to credit, and business mentoring). There needs to be strong, ongoing support for communities attempting to engage in tourism enterprises for the first time, such as employing a local facilitator or contracting a community-based organisation to assist in an ongoing fashion poorer and/or marginalised groups who are trying to engage in tourism. Allowing sufficient resources and time for such work with poorer sectors of communities at every stage of the project cycle is important if pro-poor tourism is to be realised, as was noted in Chapter 7.

Looking Beyond Economic Benefits

It is time that those discussing PPT overtly stated what they see as poverty, and how tourism can help to alleviate this scourge on humanity. Despite the continued growth of tourism globally, there are still high levels of poverty in many parts of the world. Thus a clear understanding of poverty, and what tourism can (and cannot) be expected to achieve in terms of poverty alleviation, is very much needed in PPT discourse. The conventional definition of PPT could be seen as akin to taking a welfarist approach to development whereby the poor could be seen simply as passive beneficiaries of charity and philanthropy directed at them via tourism endeavours. Zhao and Ritchie (2007) assert that this is problematic, and that a fuller understanding of poverty alleviation would position the poor as active agents of change in any strategies which emerged.

While undoubtedly financial and other economic benefits can be of great importance to poorer peoples, the discussion of the meaning of poverty in Chapter 2 of this book showed clearly the importance of understanding that poverty is not just about people lacking economic or material possessions. Rather, poverty is a very complex, multidimensional concept. Thus intangible benefits such as the development of skills, having control over a project, and increasing people's sense of pride and confidence, can be as important as gaining economic benefits from tourism from my perspective. In addition to economic benefits then, PPT should contribute to poverty alleviation in the following ways:

- Poverty is also about vulnerability; thus PPT should seek to enhance people's access to resources and build their resilience.
- Poverty is about exclusion; thus PPT should seek to enhance people's active participation in development, including decision-making.
- Poverty is about loss of dignity; thus PPT should seek to empower people and (re)establish their sense of pride and self-worth.
- Poverty is about lack of choice; thus PPT should seek to enhance people's livelihood options and help them to secure their rights.

Build Communal Benefits into Tourism Planning

As noted in Chapters 6 and 7, while PPT brings individual benefits to those directly involved in the tourism sector, its potential to provide *communal benefits* by contributing to improved services and livelihoods should not be overlooked or undervalued. Communal benefits should always be built into tourism planning to ensure positive outcomes for all sectors of a community. In some cases, for example, communities have been happy with tourism development even if not directly involved in tourism activities because it has improved roads in their area and thus transport to markets, it has led to better water and electricity supplies, or it has resulted in greater social stability by providing employment for young people who had previously had to migrate out of the area to find work.

A recent UNWTO report (2006a: 5) cites numerous examples of communal benefits arising from infrastructural improvements in pro-poor tourism projects, such as creation or upgrading of roads, bridges, water supplies, irrigation systems, recreational facilities, electricity, communication networks, lighting, sanitation systems, transportation networks, or education and health facilities. Protection of natural and cultural resources might be another communal benefit. In the pilot project for the development of mountain tourism in the High Atlas, Morocco, the opening up of a new valley for tourism required the creation of roads and installation of telecommunications, electricity, gas, and better drinking water supplies, all of which has substantially enhanced living standards of local residents (UNWTO 2006a: 102).

Build Good Networks with the Private Sector

The greatest challenge to achieving pro-poor tourism is to gain support from the private sector. However, increasing interest from travellers in ethical tourism coupled with pressure on companies to demonstrate CSR (corporate social responsibility) should help when encouraging reforms. With good planning and incentives, a wide range of private sector organisations, from hotels and resorts, to tour companies, tourism associations, and chambers of commerce, could be encouraged to support initiatives such as fair labour conditions and good training for workers, mentoring of the owners of microenterprises, making linkages with providers of alternative tourism experiences (e.g. resort clients being encouraged to experience village-run bamboo rafting adventures), establishment of a community development fund to benefit those in surrounding communities, and to change procurement practices so that more local goods and services are sourced, such as produce, furnishings and security services.

According to Harrison, the likelihood of having effective PPT relies heavily on efficient and effective governance structures, a "developmental state" that can provide an enabling environment in which the efforts of government departments, aid agencies and the private sector can be facilitated and coordinated (Harrison 2008: 863). In addition, development agencies should not shy away from the private sector. This book has provided evidence of constructive engagement between agencies such as SNV, GTZ and Tourism Concern with the private sector.

Divergent Voices Shaping Tourism to be More Pro-poor

As noted in Chapter 2, post-development thinking suggests that we need to move beyond simple binaries which suggest that tourism is either 'good' or 'bad', and instead seek to understand it in all of its complexity. Tourism is neither a saviour that can deliver social and economic development in every instance, nor is it a monolithic force bringing impending doom to peoples around the world. Rather, people can resist tourism, manipulate or otherwise transform it to their own benefit.

Those agencies working to ensure that tourism can contribute effectively to poverty alleviation through transforming aspects of the industry would appear to support the view that ' . . . it may be possible to reconstruct the modernist project of development in a more accountable, diverse, and just way' (Blaikie 2000: 1047). In this light, it is interesting to note that even some of the greatest sceptics re the 'new' forms of tourism are starting to see that PPT may have something to offer:

There exists the possibility that some Third World communities will take a degree of control over their own exploitation of tourism, and particularly new forms of tourism, which will represent, at least for them, a rebalancing of power. In this regard the pro-poor tourism initiatives ... provide some small cause for optimism. (Mowforth and Munt 2009: 377)

Thus problems inherent in the neoliberal logic behind some pro-poor development initiatives need not suggest that PPT is defunct. If we understand tourism as a system involving multiple dimensions and a wide range of stakeholders, we should be able to appreciate how it can be driven, not just by neoliberal growth motives, but also by the social and environmental interests of various sectors of society, including the poor (Wearing et al. 2005). Higgins-Desbiolles (2006) suggests that, rather than viewing tourism narrowly as an industry [driven by profits], we should consider that tourism can be seen as a social force, with due attention to the importance of governments and communities in shaping tourism that is driven by social concerns.

A post-development approach to PPT supports us looking at tourism more as a system, and potentially, as a social force. This could thus involve:

- Recognition of tourism's place in supporting social movements such as that in Chiapas, where the indigenous Mayan people rejected Mexican state involvement in their affairs. As explained in Chapter 4, tourism contributes to this post-development expression both by: a) bringing people to Chiapas on 'solidarity tours' to learn about their struggle for independence, and b) generating revenue to support the movement.
- NGOs supporting communities who are trying to *prevent* development of tourism—what Bond (2005) refers to as 'organic' social struggles which signify communities' resistance to certain developments such as those handing out leaflets protesting at charter flights at Goan airports (Lea 1993: 709).
- Donors and NGOs providing support via capacity building, access to information, publicity for certain causes, or credit, to those who are trying to shape tourism development in ways which will maximise gains to the poor. For example, Tourism Concern has been involved in initiatives to support the rights of porters in mountain areas and the rights of tourism sector workers globally.[6]
- Initiatives to transform mainstream tourism providers or to challenge the modus operandi of the tourism industry (e.g. the Fair Trade in Tourism movement discussed in Chapter 5), or the monitoring of tourism policy and large tourism enterprises in India by the NGO Equations.

We must also consider divergent voices at the local level. PPT is supposed to engage a wide range of stakeholders but the biggest challenge to this

urring in practice is often the relative lack of power of those stake-
ders who are most likely to experience negative effects of tourism: local
communities. Governments can to some extent facilitate a stronger role for
communities in planning for tourism development by actively seeking out
their voices on tourism planning matters and responding to their concerns
through appropriate processes (Scheyvens 2002; Timothy 2007).

Thus, as Carbone (2005: 562) argues, 'tourism planning should be based
on "bottom-up globalization", which engages in distributive justice by
entrusting more decision-making power in local communities'. Similarly,
Dann (1999: 26) notes that tourism specialists have recognised a need for
greater democratization of tourism, including 'resident responsive tourism'
with participation from those at grassroots level. This requires adequate
awareness-raising among the local population in tourism destination areas,
both about the benefits of tourism as well as potential problems which they
may need to anticipate and seek to control. Residents cannot go on to contribute to community tourism monitoring forums, planning committees or
the like without such information.

One way to encourage more local control is to engage communities in
monitoring or any research which takes place. The Makuleke community,
who won back part of the Kruger National Park in South Africa in a land
claim in 1996, are trying to ensure this happens by asking that researchers
involve young people from their community as research assistants. Another
strategy for active involvement is to have community representatives sitting
on local agencies which plan for tourism development, as occurs in the
Annapurna Conservation Area Project.

Such awareness-raising and participation in planning by communities
can seriously challenge the balance of power in areas popular with tourists. In French Polynesia, for example, residents from the island of Moorea
managed to stop the development of a foreign-owned luxury resort which
had been approved by a corrupt official, who has since been sent to jail
(d'Hauteserre 2003). In the Caribbean, a hotel development was stopped
because of local protests even though permission had been given by the
government (Pugh 2006). Also where tourism development does go ahead,
there are some very good examples of local communities exerting considerable power over this process and consequently gaining a number of benefits, as with traditional landowners associated with Mana Island resort,
Fiji (Sofield 2003: Chapter 9).

FINAL WORD

In this book I have attempted to shed light on some of the debates around
tourism in developing countries, paying particular attention to whether
tourism can contribute effectively to eliminating one of the great, intrac-
table scourges on our planet: poverty. Tacit acceptance of continuing high

rates of poverty and growing inequality is a challenge to notions of a common humanity. While presenting different perspectives on this issue, the book has finished on a hopeful note as there are clear examples of engagement with tourism leading to significant, positive changes in people's lives and of communities seeking to engage further with tourism development to meet their own objectives.

Overall there needs to be more debate about the value of PPT as an approach to poverty reduction. To date, insufficient critical views on PPT have been aired. This belies the reality, that is, while there are certainly circumstances in which tourism has helped to alleviate poverty, there are also situations in which it has deepened the fissures separating rich and poor, and where it has impoverished people culturally, socially or environmentally, even when the economic benefits have been real. There should not be a consensus that tourism reduces poverty, akin to the poverty consensus, as debate is critical if we are to gain a full understanding of both tourism's potential and its limitations as a means of enhancing the well-being of poor people all around the globe.

As an approach to development, PPT is in many ways inspiring and also ambitious. It seeks change at multiple levels, and across a wide range of actors, which implies it cannot be addressed in a piecemeal or tokenistic way. This explains the limitations of many PPT initiatives to date. A key challenge remaining is to ascertain how tourism can contribute not just to the economic well-being of the poor, but how it can challenge poverty more generally by reducing the vulnerability of the poor, helping them to gain more control over resources, empowering them and assisting them to claim their rights.

Notes

NOTES TO THE ACKNOWLEDGEMENTS

1. See www.snv.org.la/ecoadvsrv.htm (accessed 18 May 2009).

NOTES TO CHAPTER 1

1. Note that all $ values in this book refer to United States dollars, unless otherwise stated.
2. One notable exception is the articles published in the special issue of *Current Issues in Tourism* on pro-poor tourism (Volume 10, issues 2 & 3, 2007). See also the special issue of *Third World Quarterly* 29(5) 2008, which focused on tourism, poverty and development, and the latest edition of *Tourism and Sustainability* (Mowforth and Munt 2009). Jon Mitchell and Caroline Ashley, two key proponents of PPT, also published a book in 2010 named *Tourism and Poverty Reduction: Pathways to Prosperity* but this focuses more on the value of PPT.
3. While tourism growth internationally seems dramatic, Telfer and Sharpley (2008: 17) point out that the overall rate of growth in international tourism arrivals has diminished over time, from an average annual 10.6 percent increase in arrivals over the 1950s, to 4.2 percent growth in the 1990s.
4. Note that terms such as 'developing country' used here will be explained later in this chapter.
5. Arrivals in 2009 were lower than anticipated in all regions except Africa due to the global economic recession and A(H1N1) influenza.
6. See Chapter 7 for further discussion of the merits of both domestic and regional tourism.
7. Interestingly, the 50 LDCs put a submission in to the 2009 Copenhagen climate change conference that an aviation levy should be introduced and then used to support the world's poorest countries in adopting climate change measures (Harold Goodwin's blog: http://haroldgoodwin.wordpress.com/).
8. See www.scoop.co.nz/stories/WO0905/S00280.htm (accessed 3 December 2009).
9. See www.rollingrains.com/2008/11/responsible-tourism-at-wtm.html (accessed 3 March 2010).
10. See www.oecd.org/dac/ for a full list of recipients of ODA.
11. See www.oecd.org/dac/stats for the latest available statistics on all ODA recipient countries.

NOTES TO CHAPTER 2

1. While views of the causes of the global financial crisis are varied, many commentators, including the Australian prime minister, said much of the blame lies in corporate greed. See www.smh.com.au/business/blame-financial-crisis-on-corporate-greed—rudd-20091015-gz5p.html (accessed 20 April 2010).
2. This is BP's own 'worst case scenario' estimate. Seewww.reuters.com/article/idUSN1416392020100620 (accessed 23 June 2010).
3. See www.usatoday.com/news/world/2007-02-17-un-hunger_x.htm (accessed 23 June 2010).
4. See www.news-medical.net/news/2004/08/23/4270.aspx (accessed 3 March 2009).
5. See www.tourismconcern.org.uk/index.php?page=sun-sand-sea-sweatshops.
6. Note that the notion of tourism as a human right was advanced long ago. Thomas Cook devised tours to allow the working classes to engage in leisure pursuits. Then in 1948, the UN Universal Declaration of Human Rights asserted that all people should have the right to travel, leisure, rest and paid holidays (Higgins-Desbiolles 2006: 1199). Just recently the EU has put forward the notion of subsidized holidays for European people who are poor and marginalized, claiming that this is their human right. The EU commissioner for enterprise and industry asserted that 'Travelling for tourism today is a right. The way we spend our holidays is a formidable indicator of our quality of life (*Montreal Gazette* 2010).
7. Note that here I am focusing specifically on the emergence of pro-poor tourism as an approach to development from the late 1990s onwards. I am certainly not suggesting that this is the first time that tourism and poverty alleviation were linked. One early reference was an official statement in the Manila Declaration (WTO 1980: 1): 'world tourism can contribute to the establishment of a new international economic order that will help to eliminate the widening economic gap between developed and developing countries and ensure the steady acceleration of economic and social development and progress, in particular in developing countries'.
8. NB the PPT Partnership website, www.propoortourism.org.uk, lists a wide range of publications which are mostly accessible online.
9. Thus all World Tourism Organizations prior to 2003 which are cited in this book will be noted as 'WTO', while those published from 2003 onwards will be cited as UNWTO.
10. For a very good overview of how development theory influences thinking about tourism, see Telfer and Sharpley (2008: Chapter 1). In this book the focus is more directly on conceptualizing links between poverty and tourism.
11. Further discussion of alternative approaches to tourism, and concern about a community-based approach which fails to challenge mainstream tourism, is provided in Chapter 3.
12. The dominant, neoliberal policy prescriptions that informed a lot of development work in the 1980s and 1990s came out of organisations based in Washington DC, notably the IMF, World Bank and US Treasury.
13. Referred to by some as the Post-Washington Consensus.
14. Wearing et al. (2005) suggest that post-structuralist ideas have inspired NGOs working in the area of tourism and development.
15. See Make Poverty History campaign materials: www.makepovertyhistory.org/docs/MPHassembly1.pdf (accessed 15 April 2009).

NOTES TO CHAPTER 3

1. Not all tourism researchers feel that measures of leakages are appropriate and they claim leakages have been exaggerated. See further discussion in the section 'Criticisms are based on broad generalisations' later in this chapter.
2. This is similar to the concept of protected areas as 'islands of prosperity in a sea of poverty', as seen in Figure 3.2 later in this chapter.
3. See also the section on 'Fluctuations in tourism' in Chapter 1.
4. Refer back to Chapter 2's discussion on 'alternative tourism'.
5. See also the section called 'Avoid common biases' in Chapter 7, which discusses how many development agencies have had unrealistic expectations of alternative tourism and argues that they should look beyond small-scale alternatives and seek to change mainstream tourism.
6. Note that the notion that individual tourists can 'bring positive change' will be discussed further in Chapter 4's section on Voluntourism.
7. See Chapter 4 on voluntourism and Chapters 6 and 7 for some more positive perspectives on the potential of alternative forms of tourism.
8. This example also shows that any agency promoting the introduction of tourism to an area needs to be aware of the historical and social context and how such factors might impinge on a community's ability to take control of tourism development.
9. The contrary argument would question what happened to the other 86 percent of the tourist spend in the Gambia. Presumably there are further opportunities to maximise the local multiplier effects from tourism.
10. One downside to this, however, is that when companies have a management contract to run a hotel or resort in a developing country, they are likely to be more interested in turning a profit in the short term rather than in building long-term, positive relationships with communities nearby.

NOTES TO CHAPTER 4

1. Clearly not all tours to Soweto were as interactive in the past; however, in 2004 the Soweto Tourism Association decided to launch a "Get off the bus!" campaign. As Hjemdahl (2008: 87) explains, 'They wanted to make sure tourists don't just whiz through the township, but get out and meet the people, stay longer and spend money in Soweto'.

NOTES TO CHAPTER 5

1. It is thus somewhat disappointing that in the UNWTO's (2006) compilation of good practice in poverty alleviation through tourism, most of the examples identified are of small-scale, community-based or alternative tourism enterprises.
2. See sd2008.tuitravelplc.com/tui-sd/pages/workstreams/destinations/destination2 (accessed 30 May 2010).
3. Note that the military junta changed Burma's name to Myanmar, but most pro-democracy groups still prefer to use 'Burma'.
4. The official death toll was 13, but others estimated that 30–40 monks and 50–70 civilians were killed (UN News Centre 2007).

5. 'Value chain analysis' or VCA is a tool increasingly being applied in studies of the impacts of tourism, and measurement of its pro-poor impacts: 'Undertaking VCA in a tourist destination requires estimating the value of total tourist expenditure and disaggregating this into the different functional areas (i.e. accommodation, food and beverages, shopping, transport, excursions, etc.) where spending takes place' (ODI 2007: 1). It has become popular in PPT as a means of identifying gaps where there might be more opportunities for the poor to benefit from tourism (Ashley and Mitchell 2008).

6. Note that Wilderness Safari's website indicates that the Damaraland Camp is now 'owned and largely run by the local community'. www.wilderness-safaris.com/namibia_kunene/damaraland_camp/ (accessed 19 April 2010).

7. NB in 2008, Conservation Corporation Africa changed its name to '&Beyond Africa'.

8. Around 20 employees with specialist skills were brought in from outside the area, while the rest were locals.

9. See rttf.ca/index.php?p=conf&cid=2.

10. See Box 3.1 in Chapter 3, which discusses difficulties women had in accessing economic opportunities in association with a development project around Gunung Rinjani National Park.

NOTES TO CHAPTER 6

1. This author was also told of a particular country which has seen rapid growth of coastal development of all-inclusive accommodation, where the central government had taken over the consent process for new developments. It appears that in this case local government officials had been turning down applications due to potential environmental and social impacts, but central government stepped in, feeling it needed to create a better 'enabling environment' for investment in tourism.

2. Following publication by SNV and the Sustainable Cooperative Research Centre (Australia) of *Tourism Legislation and the Millennium Development Goals,* the president of Uganda also made a commitment to introduce legislation in support of the MDGs (IIPT 2007).

3. One tool that could help to identify areas where better linkages could be made between tourism and related sectors is the Tourism Satellite Account. Tourism Satellite Accounts, introduced by the WTTC in 1998, have been developed for over 170 countries around the world. They are essentially a means for individual countries to more accurately measure the contribution of the tourism industry to economic development. Tourism is not defined as an industry in national accounts; thus a Tourism Satellite Account allows countries to estimate tourism's contribution to the economy by 'counting' the tourism-related spend from other industries such as transport, accommodation, recreation, food and beverage services (Roe et al. 2004: 9). Once in place a satellite account should be able to provide information on the benefits of tourism, including multiplier effects, and direct and indirect employment it generates, as well as determining how high leakages are. Tourism satellite accounts thus distinguish between benefits of the 'travel and tourism *industry*', which accounts for all economic activities involving direct contact with tourists (e.g. provision of accommodation, meals, tours and souvenirs), from the 'travel and tourism *economy*', which includes a broader range of goods and services which are supplied to the tourism sector, from sale of produce from farmers to hotels, to construction of tourism infrastructure

and furniture for tourist accommodation (ESCAP 2007: 5–6). Having functioning tourism satellite accounts in developing countries can thus provide a broader overview of the ways in which tourism is contributing to economic development, as well as identifying gaps such as areas where there could be increased purchasing of local goods and services by the industry.

4. In other cases, however, governments provide generous tax exemptions in order to encourage foreign investment in tourism. For example, in Egypt some companies have been granted tax exemptions for 20 years (see Richter and Steiner, 2008).
5. This is called a 'build-operate-transfer' arrangement (UNWTO 2006: 133).
6. See www.raonline.ch/pages/bt/ecdu/bt_ecostats005.html (accessed 10 June 2010).

NOTES TO CHAPTER 7

1. For the full text of the Global Code of Ethics for Tourism, see www.world-tourism.org/pressrel/CODEOFE.htm.
2. See www.unwto.org/step/about/en/step.php?op=1 (accessed 13 June 2010).
3. See www.unwto.org/step/projects/en/projectsCountry.php (accessed 13 June 2010). Note that limits to community-based tourism were discussed in relation to Table 3.1.
4. www.adb.org/projects/summaries.asp?browse=1&type=&query=tourism.
5. NB Dates apply to either a single year (e.g. 1997) or multiple-year projects (e.g. 1997+).
6. See www.snvworld.org/en.ourwork/Pages/tourism.aspx (accessed 18 May 2009).
7. Note that these figures were accurate as of 2005, but there has since been further growth. Jonathan Mitchell of the Overseas Development Institute estimated that by 2008 there were around 76 advisors (personal communication).
8. See www.snv.org.la (accessed 18 May 2009).
9. See www.snv.org.la (accessed 18 May 2009).
10. See www.snv.org.la/ecoadvsrv.htm (accessed 18 May 2009).
11. See travaid.org.

NOTES TO CHAPTER 8

1. Approximately 1.2 billion people live on less than $1/day (UNDP Annual Report, 2008).
2. It is fair to add, however, that given the low exports from many of these countries, tourism receipts can still be a very important source of foreign exchange (Blake et al. 2008: 109).
3. When researching the poor linkages between hotel chefs and farmers in Quintana Roo, Mexico, Torres and Momsen found that 'This is mainly due to a lack of communication and the deep mistrust that exists between farmers, who are generally Maya, and the local non-Maya entrepreneurial elites and tourism industry suppliers and hotel buyers' (2004: 301).
4. The Tourism Development Authority sold coastal land in remote areas to private investors at $1 per square metre. The government then changed the status of this land, making it a developmental area. Banks valued the land at

$100 per square metre and allowed investors to use it as titles for loans, leading to the development of many hotels. Some hotels had paid off these loans within two years and thereafter, reaped huge profits (Richter and Steiner 2008: 955).

5. Discussing how 'tourism is a powerful symbol of wealth and privilege . . . ' (2004: 170), Jaakson argues that this is why tourists have been targeted by terrorists in a number of different contexts.

6. See www.tourismconcern.org.uk.

Bibliography

Abdulsamad, A. 2004 Maldives. *Just Change* 1:12, Wellington: Development Resource Centre.

Acott, T. G., La Trobe, H. L. and Howard, S. H. 1998 An evaluation of deep ecotourism and shallow ecotourism *Journal of Sustainable Tourism* 6(3): 238–253.

Adams, J. S. and McShane, T. O. 1992, *The Myth of Wild Africa: Conservation Without Illusion*, Norton and Co., New York.

Akama, J. S. 2004, Neocolonialism, dependency and external control of African's tourism industry: a case study of wildlife safari tourism in Kenya, in C. M. Hall and H. Tucker (eds) *Tourism and Postcolonialism: Contested Discourses, Identities and Representations*, Routledge, London: pp. 140–152.

———. 1999, The evolution of tourism in Kenya, *Journal of Sustainable Tourism*, 7(1): pp. 6–25.

Akama, J. S. and Kieti, D. 2007, Tourism and socio-economic development in developing countries: a case study of Mombasa Resort in Kenya, *Journal of Sustainable Tourism* 15(6): pp. 735–748.

Akindola, R. B. 2009, Towards a definition of poverty: poor people's perspectives and implications for poverty reduction, *Journal of Developing Societies,* 25(2): pp. 121–150.

Albuquerque, K. and McElroy, J. 1995, Alternative tourism and sustainability, in M. Conlin and T. Baum (eds) *Island Tourism: Management, Principles and Practice*, Wiley, New York: pp. 23–32.

Alcantara, N. 2008, Tourism 'imagines' responsibility at WTM, *eTurboNews* Global Travel Industry News, www.eturbonews.com/6211/tourism-imagines-reponsibility-wtm (accessed 27 November 2008).

Ashe, J. W. 2005, Tourism investment as a tool for development and poverty reduction: the experience in Small Island Developing States (SIDS), The Commonwealth Finance Ministers Meeting, 18–20 September 2005, Barbados.

Ashley, C. 2002 Methodology for Pro-Poor Tourism Case Studies. PPT Working Paper No.10, Overseas Development Institute, London.

———. 2006, Participation by the poor in Luang Prabang tourism economy: current earnings and opportunities for expansion, Working Paper 273, Overseas Development Institute, London.

———. 2005, The Indian Ocean tsunami and tourism, *Opinions* 33, Overseas Development Institute, London.

Ashley, C. and Ashton, J. 2006, Can the private sector mainstream pro-poor tourism? *id21insights* 62: p. 3.

Ashley, C., Goodwin, H., McNab, D., Scott, M. and Chavos, L. 2006, Making tourism count for the local economy in the Caribbean: guidelines for good practice, Pro-Poor Tourism Partnership and the Caribbean Tourism Association, Barbados.

Ashley, C. and Haysom, G. 2006, From philanthropy to a different way of doing business: strategies and challenges in integrating pro-poor approaches into tourism business, *Development Southern Africa* 23(2): pp. 265–280.

———. 2004, From philanthropy to a different way of doing business: strategies and challenges in integrating pro-poor approaches into tourism business. Submission to ATLAS Africa conference, Pretoria, October 2004, http://www.propoortourism.org.uk/Publications%20by%20partnership/propoor_business_ATLASpaper.pdf (accessed 20 June 2009).

Ashley, C. and Mitchell, J. 2008, Doing the right thing approximately not the wrong thing precisely: challenges of monitoring impacts of pro-poor interventions in tourism value chains, Working Paper 291, Overseas Development Institute, London.

Ashley, C. and Roe, D. 2002, Making tourism work for the poor: strategies and challenges in southern Africa, *Development Southern Africa* 19(1): pp. 61–82.

———. 1998, *Enhancing Community Involvement in Wildlife Tourism: Issues and Challenges*, IIED Wildlife and Development Series No. 11. International Institute for Environment and Development, London.

Ashley, C., Roe, D. and Goodwin, H. 2001, Pro-Poor Tourism: Putting Poverty at the Heart of the Tourism Agenda, *Natural Resource Perspectives*, Number 51, Overseas Development Institute, London.

Asia Travel Tips 2005, 'Use tourism on war on poverty' world leaders urged, 15 September 2005, www.asiatraveltips.com/print05cgi?file=159-Tourism.shtml (accessed 3 July 2006).

Asian Development Bank 2005 *The Greater Mekong Subregion Tourism Sector Strategy* Asian Development Bank, Manila.

Asiedu, A. 2005, Some benefits of migrants' return visits to Ghana, *Population, Space and Place* 11(1): pp. 1–11.

Atkinson, B. 2007, The travelling kind, *AA Directions Magazine* Winter 2007: pp. 70–71.

Australian Department of Foreign Affairs and Trade 2000, Republic of the Fiji Islands: Country Brief, October 2000, http://www.dfat.gov.au/geo/fiji/fiji_brief.html (accessed 17 April 2001).

Awaritefe, O. 2004, Motivation and other considerations in tourist destination choice: a case study of Nigeria, *Tourism Geographies* 6(3): pp. 303–330.

Aziz, H. 1999, Whose culture is it anyway? *In Focus* Spring: pp. 14–15.

Baker, K. and Coulter, A. 2007, Terrorism and tourism: the vulnerability of beach vendors' livelihoods in Bali, *Journal of Sustainable Tourism* 15(3): pp. 249–266.

Barnett, T. 2008, Influencing tourism at the grassroots level: the role NGO Tourism Concern, *Third World Quarterly* 29(5): pp. 995–1002.

Barrowclough, D. 2007, Foreign investment in tourism and small island developing states, *Tourism Economics* 13(4): pp. 615–638.

Bartis, H. H. 1998, A national black heritage trail in the Eastern Cape Province, South Africa: is it an option? in D. Hall and L. O'Hanlon (eds) *Rural Tourism Management: Sustainable Options,* Conference Proceedings, 9–12 September, Scottish Agricultural College, Auchincruive: pp. 17–28.

Beban-France, A. and Brooks, J. 2008, *Guide to International Development Terms and Acronyms: Pacific Focus,* Development Resource Centre, Wellington.

Bebbington, A. 2007, Social movements and the politicization of chronic poverty, *Development and Change* 38(5): pp. 793–818.

Becken, S., Simmons, D. and Frampton, C. 2003, Energy use associated with different travel choices, *Tourism Management* 24(3): pp. 267–277.

Beddoe, C. 2004, *Labour Standards, Social Responsibility and Tourism,* Tourism Concern, London.

Benavides, D. D. and Pérez-Ducy, E. (eds) 2001, *Tourism in the Least Developed Countries*, World Tourism Organization and UNCTAD, Brussels.

Berno, T. 2006, Bridging sustainable agriculture and sustainable tourism to enhance sustainability, in G. Mudacumura, D. Mebratu and M. Haque (eds) *Sustainable Development Policy and Administration*, Taylor & Francis, Boca Raton, FL: pp. 207–231.

Bianchi, R. 2004, Restructuring and the politics of sustainability: a critical view from the European periphery (the Canary Islands), *Journal of Sustainable Tourism* 12(6): pp. 495–529.

Binns, T. and Nel, E. 2002, Tourism as a local development strategy in South Africa, *Geographical Journal* 168: pp. 235–247.

Blaikie, P. 2000, Development, post-, anti-, and populist: a critical review, *Environment and Planning A* 32: pp. 1033–1050.

Blake, A., Arbache, J. S., Sinclair, M. T. and Teles, V. 2008, Tourism and poverty relief, *Annals of Tourism Research* 35(1): pp. 107–126.

Bond, P. 2005 Capitalism: degrading and destructive. Presentation to the *Capitalism Nature Socialism* conference, York University, Toronto, 22 July 2005.

———. 2006, Global governance campaigning and MDGs: from top-down to bottom-up anti-poverty work, *Third World Quarterly* 27(2): pp. 339–354.

Boniface, B. and Cooper, C. 1994, *The Geography of Travel and Tourism*, Butterworth Heinemann, Oxford.

Bonner, R. 1993, *At the Hand of Man: Peril and Hope for Africa's Wildlife*, Alfred A Knopf, New York.

Bowden, J. 2005, Pro-Poor Tourism and the Chinese experience, *Asia Pacific Journal of Tourism Research* 10(4): pp. 379–398.

Boyd, S. 1997, Egos and elephants, *New Internationalist* March: pp. 16–17.

Bradt, H 1995 Better to travel cheaply? *The Independent on Sunday* 12 February: 49–50.

Brazier, C. 2008, What is ethical travel? *New Internationalist* March: pp. 15–16.

Breen, C., Mander, M., A'Bear, D., Little, T. and Pollett, T. 1992, Social conceptions of the roles and benefits of national parks, Occasional Paper 119, Institute of Natural Resources, Pietermaritzburg.

Brennan, F. and Allen, G. 2001, Community-based ecotourism, social exclusion and the changing political economy of KwaZulu-Natal, South Africa, in D Harrison (ed) *Tourism and the Less Developed World: Issues and Case Studies*, CABI Publishing, New York: pp. 203–221.

Briedenham, J. 2004, Corporate social responsibility in tourism: a tokenistic agenda? *In Focus* 52: p. 11.

Briedenham, J. and Wickens, E. 2004, Tourism routes as a tool for the economic development of rural areas—vibrant hope or impossible dream? *Tourism Management* 25(1): pp. 71–79.

Briguglio, L. 1995, Small island states and their economic vulnerabilities, *World Development*, 23(9): pp. 1615–1632.

Britton, S. 1982, The political economy of tourism in the third world, *Annals of Tourism Research* 9(3): pp. 331–358.

Britton, S. and Clarke, W. 1987, *Ambiguous Alternative: Tourism in Small Developing Countries*, University of the South Pacific, Fiji.

Brohman, J. 1996, New directions in tourism for the Third World, *Annals of Tourism Research* 23(1): pp. 48–70.

Brown, D. 1998, In search of an appropriate form of tourism for Africa: lessons from the past and suggestions for the future, *Tourism Management* 19(3): pp. 237–245.

Brown, F. and Hall, D. 2008, Tourism and development in the global South: the issues, *Third World Quarterly* 29(5): pp. 839–849.

Brunet, S., Bauer, J., De Lacy, T. and Tshering, K. 2001, Tourism development in Bhutan: tensions between tradition and modernity, *Journal of Sustainable Tourism* 9(3): pp. 243–263.

Brunt, P. and Courtney, P. 1999, Host perceptions of sociocultural impacts, *Annals of Tourism Research* 26(3): pp. 493–575.

Burns, P. M. 2004, Tourism planning: a third way? *Annals of Tourism Research* 31(1): pp. 24–43.

———. 1999a, Dealing with dilemmas, *In Focus* 33: pp. 4–5.

———. 1999b, Paradoxes in planning: tourism elitism or brutalism? *Annals of Tourism Research* 26(2): pp. 329–348.

Burns, P. M .and Barrie, S. 2005, Race, space and 'our own piece of Africa': doing good in Luphisi village, *Journal of Sustainable Tourism* 13(5): pp. 468–485.

Burns, P. M. and Holden, A. 1995, *Tourism: A New Perspective*, Prentice Hall, Hemel Hempstead.

Butcher, J. 2006, A response to 'Building a Decommodified Research Paradigm in Tourism: The Contribution of NGOs' by Stephen Wearing, Matthew McDonald and Jess Ponting, Journal of Sustainable Tourism, Vol. 13, No. 5: pp. 424–455, *Journal of Sustainable Tourism* 14(3): pp. 307–310.

———. 2003, *The Moralisation of Tourism: Sun, Sand . . . and Saving the World?* Routledge, New York.

Butler, R. 1990, Alternative tourism: pious hope or trojan horse? *Journal of Travel Research* 28(3): pp. 40–45.

Cappelli, G. 2006, *Sun, Sea, Sex and the Unspoilt Countryside: How the English language makes tourists out of readers*, Pari Publishing, Grosseto, Italy.

Carbone, M. 2005, Sustainable tourism in developing countries: poverty alleviation, participatory planning, and ethical issues, *The European Journal of Development Research* 17(3): pp. 559–565.

Carlisle, L. 1997, Conservation Corporation: an integrated approach to ecotourism, in G Creemers (ed) *Proceedings of a Workshop on Community Involvement in Tourism,* Natal Parks Board and KwaZulu-Natal Tourism Authority, Pietermaritzburg: pp. 6–7.

Carney, D. (ed) 1998, *Sustainable Rural Livelihoods: What Contribution Can We Make?* Department for International Development, London.

Carruthers, D. 2001, From opposition to orthodoxy: the remaking of sustainable development, *Journal of Third World Studies* 18(2): pp. 93–112.

Carruthers, J. 1997, Nationhood and national parks: comparative examples from the post-imperial experience, in T. Griffiths and L. Robin (eds) *Ecology and Empire: Environmental History of Settler Societies,* Melbourne University Press, Melbourne: pp. 125–138.

Cater, E. 1995, Consuming spaces: global tourism, in J. Allen and C. Hamnett (eds) *A Shrinking World? Global Unevenness and Inequality*, Oxford University Press, Oxford, in association with the Open University, Milton Keynes: pp. 183–231.

Chambers, R. and Conway, G. 1992, Sustainable rural livelihoods: practical concepts for the 21st century, Discussion Paper No. 296, Institute of Development Studies, University of Sussex, Brighton.

Chand, S. and Levantis, T. 2000, The Fiji coup: a spate of economic catastrophes, *Pacific Economic Bulletin* 15(1): pp. 27–33.

Cheong, S. and Miller, M. 2000, Power and tourism: a Foucauldian observation, *Annals of Tourism Research* 27(2): pp. 371–390.

Cherry, M. 1993 Phinda: making ecotourism profitable for the people. *Sunday Times* Johannesburg, 30 May: 35.

Chok, S., Macbeth, J. and Warren, C. 2007, Tourism as a tool for poverty alleviation: a critical analysis of 'pro-poor tourism' and implications for sustainability, in C M Hall (ed) *Pro-poor Tourism: Who Benefits?* Cromwell Press, Clevedon: pp. 34–55.

Christie, I. 2002, Tourism, growth and poverty: framework conditions for tourism in developing countries, *Tourism Review* 57(1&2): pp. 35–41.

Christie, I. T. and Sharma, A. 2008, Research note: Millennium Development Goals—what is tourism's place? *Tourism Economics* 14(2): pp. 427–430.

Church, A. and Coles, T. 2007, Tourism and the many faces of power, in A Church and T Coles (eds) *Tourism, Power and Space,* Routledge, London: pp. 269–282.

Clancy, M. 1999, Tourism and development: evidence from Mexico, *Annals of Tourism Research* 26(1): pp. 1–20.

Cling, J. 2003, A critical review of the World Bank's stance on poverty reduction, in J. Cling, M. Razafindrakoto and F. Roubaud (eds) *New International Poverty Reduction Strategies*, Routledge, London: pp. 21–50.

Cloke, P. 2000, Tourism, geography of, in R. Johnston, D. Gregory, G. Pratt and M. Watts (eds) *The Dictionary of Human Geography,* Blackwell, Oxford: pp. 840–843.

Coghlan, A. 2006, Volunteer tourism as an emerging trend or an expansion of ecotourism? A look at potential clients' perceptions of volunteer tourism organisations, *International Journal of Nonprofit and Voluntary Sector Marketing* 11: pp. 225–237.

Cohen, E. 2002, Authenticity, equity and sustainability in tourism, *Journal of Sustainable Tourism* 10(4): pp. 267–276.

Colantonio, A. and Potter, R. B. 2006, The rise of urban tourism in Havana since 1989, *Geography* 19(1): pp. 23–33.

Cole, S. 2008, *Tourism, Culture and Development: Hopes, Dreams and Realities in East Indonesia,* Channel View Publications, Clevedon.

———. 2006, Information and empowerment: the keys to achieving sustainable tourism, *Journal of Sustainable Tourism* 14(6): pp. 629–644.

Coles, T. and Church, A. 2007, Tourism, politics and the forgotten entanglements of power, in A Church and T Coles (eds) *Tourism, Power and Space,* Routledge, London: pp. 1–42.

Coles, T. and Timothy, D. J. 2004, *Tourism, Diasporas and Space,* Routledge, London.

Cornelissen, S. 2005, Tourism impact, distribution and development: the spatial structure of tourism in the Western Cape province of South Africa, *Development Southern Africa* 22(2): pp. 163–185.

Cross Cultural Solutions 2009 Mission, Vision, Values: Providing the Focus for our Organization. http://www.crossculturalsolutions.org/about/mission-vision-values.aspx (accessed 3 February 2009)

Dann, G. 2002, Tourism and development, in V. Desai and R. Potter (eds) *The Companion to Development Studies,* Arnold, London: pp. 236–239.

———. 1999, Theoretical issues for tourism's future development: identifying the agenda, in D. G. Pearce and R. Butler (eds) *Contemporary Issues in Tourism Development,* Routledge, London: pp. 13–30.

David, R., Sekartjakrarini, S. and Braun, A. 2005, Gunung Rinjani National Park Project: Rinjani Trek Ecotourism Programme, Lombok—Indonesia: a participatory evaluation, New Zealand Agency for International Development, Wellington (Unpublished report).

Davis, J. B. 2001, Commentary: tourism research and social theory—expanding the focus, *Tourism Geographies* 3(2): pp. 125–134.

de Kadt, E. 1992, Making the alternative sustainable: lessons from development for tourism, in V. Smith and W. Eadington (eds) *Tourism Alternatives: potential and Problems in the Development of Tourism,* University of Pennsylvania Press, Philadelphia: pp. 47–75.

——. 1990, *Making the Alternative Sustainable: Lessons from Development for Tourism,* DP 272, Institute of Development Studies, Sussex.

——, (ed) 1979, *Tourism: Passport to Development?* Oxford University Press, New York.

Deloitte & Touche 1999, *Sustainable Tourism and Poverty Elimination: A Report for the Department of International Development,* IIED and ODI, London.

Deng, Z. 2000, 'Pattern of East Asia' and government-led strategy in tourism development, *Academic Forum* 3: pp. 47–50.

Dent, M. and Peters, B. 1999, *The Crisis of Poverty and Debt in the Third World,* Ashgate, Aldershot.

Department for International Development (DFID) 1999, Sustainable tourism and poverty elimination study, Report for Department for International Development by Deloitte & Touche, IIED and ODI, London.

Dernoi, L. 1981, Alternative tourism: towards a new style in North-South relations, *International Journal of Tourism Management* 2: pp. 253–264.

Desforges, L. 2000, State tourism institutions and neo-liberal development: a case study of Peru, *Tourism Geographies* 2(2): pp. 177–192.

Devereux, P. 2008, International volunteering for development and sustainability: outdated paternalism or a radical response to globalisation? *Development in Practice* 18(3): pp. 357–370.

D'Hauteserre, A. 2003, A response to 'Misguided policy initiatives in small-island destinations: why do up-market tourism policies fail?' by Dimitri Ioannides and Briavel Holcomb, *Tourism Geographies* 5(1): pp. 49–53.

Dhivehi Observer 2005, Hilton hits on Mandhoo: no room for ethics in Maldives resort, *Dhivehi Observer,* 6 November 2005, www.dhivehiobserver.com/speical reports/Mandhoo-Hilton/Hilton_Maldives_Resort.htm (accessed 5 June 2008).

Dieke, P. 1993, Tourism and development policy in the Gambia, *Annals of Tourism Research* 20: pp. 423–449.

Dombroski, K. 2006, *Reconciling Tourism, Cultural Change and Empowerment in a Tibetan Host Community,* Master's thesis in Development Studies, Massey University, Palmerston North.

Domroes, M. 2001, Conceptualising state-controlled resort islands for an environment-friendly development of tourism: the Maldivian experience, *Singapore Journal of Tropical Geography* 22(2): pp. 122–137.

Donaldson, J. A. 2007, Tourism, development and poverty reduction in Guizhou and Yunnan, *The China Quarterly* 190: pp. 333–351.

Duffy, R. 2002, *A Trip Too Far: Ecotourism, Politics and Exploitation,* Earthscan, London.

Duong, L. B. 2002, Vietnam children in prostitution in Hanoi, Hai Phong, Ho Chi Minh City and Can Tho: a rapid assessment, International Labour Organization, Bangkok.

Echtner, C. M. and Prasad, P. 2003, The context of Third World tourism marketing, *Annals of Tourism Research* 30(3): pp. 660–682.

Endo, K. 2006, Foreign direct investment in tourism—flows and volumes, *Tourism Management* 27: pp. 600–614.

Enloe, C. 1990, *Bananas, Beaches and Bases: Making Feminist Sense of International Politics,* University of California Press, Berkeley.

Epler Wood, M. and Leray, T. 2005, Corporate Responsibility and the Tourism Sector in Cambodia, World Bank Group, Washington DC.

Equations 2009 Equitable Tourism Options, http://www.equitabletourism.org (accessed 3 September 2009).

Erb, M. 2003, Uniting the bodies and cleansing the village: conflicts over local heritage in a globalizing world, *Indonesia and the Malay World* 31(89): pp. 129–139.

————. 2000, Understanding tourists: interpretations from Indonesia, *Annals of Tourism Research* 27(3): pp. 709–736.

Erbelei, W. 2000, Taking the lead in the fight against poverty: World Bank and IMF speed implementation of their new strategy, *Development and Cooperation* 3: pp. 23–24.

ESCAP 2007, Regional study of the role of tourism in socioeconomic development, 63rd Session, 22–27 May 2007, Almaty, Kazakhstan.

————. 2003, *Poverty Alleviation through Sustainable Tourism Development*, United Nations, New York.

eTurboNews 2009a, Volunteer vacation sales up 28 percent, 13 April 2009, http://www.eturbonews.com/8765 (accessed 15 April 2009).

————. 2009b, Increased budget for tourism in Thailand fails to reassure tourism professionals, 19 June 2009, http://www.eturbonews.com/9892 (accessed 22 June 2009).

————. 2009c, Recession taking its toll on Tanzania tourism as thousands of jobs get axed, 24 June 2009, http://www.eturbonews.com/9882 (accessed 30 June 2009).

————. 2009d, Re-engineering UNWTO is the way forward, Rifai says, 6 March 2009, http://www.eturbonews.com/9595 (accessed 4 June 2009).

————. 2009e, Tuvalu hopes for rising tide of tourists, (September 6 2009), http://www.eturbonews.com/print/11506 (accessed 14 September 2009).

————. 2007, 'Aerial highway' critical for poor countries', 18 November 2007, http://forimmediaterelease.net/pm/853.html (accessed 18 March 2008).

European Union 2008, The EU's relations with Maldives, http://ec.europa.eu/external_relations/maldives/intro/index.htm (accessed 5 June 2008).

Fallon, F. 2001, Conflict, power and tourism on Lombok, *Current Issues in Tourism* 4(6): pp. 481–502.

Farrington, P. 1999, All-inclusives—a new Apartheid, *In Focus* Autumn: pp. 10–11, 17.

Fingleton 2005, Privatising land in the Pacific: a defence of customary tenures, Discussion Paper No. 80, Australia Institute, Canberra.

Fleming, E. 2007, Agricultural productivity change in Pacific island countries, *Pacific Economic Bulletin* 22(3): pp. 32–47.

Forsyth, T. 1995, Business attitudes to sustainable tourism: self-regulation in the UK outgoing tourism industry, *Journal of Sustainable Tourism* 3(4): pp. 210–231.

France, L. (ed) 1997, *The Earthscan Reader in Sustainable Tourism*, Earthscan, London.

Frew, M. J. 2005, *Tourism as an Economic Development Tool for Ovalau, Fiji Islands*, Master's thesis in Development Studies, Victoria University, Wellington.

Friedmann, J. 1992, *Empowerment: The Politics of Alternative Development*, Blackwell, Cambridge.

Garland, A. 1997, *The Beach*, Penguin, London.

Garrod, B. 2003, Local participation in the planning and management of ecotourism: a revised model approach, *Journal of Ecotourism* 2(1): pp. 33–53.

Garrod, B. and Fyall, A. 1998, Beyond the rhetoric of sustainable tourism? *Tourism Management* 19(3): pp. 199–212.

Ghimire, K. 2001, The growth of national and regional tourism in developing countries: an overview, in K. Ghimire (ed) *The Native Tourist: Mass Tourism Within Developing Countries*, Earthscan, London: pp. 1–29.

Goodwin, H. 2008, Pro-poor tourism: a response, *Third World Quarterly* 29(5): pp. 869–871.

————. 2007, Pro-Poor Tourism: Annual Register 2007, http://www.propoortourism.org.uk/pptpar2007.pdf (accessed 20 March 2009).

————. 2006, Community-based tourism: failing to deliver? *id21 Insights* 62: p. 6 (available online: www.id21.org/insights).

————. 1998, Background paper for the workshop on sustainable tourism and poverty elimination in preparation for the 1999 session of the Commission on Sustainable Development, DFID and DTER, London.

Goodwin, H., Kent, I., Parker, K. and Walpole, M. 1998, *Tourism, Conservation and Sustainable Development: Case Studies from Asia and Africa*, Wildlife and Development Series No. 12, International Institute for Environment and Development, London.

Gössling, S., Peeters, P. and Scott, D. 2008, Consequences of climate policy for international tourist arrivals in developing countries, *Third World Quarterly* 29(5): pp. 873–901.

Gössling, S., Schumacher, K., Morelle, M., Berger, R. and Heck, N. 2004, Tourism and street children in Antananarivo, Madagascar, *Tourism and Hospitality Research* 5(2): pp. 131–149.

Goudie, S. C., Khan, F. and Kilian, D. 1999, Transforming tourism: black empowerment, heritage and identity beyond apartheid, *South African Geographical Journal* 81(1): pp. 22–31.

Gray, N. J. and Campbell, L. M. 2007, A decommodified experience? Exploring aesthetic, economic and ethical values for volunteer ecotourism in Costa Rica, *Journal of Sustainable Tourism* 15(5): pp. 463–482.

Green, M. and Hulme, D. 2005, From correlates and characteristics to causes: thinking about poverty from a chronic poverty perspective, *World Development* 33(6): pp. 867–879.

Gurung, D. B. and Seeland, K. 2008, Ecotourism in Bhutan: extending its benefits to rural communities, *Annals of Tourism Research* 35(2): pp. 489–508.

Hadjor, K. 1993, *The Penguin Dictionary of Third World Terms,* Penguin, Harmondsworth.

Hall, C. and Page, S. 1999 *The Geography of Tourism and Recreation: Environment, Place and Space.* Routledge, London.

Hall, C. M. 2007a, Pro-poor tourism: do 'tourism exchanges benefit primarily the countries of the South'? *Current Issues in Tourism* 10(2&3): pp. 111–118.

————. 2007b, Tourism, governance and power, in A Church and T Coles (eds) *Tourism, Power and Space,* Routledge, London: pp. 255–268.

————. 1998, Making the Pacific: globalization, modernity and myth, in G Ringer (ed) *Destinations: Cultural Landscapes of Tourism*, Routledge, London: pp. 140–153.

————. 1994, *Tourism and Politics: Policy, Power and Place*, John Wiley and Sons, Chichester.

Hall, C. M. and Butler, R. 1995, In search of common ground: reflection on sustainability, complexity and process in the tourism system, *Journal of Sustainable Tourism* 3(2): pp. 99–105.

Hall, C. M. and Page, S. J. 1996, Australia's and New Zealand's role in Pacific tourism: aid, trade and travel, in C. M. Hall and S. J. Page (eds) *Tourism in the Pacific: Issues and Cases*, International Thomson Business Press, London: pp. 161–189.

Hall, C. M. and Tucker, H. (eds) 2004, *Tourism and Postcolonialism: Contested Discourses, Identities and Representations,* Routledge, London.

Hall, D. and Brown, F. 2008, Finding a way forward: an agenda for research, *Third World Quarterly* 29(5): pp. 1021–1032.

————, (eds) 2006, *Tourism and Welfare: Ethics, Responsibility and Sustained Well-being,* CABI, Wallingford.

Hamm, B. 2001, A human rights approach to development, *Human Rights Quarterly* 23: pp. 1005–1031.

Hampton, M. 2005, Heritage, local communities, and economic development, *Annals of Tourism Research* 32(3): pp. 735–759.

Harrison, D. 1999 A Cultural Audit of Turtle Island, Fiji. Centre for Leisure and Tourism Studies, University of North London.

———. 2008, Pro-poor tourism: a critique, *Third World Quarterly* 29(5): pp. 851–868.

———. 2003, Themes in Pacific Island tourism, in D Harrison (ed) *Pacific Island Tourism,* Cognizant Communication Corporation, New York: pp. 1–23.

———, (ed) 2001, *Tourism and the Less Developed World: Issues and Case Studies,* CABI Publishing, New York.

———, (ed) 1992, *Tourism and the Less Developed Countries,* Wiley, Chichester.

Harrison, D. and Schipani, S. 2007, Lao tourism and poverty alleviation: community-based tourism and the private sector, in C. M. Hall (ed) *Pro-poor Tourism: Who Benefits?* Cromwell Press, Clevedon: pp. 84–119.

Hart, G .2001, Development critiques in the 1990s: *cul de sacs* and promising paths, *Progress in Human Geography* 25(4): pp. 649–658.

Hawkins, D. E. and Mann, S. 2007, The World Bank's role in tourism development, *Annals of Tourism Research* 34(2): pp. 348–363.

Haynes, K. 2004, Briefing on the Maldives: lost in paradise, 6 August 2004, Tourism Concern, London.

Herald News Desk 1999, JGF will oppose upmarket tourism, *The Herald,* 27 September.

Hickey, S. 2008, The return of politics in development studies I: getting lost within the poverty agenda? *Progress in Development Studies* 8: pp. 349–358.

Higgins-Desbiolles, F. 2006, More than an 'industry': the forgotten power of tourism as a social force, *Tourism Management* 27: pp. 1192–1208.

Hitchcock, R. and Brandenburgh, R. 1990, Tourism, conservation, and culture in the Kalahari Desert, Botswana, *Cultural Survival Quarterly* 14(2): pp. 20–24.

Hjemdahl, K. M. 2008, Tourism as an important weapon against poverty? *Ethnologia Scandinavica* 38: pp. 81–93.

Holcomb, J., Upchurch, R. and Okumus, F. 2007, Corporate social responsibility: what are the top hotel companies reporting? *International Journal of Contemporary Hospitality Management* 19(6): pp. 461–475.

Holden, Peter (ed) 1984, *Alternative Tourism,* Report of the workshop on alternative tourism with a focus on Asia, Chiang Mai, Thailand, April 26–May 8, Ecumenial Council on Third World Tourism, Bangkok.

Hong, E. 1985, *See the Third World While It Lasts: The Social and Environmental Impact of Tourism with Special Reference to Malaysia,* Consumers' Association of Penang, Penang.

Hughes, H. 2004, The Pacific is viable!, Issue Analysis No 53, Centre for Independent Studies, Sydney, www.cis.org.au (accessed 20 May 2008).

Husbands, W. and Harrison, L. C. 1996, Practicing (sic) responsible tourism: understanding tourism today to prepare for tomorrow, in L. C. Harrison and W Husbands (eds) *Practicing Responsible Tourism: International Case studies in Tourism Planning, Policy, and Development,* Wiley, New York.

Hutnyk, J. 1996, *The Rumour of Calcutta: Tourism, Charity and the Poverty of Representation,* Zed, London.

International Institute for Environment and Development (IIED) 2001, *The Future is Now,* IIED, London.

International Institute for Peace through Tourism 2007, Uganda to be world's first nation to adopt tourism legislation in support of UN MDG, http://www.iipt.org/media/media%20release%20june.html (accessed 1 October 2007).

———. 2004, *January Newsletter,* http://www.iipt.org/newsletter/enewsletter2004/January2004.html (accessed 1 December 2004).

International Monetary Fund (IMF) 2008, *World Economic Outlook Database*, October 2008, http://imf.org/external/pubs/ft/weo/2008/02/weodata/index. aspx (accessed 15 January 2009).

Irvine, D. 2007, Trend watch: disaster tourism, CNN World Weekly, 28 September 2007, http://www.cnn.com/2007/WORLD/europe/09/27/ww.trends.disaster-tourism (accessed February 3 2009).

Jaakson, R. 2004, Globalisation and neo-colonialist tourism, in C M Hall and H Tucker (eds) *Tourism and Postcolonialism: Contested Discourses, Identities and Representations*, Routledge, London: pp. 169–183.

Jafari, J. 2001, The scientification of tourism, in V. L. Smith and M. Brent (eds) *Hosts and Guests Revisited: Tourism Issues of the 21st Century*, Cognizant Communication, New York: pp. 28–41.

James, G. 2004, Riding the wave: working within a globalised tourism economy, *Tourism In Focus* 52: pp. 12–13.

Japardy, P. 2010, *The Private Sector and Gunung Rinjani National Park: An Examination of Tourism's Contribution to Development*, VDM Verlag, Germany.

Jayaraman, T. K. 1999, Private sector development and competition in the South Pacific: a case study of Vanuatu, *South Pacific Study* 19(1–2): pp. 1–22.

Jeffrey, P. 1999, Rebuilding brigades, *Latinamerica Press* 31(33): p. 4.

Jennings, S. 2007, South Africa's finest, *Vista: The Volunteer View on International Development*, Volunteer Service Abroad, Wellington.

Kalisch, A. 2001, *Tourism as Fair Trade: NGO Perspectives*, Tourism Concern, London.

Karammel, .S and Lengefeld, K. 2006, Can all-inclusive tourism be pro-poor? *id21insights* 62: p. 5.

Kendal, R. 2007, Disaster tourism, iafrica.com, http://travel.iafrica.com/destin/658102.htm (accessed Feb 3 2009).

Kennedy, K. 2008, *Non-governmental Organizations (NGOs) and Tourism: A Partnership for Poverty Reduction in Developing Countries*, MSc thesis in Geography, Central Connecticut State University, New Britain, Connecticut.

Khan, M. 1997, Tourism development and dependency theory: mass tourism vs. ecotourism, *Annals of Tourism Research* 24(4): pp. 988–991.

Kindon, S. 2001, Destabilising 'maturity': women as tourism producers in Southeast Asia, in Y. Apostolopoulos, S. Sonmez and D. Timothy (eds) Women as Producers and Consumers of Tourism in Developing Regions, Praeger, Westport: pp. 73–92.

King, B. and Berno, T. 2002, Tourism and civil disturbances: an evaluation of recovery strategies in Fiji, 1987–2000, *Journal of Hospitality and Tourism Management* 9(1): pp. 46–61.

Kingsbury, P. T. 2006, Corporate environmental sustainability: Sandals resorts international in Jamaica, in J. Pugh and J. Momsen (eds) *Environmental Planning in the Caribbean*, Ashgate, Burlington: pp. 111–127.

Kinnaird, V., Kothari, U. and Hall, D. 1994, Tourism: gender perspectives, in V. Kinnaird and D. Hall (eds) *Tourism: A Gender Analysis*, John Wiley & Sons, New York: pp. 1–33.

Kirsten, M. and Rogerson, C. M. 2002, Tourism, business linkages and small enterprise development in South Africa, *Development Southern Africa* 19(1): pp. 29–59.

Koch, E. 1997, A vision of tourism for the new southern Africa: why tourism matters, Paper prepared for the launch of Action for Southern Africa's People-First Tourism campaign, 5 July 1997.

Koch, E., de Beer, G. and Elliffe, S. 1998, SDIs, tourism-led growth and the empowerment of local communities, *Development Southern Africa* 15(5): pp. 809–826.

Konadu-Agyemang, K. 2001, Structural adjustment programmes and the international tourism trade in Ghana, 1983–99: some socio-spatial implications, *Tourism Geographies* 3(2): pp. 187–206.

Kontogeorgopoulos, N. 2004, Conventional tourism and ecotourism in Phuket, Thailand: conflicting paradigms or symbiotic partners? *Journal of Ecotourism* 3(2): pp. 87–108.

Koro, E. 1999a, Zimbabwe's CAMPFIRE programme promotes conservation and development, *Resource Africa* 1(8): p. 3.

Krippendorf, J. 1987, *The Holidaymakers*, Butterworth-Heinemann, Oxford.

Lancaster, J. 2007, Next stop, squalor, *Smithsonian* 37(12): pp. 96–105.

Lea, J. 1993, Tourism development ethics in the Third World, *Annals of Tourism Research* 20: pp. 701–715.

———. 1988, *Tourism and Development in the Third World*, Routledge, London.

Leijzer, M. 2006, SNV WTO Partnership, presentation at the WTO General Assembly 2005, SNV (Netherlands development organization).

———. 2003, *Reference Guide on Sustainable Tourism* (CD), SNV (Netherlands development organization).

Lepp, A. 2008, Tourism and dependency: an analysis of Bigodi village, Uganda, *Tourism Management* 29(6): pp. 1206–1214.

Levy, S. E. and Hawkins, D. E. 2008, Peace through tourism: commerce based principles and practices, Paper presented at the *Peace Through Commerce e-Conference*, theme 8: A Perspective from the Tourism Industry, http://api.ning.com/files/kqj8PjwXzUC0*fJJE6tpasBjQSIwiGMyReuje0glgwbc62zfLfcRGjVW3cPH-hWNkQpR*-iz8YuNrIiGrXPquCDskvCYmEj-/LevyandHawkinsJBESubmission.pdf (accessed 30 October 2009).

Lew, A. 1998, The Asia-Pacific ecotourism industry: putting sustainable tourism into practice, in C. M. Hall and A. A. Lew (eds) *Sustainable Tourism: A Geographical Perspective* Longman, Harlow: pp. 92–106.

Lew, A. A. and Wong, A. 2004, Sojourners, *guanxi* and clan associations: social capital and overseas Chinese tourism to China, in T. Coles and D. J. Timothy (eds) *Tourism, Diasporas and Space*, Routledge, London: pp. 202–214.

Lisle, D. 2008, Humanitarian trends: ethical communication in Lonely Planet guidebooks, *Review of International Studies* 34: pp. 155–172.

Luh, S. H. 2006, *'Involve Me and I Will Learn': A Study of Volunteer Tourism from Singapore*, Master of Social Sciences thesis in Geography, National University of Singapore.

Lyon, J. 2003, *Maldives* (fifth edition), Lonely Planet, Melbourne.

Lyttleton, C and Allcock, A 2002, *Tourism as a Tool for Development: UNESCO-Lao National Tourism Authority, Nam Ha Ecotourism Project*, External Review, 6–18 July 2002.

Macbeth, J. 2005, Towards an ethics platform for tourism, *Annals of Tourism Research* 32: pp. 692–695.

MacCannell, D. 1989, *The Tourist: A New Theory of the Leisure Class*, Schocken Books, New York.

Macleod, D. V. L. 2004, *Tourism, Globalisation, and Cultural Change: An Island Community Perspective*, Channel View Publications, Clevedon.

———. 1998, Alternative tourism: a comparative analysis of meaning and impact, in W Theobold (ed) *Global Tourism*, Butterworth Heinemann, Oxford: pp. 150–167.

MacNaulty, M. 2002, The role of government in successful island tourism, in *The Economic Impact of Tourism in the Islands of Asia and the Pacific: A Report on the WTO International Conference on Tourism and Island Economies*, World Tourism Organization, Madrid: pp. 28–41.

Magic Lantern Foundation 1999, Goa Under Siege (Video distributed by Tourism Concern, UK), New Delhi.

Mahadevan, R. 2009, The rough global tide and political storm in Fiji call for swimming hard and fast but with a different stroke, *Pacific Economic Bulletin* 24(2): pp. 1–23.

Malam, L. 2005, *Encounters Across Difference on the Thai Beach Scene*, PhD Thesis, Australian National University, Canberra.

Malloy, D. and Fennell, D. 1998, Codes of ethics and tourism: An exploratory content analysis, *Tourism Management* 19(5): pp. 453–461.

Mandalia, S. 1999, Getting the hump, *In Focus* 31: pp. 16–17.

Mander, M. and Steytler, N. 1997, *Evaluating Eden: Assessing the Impacts of Community Based Wildlife Management—The South African, Lesotho and Swaziland Component*, Phase 1, The World Conservation Union and International Institute for Environment and Development, London.

Mandke, P. 2007, *Understanding the Linkages between Tourism and Urban Poverty Reduction: A Sustainable Livelihoods Approach*, PhD thesis, University of Queensland, Brisbane.

Mann, M. (for Tourism Concern) 2000, *The Community Tourism Guide,* Earthscan, London.

Mann, S. 2005, Tourism and the World Bank, Paper presented at the Development Studies Association Conference, Milton Keynes, 7–9 September 2005.

Mansperger, M. 1995, Tourism and cultural change in small-scale societies, *Human Organization* 54(1): pp. 87–94.

Manyara, G. and Jones, E. 2007, Community-based tourism enterprises development in Kenya: an exploration of their potential as avenues of poverty reduction, *Journal of Sustainable Tourism* 15(6): pp. 628–644.

Marchand, M. and Parpart, J. 1995, *Feminism/Postmodernism/Development,* Routledge, London.

Marshment, M. 1997, Gender takes a holiday: representation in holiday brochures, in T. Sinclair (ed) *Gender, Work and Tourism*, Routledge, London: pp. 16–34.

Masters, T. 2006, *Maldives* (sixth edition), Lonely Planet, Melbourne.

Mbaiwa, J. E. 2005, Enclave tourism and its socio-economic impacts in the Okavango Delta, Botswana, *Tourism Management* 26(2): pp. 157–172.

McCulloch, N., Winters, L. and Cirera, X. 2001, *Trade Liberalization and Poverty: A Handbook,* Centre for Economic Policy Research, London.

McGehee, N. G. 2002, Alternative tourism and social movements, *Annals of Tourism Research* 29(1): pp. 124–143.

McGehee, N. G. and Santos, C. A. 2005, Social change, discourse and volunteer tourism, *Annals of Tourism Research* 32(3): pp. 760–779.

McIntosh, A. J. and Zahra, A. 2007, A cultural encounter through volunteer tourism: towards the ideals of sustainable tourism? *Journal of Sustainable Tourism* 15(5): pp. 541–556.

McLaren, D. 1998, *Rethinking Tourism and Ecotravel: The Paving of Paradise and What You Can Do to Stop It*, Kumarian Press, West Hartford.

McNeely, J. A., Thorsell, J. W. and Ceballos-Lascurain, H. 1992, *Guidelines: Development of National Parks and Protected Areas for Tourism*, World Tourism Organization, Madrid, and United Nations Environment Programme, Paris.

Metcalfe, S. and Kepe, T. 2008, Dealing land in the midst of poverty: commercial access to communal land in Zambia, *African and Asian Studies* 7: pp. 235–237.

Meyer, D. 2007, Pro-poor tourism: from leakages to linkages. A conceptual framework for creating linkages between the accommodation sector and 'poor' neighbouring communities, *Current Issues in Tourism* 10(6): pp. 558–583.

Michael, Muganda 2009, *Community Involvement and Participation in Tourism Development in Tanzania*, Master's Thesis in Tourism Management, Victoria University, Wellington.

Middleton, T. and Hawkins, R. 1998, *Sustainable Tourism: A Marketing Perspective*, Reed, Oxford.

Mikkelson, B. 2005, *Methods for Development Work and Research*, Sage, London.

Milne, S. 1998, Tourism and sustainable tourism: exploring the global-local nexus, in C. M. Hall and A. A. Lew (eds) *Sustainable Tourism: A Geographical Perspective*, Longman, Harlow: pp. 35–48.

———1997, Tourism, dependency and South Pacific microstates: beyond the vicious cycle? in D. G. Lockhart and D. Drakakis-Smith (eds) *Island Tourism: Trends and Prospects*, Pinter, London: pp. 281–301.

Ministry of Foreign Affairs and Trade (MFAT) 1995, *NZODA Support for Eco-Tourism in Fiji: A Report of a Study*, March 1995, Development Cooperation Division, Ministry of Foreign Affairs and Trade, Wellington.

Ministry of Tourism and Civil Aviation (MoTCA) 2007, *Maldives Third Tourism Master Plan, 2007–2011*, Malé, Republic of Maldives.

Mitchell, J. and Ashley, C. 2010, *Tourism and Poverty Reduction: Pathways to Prosperity*, Earthscan, London.

———. 2007a, *Pathways to Prosperity: How Can Tourism Reduce Poverty? A Review of Pathways, Evidence and Methods*, Overseas Development Institute, London.

———. 2007b, 'Leakage' claims: muddled thinking and bad for policy? *ODI Opinion* 81, Overseas Development Institute, London: pp. 1–2.

Mitchell, J. and Faal, J. 2007, Holiday package tourism and the poor in the Gambia, *Development Southern Africa* 24(3): pp. 445–464.

Mitchell, J., Keane, J. and J. Laidlaw 2009, *Making Success Work for the Poor: Package Tourism in Northern Tanzania*, ODI and SNV, Arusha.

Mitchell, J. and Phuc, L. C. 2007, *Final Report on Participatory Tourism Value Chain Analysis in Da Nang, Central Vietnam*, Overseas Development Institute, London.

Momsen, J. H. 1998, Caribbean tourism and agriculture: new linkages in the global era? in T. Klak (ed) *Globalization and Neoliberalism: The Caribbean Context*, Rowman and Littlefield, Lanham: pp. 115–134.

———. 1994, Tourism, gender and development in the Caribbean, in V. Kinnaird and D. Hall (eds) *Tourism: A Gender Analysis*, Wiley, Chichester: pp. 106–120.

Montreal Gazette 2010, Vacationing a human right, EU chief says, *Montreal Gazette*, http://montrealgazette.com/travel/news/Vacationing+human+right+ch ief+says (accessed 21 April 2010).

Morais, D., Yarnal C., Dong, E. and Dowler, L. 2005, The impact of ethnic tourism on gender roles: a comparison between the Bai and the Mosuo of Yunnan province, PRC, Asia Pacific Journal of Tourism Research 10(4): pp. 361–367.

Mowforth, M. and Munt, I. 2009, *Tourism and Sustainability: Development and New Tourism in the Third World* (third edition), Routledge, London.

———. 2003, *Tourism and Sustainability: Development and New Tourism in the Third World* (second edition), Routledge, London.

———. 1998, *Tourism and Sustainability: Development and New Tourism in the Third World*, Routledge, London.

Munt, I. 1994, Eco-tourism or ego-tourism? *Race and Class* 36(1): pp. 49–60.

Murphy, P. 1985, *Tourism: A Community Approach*, Methuen, New York.

Mustonen, P. 2005, Volunteer tourism: postmodern pilgrimage? *Journal of Tourism and Cultural Change* 3(3): pp. 160–177.

Narayan, D., with Patel, R., Schafft, K., Rademacher, A. and Koch-Schulte, S. 2000, *Voices of the Poor: Can Anyone Hear Us?* Published for the World Bank by Oxford University Press, New York.

Narayan, P. K. 2000, Fiji's tourism industry: a SWOT analysis, *The Journal of Tourism Studies* 11(2): pp. 15–24.

Narayan, P. K. and Prasad, B. C. 2003, Fiji's sugar, tourism and garment industries: a survey of performance, problems, and potentials, *Fijian Studies* 1(1): pp. 3–28.

Nash, D. 1996, *The Anthropology of Tourism*, Pergamon, Oxford.

——. 1977, Tourism as a form of imperialism, in V. L. Smith (ed) *Hosts and Guests: The Anthropology of Tourism*, University of Pennsylvania Press, Philadelphia: pp. 33–47.

Nepal, S. 2007, Tourism and rural settlements: Nepal's Annapurna region, *Annals of Tourism Research* 34(4): pp. 855–875.

Neto, F. 2003, A new approach to sustainable tourism development: moving beyond environmental protection, *Natural Resources Forum* 27(3): pp. 212–222.

Neumayer, E. 2004, The impact of political violence on tourism: dynamic cross-national estimation, *Journal of Conflict Resolution* 48: pp. 259–281.

New Frontiers 2008, Briefing on tourism, development and environment issues in the Mekong Subregion, 'Burning homes of the poor' *New Frontiers* 14(1): 3.

Norberg-Hodge, H. 1991, *Ancient Futures: Learning from Ladakh,* Rider, London.

Noronha, F. 1999, Culture shocks, *In Focus* Spring: pp. 4–5.

Novelli, M. and Gebhardt, K. 2007, Community based tourism in Namibia: 'reality show' or 'window dressing'? *Current Issues in Tourism* 10(5): pp. 443–479.

Nowak, J., Sahli, M. and Sgro, P. M. 2003, Tourism, trade and domestic welfare, *Pacific Economic Review* 8(3): pp. 245–258.

Öniş, Z. and Şenses, F. 2005, Rethinking the emerging post-Washington consensus, *Development and Change* 36(2): pp. 263–290.

Opperman, M. 1993, Tourism space in developing countries, *Annals of Tourism Research* 20(3): pp. 535–556.

Organization for Economic Cooperation and Development (OECD) 2010, Aid Statistics, Recipient Aid Charts, www.oecd.org/countrylist/0,3349,en_2649_3444 7_25602317_1_1_1,00.html (accessed 30 May 2010).

Osmani, S. R. 2003, Evolving views on poverty: concept, assessment, and strategy, Poverty and Social Development Papers No. 7, Asian Development Bank, Manila.

Overseas Development Institute (ODI) 2007, The impacts of tourism on rural livelihoods: Namibia's experience, Working Paper 128, ODI, London.

——. 2000, Assessing how tourism revenues reach the poor, ODI Briefing Paper 21: pp. 1–4.

Pacific and Asia Travel Association (PATA) 2008, Developing world leads global tourism growth, PATA News Extra, 10 March 2008, http://www.pata.org/patasite/index.php?id=1303 (accessed 18 March 2008).

Pagdin, C. 1995, Assessing tourism impacts in the Third World: a Nepal case study, *Progress in Planning* 44: pp. 185–266.

Papatheodorou, A. 2006 Corporate Rivalry and Market Power: Competition Issues in the Tourism Industry- An Introduction. In A Papatheodorou (ed.) *Corporate Rivalry and Market Power: Competition Issues in the Tourism Industry* I.B. Taurus and Co., London: 1-19.

Parker, S. and Khare, A. 2005, Understanding success factors for ensuring sustainability in ecotourism development in Southern Africa, *Journal of Ecotourism* 4(1): pp. 32–46.

Parnwell, M. 1998, Tourism, globalisation and critical security in Myanmar and Thailand, *Singapore Journal of Tropical Geography* 19(2): pp. 212–231.

Pattullo, P. 1996, *Last Resorts: The Cost of Tourism in the Caribbean*, Cassell, London.

Pattullo, P. and Minelli, O., for Tourism Concern 2009, *The Ethical Travel Guide: Your Passport to Exciting Alternative Holidays*, Earthscan, London.

Pelling, M. and Uitto, J. 2001, Small island developing states: natural disaster vulnerability and global change, *Environmental Hazards* 3(2): pp. 49–62.

Pera, L. and McLaren, D. 1999, Globalization, tourism and indigenous peoples: what you should know about the world's largest 'industry', Planeta.com, Exploring Ecotourism, http://www2.planeta.com/mader/ecotravel/resources/rtp/globalization.html (accessed 18 January 2000).

Phaswana-Mafuya, N. and Haydam, N. 2005, Tourists' expectations and perceptions of the Robben Island Museum—a world heritage site, *Museum Management and Curatorship* 20(2): pp. 149–169.

Phillimore, J. 1998, Gender, tourism employment and the rural idyll, in *Rural Tourism Management Sustainable Options*, International Conference, 9–12 September, SAC Auchincruive, Scotland: pp. 409–431.

Picard, M. 1993, Cultural tourism in Bali: national integration and regional differentiation, in M. Hitchcock, V. King and M. Parnwell (eds) *Tourism in South-East Asia*, Routledge, London: pp. 71–98.

Pleumarom, A. 1994, The political economy of tourism, *The Ecologist* 24(4): pp. 142–148.

Plüss, C. and Backes, M. 2002, *Red Card for Tourism? 10 Principles and Challenges for a Sustainable Tourism Development in the 21ˢᵗ Century*, DANTE (NGO network for sustainable tourism development), Freiburg.

Potter, R. 2005, 'Young, gifted and back': second-generation transnational return migrants to the Caribbean, *Progress in Development Studies* 5(3): pp. 213–236.

———. 1993, Basic needs and development in the small island states of the Eastern Caribbean, in D. G. Lockhart, D. Drakakis-Smith and J. Schembri (eds) *The Development Process in Small Island States*, Routledge, London: pp. 92–116.

Potter, R., Binns, T., Elliott, J. and Smith, D. 1999, *Geographies of Development*, Longman, Harlow.

Prasad, B. and Narayan, P. 2006, The long-run impact of coups on Fiji's economy: evidence from a computable general equilibrium model, *Journal of International Development* 19: pp. 149–160.

Pritchard, A. and Morgan, N. 2000, Constructing tourism landscapes: gender, sexuality and space, *Tourism Geographies* 2(2): pp. 115–139.

Pro-Poor Tourism Partnership 2007, *Pro-Poor Tourism: Annual Register 2007*, www.propoortourism.org.uk/annualregister07w.pdf (accessed 3 March 2008).

———. 2005a, *Pro-Poor Tourism: Annual Register 2005*, Pro-Poor Tourism Partnership, London.

———. 2005b, *Key Principles and Strategies of Pro-Poor Tourism*, Pro-Poor Tourism Partnership, London.

Pugh, J. 2006, Physical development planning in the Anglophone Caribbean: the re-articulation of formal state power, in J. Pugh and J. Momsen (eds) *Environmental Planning in the Caribbean*, Ashgate, Burlington: pp. 111–127.

Putnam, R. D. 1995, Bowling alone: America's declining social capital, *Journal of Democracy* 6(1): pp. 65–78.

Radcliffe, S. (ed) 2006, *Culture and Development in a Globalizing World: Geographies, actors and paradigms*, Routledge, London.

Raguraman, K. 1998, Troubled passage to India, *Tourism Management* 19(6): pp. 533–543.

Rangan, H. 1996, From Chipko to Uttaranchal, in R. Peet and M. Watts (eds) *Liberation Ecologies: Environmental, Development, Social Movements*, Routledge, New York: pp. 205–226.

Rao, M. 2002, Challenges and issues for tourism in the South Pacific island states: the case of Fiji Islands, *Tourism Economics* 8(4): pp. 401–429.

Rawls, J. 1973, *A Theory of Justice*, Oxford University Press, Oxford.

Raymond, E. M. and Hall, C. M. 2008, The development of cross-cultural (mis) understanding through volunteer tourism, *Journal of Sustainable Tourism* 16(5): pp. 530–543.

Redman, D. 2009, *Tourism as a Poverty Alleviation Strategy: Opportunities and Barriers for Creating Backward Economic Linkages in Lang Co, Vietnam*, Master's thesis in Development Studies, Massey University, Palmerston North.

Reid, D. G. 2003, *Tourism, Globalization and Development: Responsible Tourism Planning*, Pluto Press, London.

Reid, R., Bindloss, J. and Butler, S. 2009, *Myanmar (Burma)*, Lonely Planet, Melbourne.

Rice, A. 2005, *Post-tsunami Reconstruction and Tourism: A Second Disaster?* Tourism Concern, London.

Richter, L. K. 2001, Tourism challenges in developing nations: continuity and change at the millennium, in D. Harrison (ed) *Tourism and the Less Developed World: Issues and Case Studies*, CABI Publishing, New York: pp. 47–59.

———. 1995, Gender and race: neglected variables in tourism research, in R. Butler and D. Pearce (eds) *Change in Tourism: People, Places, Processes*, Routledge, London: pp. 71–91.

———. 1983, Political implications of Chinese tourism policy, *Annals of Tourism Research* 10(3): pp. 395–413.

Richter, T. and Steiner, C. 2008, Politics, economics and tourism development in Egypt: insights into the sectoral transformations of a neo-patrimonial rentier state, *Third World Quarterly* 29(5): pp. 939–959.

Riley, P. 1988, Road culture of international long-term budget travellers, *Annals of Tourism Research* 15: pp. 313–328.

Ringer, G. 1998, Introduction in G. Ringer (ed) *Destinations: Cultural Landscapes of Tourism*, Routledge, London: pp. 1–16.

Rivett-Carnac, K. 2006, Black economic empowerment: the South African approach, *id21 insights*, http://www.id21.org/insights/insights62/art02.html (accessed 12 June 2006).

Robertson, P. 2010, Islands in the sun, *Currents*, NZAID Magazine, February 2010: pp. 10–15.

Rockell, D. 2007, *Development Possibilities and Customary Land Tenure in the Pacific*, Master's thesis in Development Studies, Massey University, Palmerston North.

Roe, D., Ashley, C., Page, S. and Meyer, D. 2004, Tourism and the poor: analysing and interpreting tourism statistics from a poverty perspective, PPT Working Paper No. 16, Pro-Poor Tourism Partnership, London.

Roe, D., Goodwin, H. and Ashley, C. 2002, The tourism industry and poverty reduction: a business primer, PPT Briefing No. 2, Pro-Poor Tourism Partnership, London.

Rogerson, C. M. 2002, Urban tourism in the developing world: the case of Johannesburg, *Development Southern Africa* 19(1): pp. 169–190.

Ross, J. 1999, The 'revolutionary tourist', *Latinamerica Press* 31(33): p. 5.

Save the Children 2010, *Women on the Front Lines of Health Care: State of the World's Mothers 2010*, http://www.savethechildren.org/publications/state-of-the-worlds-mothers-report/SOWM-2010-Women-on-the-Front-Lines-of-Health-Care.pdf (accessed 21 April 2010).

Schellhorn, M. 2007, *Rural Tourism in the 'Third World': The Dialectic of Development—The Case of Desa Senaru at Gunung Rinjani National Park in Lombok Island,* PhD thesis, Lincoln University, Christchurch.

Scheyvens, R. 2007a, Exploring the tourism poverty nexus, in C. M. Hall (ed) *Pro-poor Tourism: Who Benefits?* Cromwell Press, Clevedon: pp. 121–141.

———. 2007b, Poor cousins no more: valuing the development potential of domestic and diaspora tourism, *Progress in Development Studies* 7(4): pp. 307–325.

———. 2006, *Desk Study for NZAID on Alternative Forms of Tourism Including Ecotourism, Nature Tourism and Pro-Poor Tourism,* Massey University, Palmerston North.

———. 2005, Growth of beach *fale* tourism in Samoa: the high value of low-cost tourism, in C. M. Hall and S. Boyd (eds) *Nature-Based Tourism in Peripheral Areas: Development or Disaster?* Channelview Publications, Clevedon: pp. 188–202.

———. 2003, Local involvement in managing tourism, in S. Singh, D. J. Timothy and R Dowling (eds) *Tourism in Destination Communities,* CABI Publishing, Wallingford: pp. 229–252.

———. 2002a, *Tourism for Development: Empowering Communities,* Prentice Hall, Harlow.

———. 2002b, Backpackers and local development in the Third World, *Annals of Tourism Research* 29(1): pp. 144–164.

———. 1999, Ecotourism and the empowerment of local communities, *Tourism Management* 20(2): pp. 245–249.

Scheyvens, R. and Russell, M. 2010, *Sharing the Riches of Tourism: Summary Report, Fiji,* Massey University, Palmerston North.

Schilcher, D. 2007a, Growth versus equity: the continuum of pro-poor tourism and neoliberal governance, in C. M. Hall (ed) *Pro-poor Tourism: Who Benefits?* Cromwell Press, Clevedon: pp. 56–83.

———. 2007b, *Supranational Governance of Tourism: Aid, Trade and Power Relations Between the European Union and the South Pacific Island states,* PhD thesis, University of Otago.

Schipani, S. and Oula, T. 2006, Government support in Lao PDR: how effective is it? *id21 Insights* 62: p. 4 (available online: www.id21.org/insights).

Scott, C. 2008, Creating a buffer fund to help farmers access the hotel trade in St Lucia, http://www.unctad.info/upload/SUC/SCFBarbadosWorkshop/ScottDoc.PDF (accessed 14 March 2010).

Sen, A. 2000, Social exclusion: concept, application, and scrutiny, Social Development Papers No. 1, Asian Development Bank, Manila.

———. 1999, *Development as Freedom,* Oxford University Press, Oxford.

———. 1993, Capability and well-being, in M. Nussbaum and A. Sen (eds) *The Quality of Life,* Clarendon Press, Oxford: pp. 30–53.

Shah, K. and Gupta, V. (and C. Boyd, ed) 2000, *Tourism, the Poor and Other Stakeholders: Experience in Asia,* Overseas Development Institute and Tourism Concern, London.

Sharpley, R. 2007, Tourism in the Gambia—ten years on, in J. Tribe and D. Airey (eds) *Developments in Tourism Research,* Elsevier, Amsterdam: pp. 49–61.

Siddique, M. and Ghosh, R. 2003, Tourism in the Indian Ocean region, in R. Ghosh, M. Siddique and R. Gabbay (eds) *Tourism and Economic Development: Case Studies from the Indian Ocean Region,* Ashgate, Aldershot: pp. 8–18.

Silltoe, P. 1997, Pacific values and the economics of land-use: a response to Bayliss-Smith, *Environment and Development in the Pacific Islands,* University of Papuan New Guinea Press, Port Moresby: pp. 171–184.

Simms, A. 2005, *Tourism: Creating a Framework for a Vehicle for Economic Development in Underdeveloped Societies,* Master's thesis, Brown University, Rhode Island.

Simpson, K. 2004, 'Doing development': the gap year, volunteer-tourists and a popular practice of development, *Journal of International Development* 16: pp. 681–692.

Sindiga, I. 1995, Wildlife-based tourism in Kenya: land use conflicts and government compensation policies over protected areas, *Journal of Tourism Studies* 6(2): pp. 45–55.

Singh, T. V. 2002, Altruistic tourism: another shade of sustainable tourism—the case of Kanda Community, *Tourism* 50(4): pp. 361–370.

Singh, T. V. and Singh, S. 1999, Coastal tourism, conservation, and the community: case of Goa, in T. V. Singh and S. Singh (eds) *Tourism Development in Critical Environments*, Cognizant Communication, New York: pp. 65–76.

Slatter, C. 2006, The Con/Dominion paying the price of investment and land liberalisation in Vanuatu's tourism industry. www.oxfam.org.nz/imgs/whatwedo/mtf/onz_vantourism_final.pdf. Oxfam, Auckland.

Smith, M. and Duffy, R. 2003, *The Ethics of Tourism Development*, Routledge, London.

Smith, V. L. 1977, *Hosts and Guests: The Anthropology of Tourism*, University of Pennsylvania Press, Philadelphia.

Smith, V. L. and Eadington, W. R. 1992, *Tourism Alternatives: Potentials and Problems in the Development of Tourism*, University of Pennsylvania Press, Philadelphia.

SNV n.d., Sustainable tourism: SNV practice area, SNV (Netherlands Development Organisation), The Hague.

Sobania, I. 1999 *Turning Green? A Case Study of Tourism Discourses in Germany in Relation to New Zealand* Master's Thesis, Waikato University, Hamilton (NZ).

Socialist Republic of Vietnam 2005, *Law on Tourism*, National Assembly, Vietnam.

Sofield, T. 2003, *Empowerment for Sustainable Tourism Development*, Pergamon, Oxford.

———. 1993, Indigenous tourism development, *Annals of Tourism Research* 20: pp. 729–750.

Sofield, T., Bauer, J., De Lacy, T., Lipman, G. and Daugherty, S. 2004, *Sustainable Tourism ~ Eliminating Poverty: An Overview*, Cooperative Research Centre for Sustainable Tourism, Australia.

Solomon, R. 2009, *The Challenge and Prospects of Tourism in Goa*, http://www.equitabletourism.org/stage/files/fileDocuments529_uid10.pdf (accessed 12 June 2010).

Spenceley, A. and Goodwin, H. 2007, Nature-based tourism and poverty alleviation: impacts of private sector and parastatal enterprises in and around Kruger National Park, South Africa, *Current Issues in Tourism* 10(2&3): pp. 255–277.

Standing, G. 2007, Decent workplaces, self-regulation and CSR: from puff to stuff? Working Paper 62, United Nations Department of Economic and Social Affairs, New York, http://www.un.org/esa/desa/papers/2007/wp62_2007.pdf (accessed 10 May 2010).

Stefanova, M. 2008, The price of tourism: land alienation in Vanuatu, *Justice for the Poor* 2(1): pp. 1–4, http://siteresources.worldbank.org/INTJUSFORPOOR/Resources/J4PBriefingNoteVolume2Issue1.pdf (accessed 13 June 2009).

Storey, D., Bulloch, H. and Overton, J. 2005, The poverty consensus: some limitations of the 'popular agenda', *Progress in Development Studies* 5(1): pp. 30–44.

Strategic Management Solutions 2004, Market scoping-feasibility study for agribusiness development in Siem Reap province, Cambodia, prepared for NZAID, February 2004.

Stronza, A. 1999, Learning both ways: lessons from a corporate and community ecotourism collaboration, *Cultural Survival Quarterly* 23(2): pp. 36–39.

Sultana, N. 2002, Conceptualising livelihoods of the extreme poor, Working Paper 1, January 2002, Department for International Development, London.

Sunday Star Times 2009, Helping hand, *Sunday Star Times* August 2: p. A13.

Sutcliffe, W. 1999, *Are You Experienced?* Penguin, London.

Tampe, M. and Lengefeld, K. 2007, *Tourism as a Field of Activity in German Development Cooperation: A Basic Overview, Priority Areas for Action and Strategic Recommendations*, GTZ, Eschborn, Germany.

Tarplee, S. 2008, After the bomb in a Balinese village, in J Connell and B Rugendyke (eds) *Tourism at the Grassroots: Visitors and Villagers in the Asia-Pacific*, Routledge, London: pp. 148–163.

Telfer, D. J. 2003, Development issues in destination communities, in S. Singh, D. J. Timothy and R. K. Dowling (eds) *Tourism in Destination Communities*, CABI Publishing, New York: pp. 155–180.

———. 2002, The evolution of tourism and development theory, in R. Sharpley and D. J. Telfer (eds) *Tourism and Development: Concepts and Issues*, Channel View Publications, Clevedon: pp. 35–78.

Telfer, D. J. and Sharpley, R. 2008, *Tourism and Development in the Developing World*, Routledge, London.

Teo, P. 2003, Striking a balance for sustainable tourism: implications of the discourse on globalization, *Journal of Sustainable Tourism* 10(6): pp. 459–474.

Teo, P. and Chang, T. 1998, Critical issues in a critical era: tourism in Southeast Asia, *Singapore Journal of Tropical Geography* 19(2): pp. 119–129.

Thomlinson, E. and Getz, D. 1996, The question of scale in ecotourism: case study of two small ecotour operators in the Mundo Maya region of Central America, *Journal of Sustainable Tourism* 4(4): pp. 183–200.

Thompson, D. (ed) 1995, *The Concise Oxford Dictionary of Current English*, Oxford University Press, Oxford.

Ticknell, A. 2001, Footprints on The Beach: traces of colonial adventure in narratives of independent tourism, *Postcolonial Studies* 4(1): pp. 39–54.

Times of India 2005, Tsunami spawns disaster tourism, *Times of India*, 7 January 2005. http://timesofindia.indiatimes.com/India/Tsunami_spawns_disaster_tourism/acticleshow/msid-983383,curpg-1.cms (accessed Feb 3 2009).

Timothy, D. J. 2007, Empowerment and stakeholder participation in tourism destination communities, in A. Church and T. Coles (eds) *Tourism, Power and Space*, Routledge, London: pp. 203–216.

Todaro, M. and Smith, S. 2003, *Economic Development*, Pearson Education, Harlow.

Torres, R. and Momsen, J. H. 2004, Challenges and potential for linking tourism and agriculture to achieve pro-poor tourism objectives, *Progress in Development Studies* 4(4): pp. 294–319.

Tourism Concern 2009, *Putting Tourism to Rights: A Challenge to Human Rights Abuses in the Tourism Industry*, Tourism Concern, London.

———. 2008 Guidelines and Principles for Fair Trade in Tourism network. http://www.tourismconcern.org.uk/index.php?page=fairtrade-network (accessed 20 August 2008).

———. 2002 Daw Aung San Suu Kyi on Tourism to Burma - Interview with the BBC, December 2002. http://www.tourismconcern.org.uk/index.php?page=san-suu-kyi-on-tourism (accessed 3 September 2009).

———. 1999, Adopting farmers, *In Focus* Summer: pp. 12, 19.

The Travel Foundation 2010 Travel Foundation Annual Review 2009-2010, http://www.thetravelfoundation.org.uk/assets/files/about_us/ANNUAL%20REVIEW%202009%202010.pdf . The Travel Foundation, London.

Travel Wire News 2006, UNWTO and Microsoft to boost e-tourism for development: Africa to be primary target, http://www.travelwirenews.com/news/12JUL2006.htm (accessed 13 July 2006).

———. 2005, 'Mission Africa' announced by International Council of Tourism Partners (ICTP) to help Africa sustainably triple its tourism export income by 2015, http://www.travelwirenews.com/cgi-script/csArticles/articles/000060/006054-p.htm (accessed 10 October 2005).

Turner, L. and Ash, J. 1975, *The Golden Hordes: International Tourism and the Pleasure Periphery*, Constable, London.

Twining-Ward, L. and Butler, R. 2002, Implementing STD on a small island: development and use of sustainable tourism development indicators in Samoa, *Journal of Sustainable Tourism* 10(5): pp. 363–387.

United Nations 2010, The criteria for the identification of the LDCs, www.un.org/special-rep/ohrlls/ldc/ldc%20criteria.htm(accessed 30 May 2010).

———. 2002 Development Assistance Framework for Republic of Maldives, 2003-2007. Male', Republic of Maldives. www.undp.org/execbrd/word/UNDAF-Maldives.doc (accessed January 20 2009).

United Nations Conference on Trade and Development (UNCTAD) 2007, *FDI in Tourism: The Development Dimension*, UNCTAD Current Studies on FDI and Development No. 4, United Nations, New York.

———. 1998, Developing countries could target tourism to boost economic growth, http://www.unctad.org/Templates/Webflyer.asp?docID=3243&intItemID=2068&lang=1 (accessed 9 June 1998).

United Nations Development Program (UNDP) 2009, *Human Development Report 2009*, UNDP, New York, http://hdr.undp.org/en (accessed 30 May 2010).

———. 2000, *Human Development Report 2000: Human Rights and Human Development*, UNDP, New York.

United Nations News Centre 2007, Myanmar: UN rights expert to probe allegations of abuses during crackdown, 25 October 2007, www.assiantribune.com/node/7977 (accessed 21 May 2010).

United Nations News Service 2007, UN tourism agency sets up internet platform for socially conscious travellers, http://www.un.org/apps/news/printnewsAr.asp?nid=21428 (accessed 18 March 2008).

United Nations World Tourism Organization 2010, *World Tourism Barometer: Interim Update April 2010*, UNWTO, Madrid.

———. 2009 'Tourism 2020 Vision' http://www.unwto.org/facts/eng/vision.htm (accessed 30 November 2009).

———. 2007, *UNWTO ST-EP Programme: An Initiative of the World Tourism Organization (UNWTO) in conjunction with the UNWTO ST-EP Foundation*, UNWTO, Madrid.

———. 2006a, *Poverty Alleviation Through Tourism—A Compilation of Good Practices*, UNWTO, Madrid.

———. 2006b, *Tourism and Least Developed Countries: A Sustainable Opportunity to Reduce Poverty*, UNWTO, Madrid.

———. 2006c UNWTO promotes the fight against poverty through tourism. *UNWTONEWS* 1: 9.

———. 2005a, 'Use tourism on war on poverty' world leaders urged, 15 September 2005, http://www.asiatraveltips.com/news05/159-Tourism.shtml (accessed 7 March 2006).

———. 2005b, *Report of the World Tourism Organization to the United Nations Secretary-General in preparation for the High Level Meeting on the Mid-Term Comprehensive Global Review of the Programme of Action for the Least Developed Countries for the Decade 2001–2010*, World Tourism Organization, Madrid.

———. 2004, *Tourism and Poverty Alleviation: Recommendations for Action,* UNWTO, Madrid.

Urry, J. 1990, *The Tourist Gaze: Leisure and Travel in Contemporary Societies,* Sage, London.

Utting, P. 2007, CSR and equality, *Third World Quarterly* 28(4): pp. 697–712.

Van der Duim, V. R. and Caalders, J. 2008, Tourism chains and pro-poor tourism development: an actor-network analysis of a pilot project in Costa Rica, *Current Issues in Tourism* 11(2): pp. 109–125.

Veit, R. 2009, A feasibility study of collection centres in Fiji, report prepared as a contribution to the All ACP Agricultural Commodities Programme, European Union.

———. 2007, Tourism, food imports and the potential of import-substitution policies in Fiji, paper prepared for Fiji AgTrade, Ministry of Agriculture, Fisheries and Forests.

Wearing, S. 2001, *Volunteer Tourism: Experiences that Make a Difference,* CABI, Wallingford.

Wearing, S., McDonald, M. and Ponting, J. 2005, Building a decommodified research paradigm in tourism: the contribution of NGOs, *Journal of Sustainable Tourism* 13(5): pp. 424–439.

Weaver, D. 2001, Mass tourism and alternative tourism in the Caribbean, in D Harrison (ed) *Tourism and the Less Developed World: Issues and Case Studies,* CABI Publishing, Wallingford: pp. 161–174.

———. 1998, Peripheries of the periphery: tourism in Tobago and Barbuda, *Annals of Tourism Research* 25(2): pp. 292–313.

Weaver, D. and Oppermann, M. 2000, *Tourism Management,* Wiley, Brisbane.

Wells, M. 1996, The economic and social role of protected areas in the new South Africa, Policy Paper 26, Overseas Development Institute, London and Land and Agriculture Policy Centre, Johannesburg.

Wels, H. 2004, About romance and reality: popular European imagery in postcolonial tourism in southern Africa, in C. M. Hall and H. Tucker (eds) *Tourism and Postcolonialism: Contested Discourses, Identities and Representations,* Routledge, London: pp. 76–94.

Wen, J. J. and Sinha, C. 2009, The spatial distribution of tourism in China: trends and impacts, *Asia Pacific Journal of Tourism Research* 14(1): pp. 93–104.

Wenham, R. and Wenham, J. 1984, Just travel: an experiment in alternative tourism, in P. Holden (ed) *Alternative Tourism,* Report of the workshop on alternative tourism with a focus on Asia, Chiang Mai, Thailand, 26 April–8 May, Ecumenial Council on Third World Tourism: pp. ATCM09/1-ACTM09/4, Bangkok.

Wheat, S. 1999a, To go or not to go to Indonesia? *In Focus* 33: p. 5.

———. 1999b, Tourism Concern interview, *In Focus* 33: pp. 16–17.

Wilkin, P. 2002, Global poverty and orthodox security, *Third World Quarterly* 23(4): pp. 633–645.

Wilkinson, P. 1989, Strategies for tourism in island microstates, *Annals of Tourism Research* 16: pp. 153–177.

Wilkinson, S. 2008, Cuba's tourism 'boom': a curse or a blessing? *Third World Quarterly* 29(5): pp. 979–993.

Williams, S. 1998, *Tourism Geography,* Routledge, London.

Wilson, D. 1997, Paradoxes of tourism in Goa, *Annals of Tourism Research* 24(1): pp. 52–75.

Wood, K. and House, S. 1991, *The Good Tourist,* Mandarin, London.

Wood, R. 1998, Bali: cultural tourism and touristic culture, *Annals of Tourism Research* 25(3): pp. 770–771 .

World Bank 1997, *Advancing Sustainable Development: The World Bank and Agenda 21,* World Bank, Washington DC.

World Tourism Organization (WTO) 1998, *Tourism: 2020 Vision—Executive Summary Updated*, World Tourism Organization, Geneva.

———. 1980, *Manila Declaration on World Tourism*, World Tourism Organization, Madrid.

World Travel and Tourism Council (WTTC) 2010, *World Travel and Tourism Council: Progress and Priorities 2009–10*, WTTC, London.

———. 2009, Economic data search tool, http://www.wttc.org/eng/tourism_research/tourism_impact_data_and_forecast_tool (accessed 7 April 2010).

World Wildlife Fund (WWF) 2000, Tourism certification struggling for credibility, Press release, http://www.wwf-uk.org/news/news148.htm (accessed 29 August 2000).

Wrelton, E. 2006, *Reality Tours to Chiapas, Mexico: The Role of Justice Tourism in Development*, Master's thesis in Development Studies, Massey University, Palmerston North.

Yahya, F., Rodney, S., Ashvin, P. and Inaz, A. 2005, Economic costs of tourism in Maldives, *Journal Tourism, Croatia* 53(2): pp. 33–44.

Yeung, Y. 1998, The promise and peril of globalization, *Progress in Human Geography* 22(4): pp. 475–477.

Ying, T. and Zhou, Y. 2007, *Community, governments and external capitals in China's rural cultural tourism: a comparative study of two adjacent* villages, *Tourism Management* 28(1): pp. 96–107.

Zhao, W. and Ritchie, B. 2007, Tourism and poverty alleviation: an integrative research framework, *Current Issues in Tourism* 10(2&3): pp. 119–143.

Zimny, Z. 2006, Realities around foreign tourism direct investment—UNCTAD Project 'Foreign Direct Investment in Tourism: Development Dimension', Presentation at the World Tourism Forum, Porto Alegre, 30 November–2 December 2006.

Zoomers, A. 2008, Global travelling along the Inca Route: is international tourism beneficial for local development? *European Planning Studies* 16(7): pp. 971–983.

Index

An environmentally friendly book printed and bound in England by www.printondemand-worldwide.com

This book is made entirely of sustainable materials; FSC paper for the cover and PEFC paper for the text pages.

#0138 - 010813 - C0 - 229/152/15 - PB